T0358837

THE
HUSBAND
POISONER

Also by Tanya Bretherton

The Suitcase Baby
The Suicide Bride
The Killing Streets

TANYA BRETHERTON

THE HUSBAND POISONER

hachette
AUSTRALIA

Published in Australia and New Zealand in 2021
by Hachette Australia
(an imprint of Hachette Australia Pty Limited)
Level 17, 207 Kent Street, Sydney NSW 2000
www.hachette.com.au

10 9 8 7 6 5 4 3 2 1

Copyright © Tanya Bretherton 2021

This book is copyright. Apart from any fair dealing for the purposes of private study, research, criticism or review permitted under the *Copyright Act 1968*, no part may be stored or reproduced by any process without prior written permission. Enquiries should be made to the publisher.

A catalogue record for this book is available from the National Library of Australia

ISBN: 978 0 7336 4245 6 (paperback)

Cover design by Christabella Designs
Cover photograph courtesy of Trevillion
Typeset in 12/18.6 pt Sabon LT Pro by Bookhouse, Sydney
Printed and bound in Australia by McPherson's Printing Group

The paper this book is printed on is certified against the Forest Stewardship Council® Standards. McPherson's Printing Group holds FSC® chain of custody certification SA-COC-005379. FSC® promotes environmentally responsible, socially beneficial and economically viable management of the world's forests.

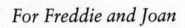

For Freddie and Joan

CONTENTS

1

THE BONOX HABIT

In October 1947, Sydney housewife Yvonne Gladys Butler planned the perfect murder. She didn't arrange an alibi, because she wouldn't need one. In fact, she felt so confident of getting away with it she left the victim's body out in plain sight and didn't bother to hide it. Yvonne believed the perfect murder was possible if it could be made to look like something else entirely and no one even realised that a crime had been committed.

Her recipe for murder was simple. In her small kitchen at 57 Ferndale Street in the working-class suburb of Newtown, she waited for the kettle to boil. She carefully measured from two small glass bottles, one labelled 'Bonox', the other 'Thall-Rat'. Although both products were described as economical and easy to use, only one was marked 'poison'.

Cooking by feel, Yvonne did not measure precisely. She tapped a small amount from each bottle into a porcelain teacup, poured boiling water over the mixture and stirred.

Her plan was now in motion.

She watched the swirling vortex of liquid and paused to ensure the mixture had dissolved. She leaned over it. Curls of steam spiralled slowly and ominously from the cup. The flame-shaped clouds of water vapour touched her nose. Satisfied that the hot brew looked and smelled like a cup of regular 'beef tea', she picked it up and walked down the hall and upstairs to the bedroom. She flicked off the hall light as she passed and the entire house fell into darkness. She handed the hot tea to her husband, Desmond, who was propped up in bed reading the newspaper by lamplight.

'Your Bonox, dear.'

●

Desmond woke early the next morning feeling sick, though not sick enough to warrant medical attention. His diarrhoea was dismissed as an upset stomach. He attributed his headache and nausea to a hangover. He went to work.

That night, Yvonne reached again for the two small glass bottles with the strange-sounding names.

The following day, Desmond felt worse; sufficiently so to take a few days off from his job as a cleaner at the Grace Bros. department store. He felt exhausted and had aches and pains, and an odd stiffness in his legs. He decided to see the local doctor. His sore throat and lethargy might be something more serious. The diphtheria bacterium was still fairly common in the community and it affected the throat. Poliomyelitis, although less common in adults, was also raised as a possibility. When the more serious diseases were ruled out, the doctor diagnosed a common cold. He prescribed bed rest. And more Bonox.

A thick, brown, concentrated paste, Bonox was known by a few different names, including beef tea, clear beef and fluid beef. It was a regular grocery item for many working-class families because it was cheap and, according to the advertising, provided all the nutrients of meat for those who could not afford to buy it fresh. Doctors recommended Bonox because, as 'pre-digested beef', it was gentle on the stomach and could be dissolved quickly in hot water. High in iron, it was frequently served to patients in recovery on hospital wards. There was even a term coined for a daily intake of liquid beef when one was recuperating: the 'Bonox habit'.

Yvonne followed the doctor's orders. She made beef tea for her husband every night.

After a few days, Desmond's lethargy and the worst of his symptoms seemed to go away. He hadn't completely recovered, but he felt better.

In Newtown's close-knit community, neighbours noticed everything. They noticed when Desmond missed work and they noticed when a doctor made a house call. The Butlers lived in a particularly cramped part of the densely populated suburb. Buildings were terraced closely together – common fences, narrow lanes and shared walls meant that families came to know far more about each other than perhaps they cared to. A neighbour could be heard coughing from next door, even when the windows were closed. Everyone knew which marriages were happy and which ones weren't; who had sons who'd gone away to war, and who had sons who hadn't come home. Many of the twenty-five families living on Ferndale Street had been there for more than a decade. Desmond and Yvonne Butler had lived there for only a few years, but everyone in the street seemed to know them – or know of them.

Families with young children were the most obvious. Babies woke up the neighbourhood as they cried for morning feeds like urban roosters crowing at dawn. Desmond, aged twenty-nine, and Yvonne, twenty-five, had two children – Raymond and Ellen. Neighbours heard baby Ellen crying and little Ray on his squeaky scooter playing in the street.

With his aquiline features, athletic figure, cleft chin, deep-set eyes and thick flop of jet hair, Desmond was hard to miss. In his dark suit and with his long, bounding legs, he cut a dramatic figure as he strode through the suburb. A quiet man, he spoke with a gravelly timbre which most thought was due to a poorly performed childhood tonsillectomy.

Desmond's laconic manner didn't stop him from communicating, though. One female neighbour described him as a 'physical man'. Others knew him as the dark-haired chap who would sidle up to women and wrap his arm around their shoulders while having a friendly chat. He was known to pinch a bottom here and there as well. Some women viewed the behaviour as playful, others as predatory. Desmond did not hide the pleasure he took in flirting with women, not even from his wife. Yvonne once said, 'He's not a cranky type. But he just can't seem to talk to a woman without pawing and mauling her. He's a real tiger.'

If Desmond was the resident tiger, Yvonne was the leopard. She was also hard to miss. Her favourite coat went down past her knees, had wide lapels, and featured a synthetic leopard-skin print. Yvonne would team this with a garish scarf around her neck, a patterned turban to restrain her wild tangle of hair, and a bold two-toned heel. She was doll like: a small-framed woman with a long, smooth face and tiny, flat features. She painted her face with precision: her blue–red satin lips were shapely, her eyes defined by a sharp brow, and the red rouge on the apple of her cheeks gave her the appearance of someone blushing shyly. Her curly hair bounced cheekily when she walked and was rolled at the front to create a fringe. Though Mattel's first Barbie doll would not be available for sale in Australia for more than a decade, with her heavy-lidded eyes, sharply contoured eyebrows and pouting lips, Yvonne's look bore an uncanny resemblance to it.

Neighbours not only noticed Yvonne and Desmond, they judged them. Like every family in Ferndale Street, the Butlers had been affected by the war. Although Desmond's army service record was long, his war stories were not heroic. In his Australian Military Forces file, the 'service and casualty' section typically used to record injuries, promotions and positions was instead devoted to listing his arrests and prosecutions.

In simple terms, Desmond Butler was a deserter.

Desmond had joined the Citizen Military Forces (CMF) in 1941 but failed to report when required. Absent without leave, he was declared an illegal absentee and was caught and sent to the detention barracks in Bendigo. Once released, he again failed to turn up for assigned duty and was again sent to detention. He faced even more charges when he was caught trying to escape. On another occasion, a search of his possessions uncovered a full naval uniform. It was an offence viewed very dimly by military officials because it was assumed that Desmond, a known deserter, was impersonating an enlisted officer of significant status and rank. The cycle of capture, punishment and release went on for two years. In April 1943, he was formally charged with desertion and convicted. It was now part of his permanent criminal record. Sentenced to two years with hard labour, he was dishonourably discharged. Crucially, he also forfeited the 797 days' pay he was owed.

With her husband in gaol and with no other way of supporting herself and Ray, who was still a baby at the time, Yvonne found work in a factory in Redfern which supplied cardboard packing for foodstuffs and artillery supplies. She organised care for Ray. Neighbours were happy to help the struggling mother making a contribution to the war effort. Yvonne carefully saved to make sure there was money to help Desmond get back on his feet when he finished his sentence.

He was released in January 1945, but struggled to find work. He quickly gambled and drank the savings in the family bank account. To make matters worse, when the war ended, Yvonne's box factory work dried up. The couple's second child, Ellen, was born in 1946. Between 1943 and 1947, Yvonne had wed and had two children, but had spent less than half her married life living with her husband. The marriage had spanned only four years but there was plenty of time for resentments to brew.

While the sound of children was regularly heard coming from the Butlers' house, so too was the sound of yelling parents. Sunday mornings were especially bad, as the couple rebuked each other for the shenanigans of Friday and Saturday nights. Yvonne's voice could be heard at fever pitch over the rooftops with the high-note emotion of a diva in a sweeping soprano solo. 'Stop running around the billiard rooms!' It might momentarily go quiet. Without fail, however, a short time later divo Desmond could be heard booming out a baritone response: 'I'm not stupid, Vonnie, I know *you're* seeing someone!' The residents of Ferndale Street had front-row seats to a working-class melodrama underscored with jealousy and revenge.

Neighbours had seen Yvonne with an older man. Herbert Wood was a well-known retired fireman from Glebe who had worked in the area for years. He was forty years older than Yvonne and widowed. When asked why he spent so much time with a young married woman with children his response was always the same: 'I'm helping her hang wallpaper.'

Rumours spread like wildfire. One neighbour told another, who told the next, who passed the information on to Desmond. Seething over the humiliation, he followed Yvonne one night to the door of Herbert Wood's home. Desmond waited for them to go in, then he waited a little longer before he finally knocked on the front door. Wood opened the door to a man with a look of absolute thunder on his face. Taciturn, even in a state of rage, Desmond simply said, 'You'll see what she's like.' Then he left.

A week or so later, Desmond went out to play cards with the boys. And Yvonne believed it to be true, until neighbour Mrs Thompson told her otherwise: Desmond was at the Surryville Dance Hall on City Road, just near the University of Sydney. Yvonne stormed straight up there in a fury and found him. It led to a very public altercation in the street. The words 'Father?!' and 'Husband?!' were screamed like questions, as if Yvonne were publicly stripping Desmond of his right to hold these titles. 'Stay home!' was shouted so loudly the words bounced off the sandstone of the surrounding university buildings. By the end of October 1947, most of Newtown appeared to be looking on, fearful of the trouble brewing in the Butler household.

2

JITTERBUG AND JUGS

AROUND 8 P.M. ON SATURDAY, 15 NOVEMBER 1947, FOUR MEN arrived at a community dance hall in the western Sydney suburb of Merrylands. They had a big night planned. Desmond Butler was accompanied by his younger brother Lionel, who was visiting from Victoria, and his two closest friends, Ronald Hicks (nicknamed Podgey) and Ronald Harding (nicknamed Ronnie). Desmond and Lionel, in particular, loved the dance hall scene. Their father had been a musician and band leader in the bayside suburbs of Albert Park and St Kilda, and the boys had grown up with rowdy big band music and rollicking musical theatre.

Unlike many of the men known to herd together in Newtown's pubs after work, the friendship between Desmond, Podgey and Ronnie had not formed because they worked together, but because they lived together. All three resided in the same neighbourhood – a block of streets off Edgeware Road which had Ferndale Street at its centre. Ronnie drove a truck and lived next door to Desmond at 59 Ferndale Street in an almost identical terrace, with his married sister Mrs Phyllis Stewart and her husband, Roy. Podgey made local deliveries of milk and ice, and raced greyhounds on the side, and lived just around the corner. The trio gambled, played cards, smoked and drank, often on the tiny porch in front of Desmond's home. It was well known to anyone that Desmond assumed the lifestyle of a single man. In fact, of the four at the dance hall that night, he was the only one who was married, and the only one with children.

When Lionel asked Desmond if Yvonne was coming, he curled his lip. 'She's got a boyfriend.'

'Do you know who he is?'

Desmond responded with disgust. 'Some old geezer in Glebe. Wood is his name. Old enough to be her father.'

That same night, Yvonne had travelled to the popular Albert Palais dance hall in Leichhardt with her mother, Dottie Bogan. It was one of the most popular entertainment venues in the city because it offered the public the full experience of a dance hall, with a stage large enough to accommodate a twenty-piece band.

Yvonne and Dottie worked nights in the supper room, serving drinks and tea, and preparing and selling sandwiches. A small-framed woman fond of colourful, tight frocks, it was Dottie's hair people noticed first. She had dyed it platinum blonde, but it was so brassy that even with the screaming trumpet and the piercing metallic notes of the trombone in full swing, her hair was still the loudest thing in the room. Dottie was cheeky and flirtatious, and playfully conspired with Yvonne like a girlfriend. The clatter and chatter of the two women behind the rattling crockery and sandwich stand only enhanced the Palais' revelrous tone. On meeting them for the first time, few realised they were mother and daughter.

To appreciate why it was significant that Desmond and Yvonne did not attend dances together, it is important to understand both the culture of dance halls and the culture of marriage in Sydney at the time. For those wanting to cut loose, dance halls provided an opportunity to do so. Swing jazz allowed improvisation and attracted people who wanted to flout convention. Old-time dances, like country or waltz, were slower and stiffer and reliant on a set sequence of movements. They were popular with older couples. But the new and wilder forms of dance – such as the 'cakewalk' and 'the black bottom' – brought irreverence with strutting and pigeon-neck movements. Racier and faster styles like the 'Lindy hop' and the 'jitterbug' were suggestive and signalled that the rules of sexual engagement had begun to change.

Men and women who were usually governed by the constraints of polite engagement found themselves able to be cheeky and flirtatious and downright sexual. Dance partners openly touched each other – and not just with their hands, or rigidly with their upper bodies; the more adventurous and athletic dancers straddled, as their bodies bounced against each other openly, breasts jiggling and hips rolling. Men dropped low to the ground, weak at the knees and slick with sweat while they bounced and kicked and wiggled. Skirts lifted outrageously as women twirled. The male body provided the solid foundation for the dance; the slapping and spanking of the double bass providing an infectious rhythm and the trumpets squealed with delight. This was sex, standing up, with clothes on. If dance halls were places to meet and size up potential partners, dance floors allowed potential mates to 'try before you buy'. The Palais had a reputation as more than a dance hall. Singles went there to find partners. It was rumoured that so many people had wed after first meeting at the Palais that the hall had a nickname – the Marriage Bureau.

The community dance halls that Desmond and his mates frequented, like the one in Merrylands, were rougher than the Palais and the Trocadero in the city. A refreshment room offered cut sandwiches, pitchers of cordial and urns of tea. Unless a liquor permit had been issued, alcohol was not permitted. However, at some of the smaller suburban dance halls, enterprising locals organised refreshments straight off the back of a truck. At Merrylands a local woodcutter had established a lucrative black market business selling cheap plonk. While inside the hall there was dancing, outside was a lorry full of sly grog, parked conveniently in a nearby street. A tarp was usually thrown roughly over the load to cover the sight of the beer bottles and wine jugs. The tray of the truck functioned as a makeshift bar and dance goers could buy warm home brew and vinegary wine, cheap, and on the sly.

Desmond may have been in the grip of dance fever, but on that night in November he was in the grip of another fever as well. On the crowded dance floor, while kicking his legs wildly, he suddenly began to feel sharp pins and needles in his feet. The prickly sensation in his toes quickly spread to his legs. As the dancers around him jerked and hopped and spun, Desmond struggled to maintain control of the lower half of his body. Before he had time to break his fall, his knees buckled and he dropped to the floor. Those around him initially dismissed his jangly movements as a wild improvisation of the jitterbug. They assumed he was drunk. Since there was no alcohol legally for sale, and half the hall was inebriated, most turned a blind eye to his plight, deciding it was best for all concerned to ignore him, lest they get into trouble. It took more time than it should have for onlookers to realise something was very wrong. His two friends, Podgey and Ronnie, and his brother Lionel eventually noticed what was going on and rushed over.

Still lying on the floor, Desmond's body was limp but he couldn't control his legs. With a man under each arm bearing his weight, he was lifted from the dance floor and dragged forward with a definite lean. Podgey was short but strong, so he shouldered much of Desmond's weight. Ronnie had seen Desmond drunk before – he'd had to drive him home on occasion – but he had never seen him this sick from booze. Lionel walked ahead, cutting a path through the crowd towards the exit.

Desmond rallied a little as he was shuffled through the crowd. But then, clearly in great pain, he started wailing loudly. 'I feel like I'm on fire!' Embarrassed by the man's hysteria, his friends moved even more quickly to get him outside.

To their dismay, Desmond's vocal distress did not subside. His voice remained panicky. He threw one hand across his face, trying to shield his eyes from the glare of the large electric flood lamp mounted outside. He flinched, squinting at the glowing orb of light. Conscious of his discomfort, his friends dragged him well away from the blaring trumpets which continued to echo out of the hall. Embarrassed by his feminine shrieks, they were rattled by seeing such a steely man as Desmond lose self-control. They felt empathy for him, but most of all they just wanted him to be quiet.

A short distance away, they propped him at the base of a tree and considered how to get him home. He seemed unable, or at least reluctant, to walk. Ronnie agreed to go to the nearest main road, hail a cab, then return for the rest of the group.

Refreshed by the cool night air, Desmond again rallied a little. Lionel and Podgey hoped for calm and for their friend to regain control of himself. Their hopes were misplaced. Legs splayed like a floppy marionette, Desmond was quieter but not silent. He began to weep. Podgey and Lionel looked awkwardly at each other with no idea what to do. All that Lionel could hear was his brother's sobbing and heavy breathing. The atmosphere was finally broken by Ronnie's return. He had successfully hailed a driver who agreed to take the men back to Newtown.

Desmond was now staring vacantly into space. This frightened Podgey even more than the screaming. He looked at his friend, sitting defeated in the dirt, and could tell he was in no condition to walk. Podgey turned to his two companions. 'I'll take his head, if you two can take the feet.' Before Lionel and Ronnie could answer, Podgey slid between Desmond's back and the tree trunk, put his arms under his mate's armpits and hoisted him up with all the expertise of a rescue vessel's crew swiftly and heroically saving a man who has fallen overboard.

The taxi wound its way through the streets of suburban Merrylands, past the many new red-brick homes being built for growing families. They passed a hospital at one point. Podgey glanced at his mate, and for a moment considered diverting the driver. But he thought better of it. It had all come on suddenly, but he had not seen Desmond be physically injured. Podgey believed if he could just get him home, he'd be fine.

Desmond grimaced with every turn in the road. Even the sensation of his leg pressing against the car seat seemed to cause him pain. Podgey asked the driver to speed up. 'Won't be too long, mate,' Podgey said to his friend.

In agony, Desmond seemed barely able to hear him.

It was around midnight when the cab finally turned off busy King Street into the block of terraces bordered by Edgeware Road in Newtown. No lights were on in any of the houses as the cab cruised up Ferndale Street and pulled up outside number 57. The lights were off and Podgey guessed that Yvonne wasn't home.

The three men hopped out of the car and conferred briefly and quietly again, with Desmond still prostrate on the back seat. There was no way to contact Yvonne, and no one wanted to leave Desmond alone. For a fleeting moment, Ronnie wondered if his sisters might be able to help. One sister, Phyllis Stewart, lived next door with her husband, Roy. His other sister, Lillian Backhouse, lived directly across the road. Ronnie thought better of it. He knew how this looked. Desmond was distressed, but he also seemed drunk, and for that he would receive no sympathy. 'He didn't have much to drink, did he?' Ronnie asked the others.

'Nah, Ron, you saw it yourself,' said Podgey. 'He barely touched the grog tonight.'

Podgey fumbled in Desmond's pocket for his keys. He then fumbled to get the key in the door. The lighting was dim, and there was a bang and crash as he tripped over a garden chair and knocked over a brass pot out the front. With the door finally open, they managed to get Desmond inside. To any neighbours who might have witnessed the scene, it would not have looked out of the ordinary: three men carrying a drunk brother-in-arms to sleep off a big one.

Inside, Ronnie headed straight for the kitchen to put the kettle on. Podgey helped Desmond out of his jacket with some difficulty and lowered him onto his bed. He slipped off his shoes, loosened his belt, unknotted his tie and removed it from his neck.

By the time Ronnie had made tea, Desmond opened his eyes, rolled over in bed and said, 'Thanks.' The men breathed a sigh of relief, but the mystery of what was wrong with him remained. They wanted to know how someone who had been so deathly ill only an hour before could be returning to normal so quickly. Desmond was no longer grimacing with pain, yet he had taken no painkillers. Privately, each of the three men wondered if his symptoms had not been quite as bad as he had made them out to be.

•

When Yvonne came home the next morning, Desmond was alone. His condition had improved slightly, but he still felt unwell. Yvonne called a local GP, Dr Cummings, a locum who had attended Desmond before. Each time, Dr Cummings could find nothing physically wrong with the man. This time was no different. He left Yvonne with the same instructions: Bonox and bed rest.

In the week following the dance, Desmond's condition worsened. In addition to pins and needles in his feet, he now had excruciating pain travelling up his legs. He had trouble keeping food down, and his stomach was on fire. Doctors came and went. None seemed to be able to offer a diagnosis. 'It seems mental,' one said. 'Typical of someone having a nervous breakdown,' said another.

Two weeks later, Desmond could barely even drink his Bonox. He spent whole days in bed. Yvonne sat with him, lighting cigarettes for him for chain-smoking when he did not feel quite so sick. He was angry. The constant pain had made him disagreeable. The couple began to argue again. Neighbours noticed.

Early one morning, around 2 a.m., Podgey was sound asleep when he heard a loud and frantic banging on his front door. He stumbled through the house in the dark and flicked on the porch light. Through the glass panel in the door he could see the silhouette of a woman. It was Yvonne. Standing in slippers and a night coat, her hair in curlers, she looked nervous and upset. Her fingers twitched as she drew deeply on her cigarette.

'Podge, you gotta come, please come. Des is really sick. He won't stop crying, I just can't stop him. He's out of his mind.'

Podgey heard Desmond's screams before he even got to the house. He was a strong man and a steady person in times of crisis, but the baseness of the cries spooked him. Podgey asked Desmond what was wrong but Desmond couldn't hear him. He went next door to number 59 to fetch Ronnie. The screaming had woken Roy and Phyllis Stewart, and Ronnie as well, but so many arguments could be heard coming from the Butlers' house that they were reluctant to interfere. When Podgey knocked, however, the couple was already awake and trying to decide what to do. Ronnie was ashamed to admit that the screaming had been frightening and had kept them at bay.

Back at number 57, Podgey took control. He lifted Desmond gently out of bed, helped him to pull a suit coat over his pyjamas, and then slid the man's limp feet into some loafers.

He sent Ronnie to flag a cab and told him to bring it to the front of the house. Podgey turned to Yvonne. Her eyes were bright red from crying. He rested his giant bear-paw hands on her narrow shoulders and tried to reassure her. 'Vonnie, me and Ronnie are taking Dessie to hospital.'

All of Ferndale Street heard Desmond Butler's blood-curdling screams that morning. As the cab drove away, Podgey looked back. Yvonne was standing in the middle of the road, her hair wild and woolly. Podgey thought she looked terrified.

•

A few hours later, another cab pulled up outside 57 Ferndale Street. Podgey ran in to tell Yvonne the news: they had taken Desmond to the Royal Prince Alfred Hospital in Camperdown, one of the biggest and best in the state, where he had been seen by some of Sydney's most experienced doctors. 'There's nothing wrong with him,' Podgey said, then paused as if he was about to say something else, but thought better of it. They had brought him home.

With Desmond now in bed on the first floor, the three friends – Ronnie, Podgey and Yvonne – sat huddled around the kitchen table at the bottom of the stairs. No one seemed to know quite what to say. Yvonne sobbed quietly into a handkerchief which was mangled in her fist. Ronnie, suddenly aware there was something heavy in his pocket, emptied the contents onto the table, and placed a bottle of liniment down with a crack. Yvonne and Podgey jumped at the sound of the glass bottle hitting the laminate. 'They said you could rub it on his legs,' Ronnie said and looked at Yvonne, frustrated that there was little else to do. Under his breath, he told Yvonne what the doctors had said. 'They thought he was shamming,' he whispered. This made Yvonne cry even harder.

'Shh, mate,' Podgey said to Ronnie. 'Why do you think I didn't say that before?'

Both Ronnie and Podgey now firmly believed that their friend was afflicted, but not with something physical. The two men closest to Desmond Butler had come to the conclusion that it was all in their friend's head.

•

Desmond stayed in bed for weeks. For long stretches he lay as if dead. Yvonne brought him food. He threw it at the wall. With little control of his bowels, the smell of faeces soon filled the house. She helped him to bathe, but this was done with a sponge in bed because she could not lift him. She sat and talked with him. She smoked with him, holding the cigarette to his lips.

But still his condition worsened.

Neighbours began to see Yvonne less and less. The Butler children – Raymond and Ellen – had been moved almost permanently to Dottie's home around the corner. Aware of the noise of Desmond's screams carrying across the neighbourhood, Yvonne called Dr Cummings again, and again. Several times that week, either Dr Cummings or one of his assistants attended the Butler home. Every time, they left with no firm diagnosis other than severe nervous tension. The man was on the brink of mental collapse, they believed, and there was little they could do.

Desmond grew so weak he could barely lift his arms above his head. This only intensified his anger and frustration. Though Yvonne brought him food and water, the only toilet was outside at the back corner of the yard. When he had enough strength, he took to crawling. Yvonne slept downstairs, and the couple yelled between floors, their voices carrying not just up the stairwell but out onto the street as well.

The noises coming from the Butler house frightened the neighbours. In the daylight it was bad enough, but at night it was chilling. One night Phyllis, who was home more than her husband and brother, heard a grunting noise coming from next door that she could not explain. The persistence of the noise worried her. She waited for it to resume, which it did, and then went outside to listen more carefully. She bent down and peered between the fence palings that separated her property from the Butlers'. To her horror, she saw Desmond within arm's reach. He was dragging his body along the ground, grunting in pain.

Neighbours now rarely saw Yvonne in Ferndale Street. When she was at home, the Butlers argued constantly. The smell of urine and faeces was like an aura surrounding their house. Yvonne wanted Desmond admitted to hospital. But the doctors continued to say there was nothing wrong with him. There seemed to be no solution in sight.

Then, in the last week of November, neighbours witnessed a strange altercation which, to this day, has never been explained. A group of friends had come to visit to cheer Desmond up and had assembled in his bedroom. Podgey and Ronnie were there, as well as Phyllis and Lillian, Ronnie's two sisters who lived next door and across the road. Phyllis's husband, Roy, had also come over. The group had dragged chairs into the bedroom and sat crowded around Desmond's bed.

Suddenly, Yvonne stormed into the room. She stood at the foot of the bed and in front of everyone shoved her arm under her skirt and plunged her hand into her underwear. She pulled out her fingers, which were smeared with blood. 'You are responsible for this, you bastard!' she yelled, waving her fingers in the air in front of her husband's face. She then turned on her heel and left without saying another word. Desmond stared after her, his face blank. The other men in the room were so shocked, they froze. Phyllis and Lillian jumped up and followed Yvonne out. Phyllis helped Yvonne pin and tighten the sanitary pad that she was wearing back into place. Yvonne said nothing more and no one seemed able to work out what on earth had prompted it all.

Later, Lillian and Phyllis speculated. Had Yvonne been pregnant? Had she miscarried? Had the stress of caring for Desmond made her lose a baby? Or was she accusing her husband of something more sinister? Had he hurt her? No one believed he could do harm. His once strong and virile body was curled into a foetal form, crumpled in his soaking and stinking sheets.

Desmond's friends continued to visit, trying to maintain a semblance of normality. They drank spirits with him, poured neat in heavy-bottomed glasses. Desmond was not steady enough to hold a glass, so Podgey held it to his lips. They lit his cigarette, though he struggled to maintain the fine motor dexterity to smoke it. He was so weak he could barely hold a hand of cards, though the men tried to help him. They propped him outside in the little strip of tiled ground, next to the untended garden, and helped him play his turn. They tried to wedge the cards between his fingers, to hold them there while other players had their turns, but the cards simply slipped from his grasp and fluttered to the ground.

A few days later, on 30 November, Yvonne banged on the front door of Podgey's house in the early hours of the morning. She had all but given up hope that the doctors could help, but asked Podgey if he could come around. 'Could you just come sit with Dessie for a while? Please, Podge. He is crying all the time.'

'I'll be right round,' Podgey said. 'You go back now, I'll follow you in a few minutes.' He grabbed a coat and threw on some pants. As he headed towards the front door, he changed his mind and went to the kitchen. He began digging through the cabinet where his mother kept her tea. Next to the caddy, there was a small white and unmarked bottle of pills. Podgey's mother suffered from high blood pressure and had been told by doctors to lay off the salt and sugar. Unable to give up sweet tea, she had turned to artificial sweetener, which came in the form of small tablets. She had decanted the tablets into a pharmacist's bottle because it was more convenient. Though they looked just like drugs from the chemist, they were nothing more than saccharine, purchased at the grocery store. Podgey slipped the bottle into his pocket and set off for the Butler house.

Podgey sat with his friend all night. He talked. Desmond wailed. Podgey was shocked, and scared, and distressed – though let none of this show. In desperation, he offered the only comfort he believed he could. He poured Desmond a huge slug of brandy and emptied a handful of the little white pills into the man's shaking hand. 'This will fix you up, mate,' he said, 'it's morphine.' When Podgey saw Desmond fall asleep shortly afterwards, he took it as further evidence that his friend was not right in the head.

•

Later that morning, Podgey went to fetch Ronnie and sat down with Yvonne to hatch yet another plan. Since Desmond had become ill, their pattern of communication with him had changed. Now used to his incoherence and stupor, family and friends had become so accustomed to being unable to talk to him they had simply stopped trying. On this day, like many others in recent times, his loved ones negotiated his fate, talking about and around him, but not to him.

'We need the hospital to take notice,' said Yvonne, standing at the foot of the bed. Desmond was in a supine position. He looked like he was in a coma.

'We'll force them to take him, Von, don't worry,' said Podgey.

'You've tried that, it didn't work. We need to do something different,' she said dismissively.

Ronnie also felt that hospital was the only solution. Living next door, he had heard Desmond screaming. It was almost constant now. Whether his friend's ailments were real, or imagined, he believed the doctors had a responsibility to do more. 'We've got to get him to hospital somehow,' he said.

'But we couldn't get him into Prince Alfred, you know that,' said Yvonne, shaking her head in frustration. She pulled a handkerchief from her pocket and crushed her face into it, holding back tears. 'How are you going to get him in this time?' The room fell quiet. 'Tell them he tried to take something,' she then said. 'Tell them he tried to take poison. Just so long as you get him into the hospital.'

The room fell quiet again. Ronnie and Podgey were clearly giving serious thought to what Yvonne had just said. To everyone's surprise, it was Desmond who finally broke the silence. His eyes had been closed, but it seemed he had been listening. In a slurred voice, he said, 'Don't worry, Vonnie, I'll tell them.' He spoke more slowly than usual, but he was lucid. 'I won't worry you anymore. I'll get into hospital.'

Ronnie and Podgey lifted Desmond out of bed. They made no real effort to dress him, although they did attempt to bend his aching limbs into a robe because this helped to cover the immodesty of the open fly in his drawstring pyjamas. It also helped to cover the smell. Ronnie and Podgey were not sure if it was his bedroom or the man that stank of faeces, but they did all they could to maintain his dignity. Meanwhile, Yvonne stuffed some clothes into a small bag.

The two men hauled Desmond down the narrow staircase, negotiated the small front door and led him through the wonky courtyard path to the street just as they had so many times before. Yvonne held the small, broken wire gate for them, and cleared the garden path as the three men staggered out to the taxi parked on the street.

Podgey sat beside the driver so he could give directions. Ronnie climbed into the back, next to what appeared to be an unconscious Desmond. Yvonne, clearly distressed, leaned in the window of the cab and in hushed tones urged again, 'Tell them, Podge, tell them he's threatening to eat poison.' Podgey nodded, and the cab took off.

Once the vehicle began to move, the vibrations set Desmond's nerves on edge. As the cab accelerated and slowed, swerved and turned, the man groaned. He wailed. He wept. Much to the dismay of his friends, this all happened very openly – and very loudly. They looked on, helpless. Desmond's body contorted. He rolled forward and placed his head between his knees. When this position didn't help he flung his body wildly about again. This time he arched his back and violently stamped his feet like a child having a tantrum. The driver, alarmed by the erratic behaviour, slowed the vehicle. Reluctant to proceed, he seemed hopeful the occupants might just get out, if given the opportunity. Podgey would not have it. He motioned the driver on.

Both Podgey and Ronnie tried to speak to Desmond, to momentarily distract him from his pain, but their efforts were in vain. Desmond seemed crazed. Podgey twisted in his seat, turning around as far as he could so his back faced the windshield, his attention focused firmly on the drama unfolding behind him. Ronnie and Podgey discussed what to do next. By now both had lost confidence in the plan they had hatched before they left. Doctors had not believed Desmond before and had attributed his physical symptoms to 'nervous tension' or 'hypochondria'. In 1947, these kinds of statements were tantamount to saying 'it's all in his head'. Both men feared the worst – that Desmond would be sent home in the same state he had been in when he left.

As the cab headed up Enmore Road towards the hospital, the two men hatched an alternate plan. Podgey directed the cabbie to drive on past RPA. But the driver objected. Podgey ignored his protests and insisted he continue through Newtown and into the city. 'Macquarie Street, please,' he said, with a grim tone. Even Podgey, a man known for his cheerful demeanour, could not disguise the fear in his voice.

The driver knew immediately where to go. Macquarie Street was well known as an important medical precinct comprising a large general hospital and numerous private practices. The driver pulled up sharply outside Sydney Hospital, killed the engine and went to get out of the car, eager to be free of the troublesome passengers. Podgey cuffed the man on the arm before he could get out. 'Drive on,' he said, 'to the Board building.' The cabbie shook his head, turned the ignition over once more and the cab roared on down Macquarie Street.

At the time, the NSW Department of Health, including a board of experts, was the highest-profile organisation in the state in the field of disease control. In the late 1940s, the Board of Health was known to employ an impressive array of scientific staff who were experts in their respective fields of medical practice and microbiology. These experts also played an active role in health promotion and ensuring the public followed their safety protocols and quarantine instructions during times of crisis. Though Podgey knew little about science, and was not a medical man, he hoped he could convince one of the officials that Desmond was the victim of an as yet unidentified and possibly dangerous new disease. When the cab pulled up outside the sandstone building and Podgey saw the word 'HEALTH' adorning the archway, he jumped out and rushed to the heavy glass doors. But they would not budge, no matter how hard he pushed them.

Through a large clear panel, he could see a man inside. He rapped on the door loudly to get his attention. Dressed in overalls, the man looked up, stared at Podgey, then shook his head firmly while mouthing the word 'closed'. It was only then that Podgey realised what day it was. In his haste, he had forgotten it was Sunday.

Podgey had left Newtown with no intention of doing what Yvonne suggested. As he returned to the cab, however, he caught a glimpse of Desmond through the window and reconsidered. His friend's face was twisted with pain and his body was lathered in sweat. Podgey felt a renewed sense of determination: he needed to do whatever was necessary. He hopped back in the cab and asked the driver to take them to the emergency entrance of the nearby Sydney Hospital. Sometime before 10 a.m., Podgey and Ronnie dragged Desmond through the hospital doors.

By 10.15 a.m., hospital staff had made their decision. They refused to admit Desmond because they could find nothing wrong with him, physically at least. The physician on duty, Dr Blackman, said there was 'no diagnosis' and that the hospital could not admit a man who was not sick. Podgey and Ronnie watched on helplessly as they saw hospital staff move to evict Desmond from the hospital bed where he'd been examined.

Podgey pulled the doctor aside. 'He's been really ill,' he told him, 'in so much pain he's been threatening to eat poisoned wheat. His wife told us so.' This was a shameful and humiliating declaration to make about someone, particularly a man. It suggested Desmond was weak, hysterical and unstable.

Podgey and Ronnie would have known that a threat of suicide would be taken seriously but it's unclear whether they understood the legal gravity of what Podgey had just said. In 1947, the threat to commit suicide was a criminal act, and therefore an entirely different set of medico-legal protocols applied. Rather than being admitted to hospital, Desmond would now be taken to prison. As soon as Podgey made the admission to the doctor, the police were called and Desmond was taken into custody.

He was transferred to Reception House near the gaol at Darlinghurst, a facility where criminals considered to be psychiatrically impaired were held and assessed. Again, Desmond wailed, wept, gnashed his teeth, and passed out. He roused, and the cycle continued. Unable to find any physical source for the man's pain, or for the weakness in his lower limbs, his distress was defined to be the result of 'nervous tension and anxiety'. It was legal grounds sufficient to certify him legally 'insane', and this meant the state could hold him against his will. It was the first diagnosis that Desmond had received that claimed to explain his unusual symptoms.

•

Later that day, a cab pulled up in Ferndale Street and Podgey and Ronnie got out. They knocked on Yvonne's door. 'They've kept him, Von,' said Podgey, deliberately censoring the horror of what they had just witnessed and trying to shield Yvonne from the humiliation and shame.

Ronnie was less delicate. 'They've locked him up. They said he's mad.'

Podgey nudged Ronnie. He knew Yvonne was prone to hysteria too – he had seen and heard her arguing with Desmond. He wanted to offer her some comfort, but words failed him. 'They'll keep him for a while,' he said eventually. 'Are you sure you're gonna be all right here?'

Yvonne didn't answer. She collapsed into Podgey's arms and cried like someone who had held back tears for a very long time.

Bonox (1947)

Ingredients

1 teaspoon Bonox

1 cup water, brought to a rolling boil

Method

Boil water. Place teaspoon of Bonox in cup and pour in boiling water. Stir vigorously until dissolved. Drink while steaming hot.

3

BLACK TEA

IN OCTOBER 1947, SYDNEY HOUSEWIFE CAROLINE GRILLS planned the perfect murder. She didn't arrange an alibi, because she wouldn't need one. In fact, she felt so confident of getting away with murder, she left the victim's body out in plain sight and didn't bother to hide it. Caroline believed the perfect murder was possible if it could be made to look like something else entirely and no one even realised that a crime had been committed.

Caroline had never met Yvonne Butler of Newtown and knew nothing about her, so it cannot be said she sought to follow her recipe. Yet two women, in the same month of the same year, living in the same city, planned to commit a murder in the very same way.

For Caroline, October was unfolding as it usually did, with a calendar of regular events. She played cards with friends on Mondays. On Fridays she visited her in-laws (relatives of her husband, Richard). And every Wednesday she travelled the eleven kilometres from her flat in Goulburn Street in the city to have lunch with her father, George Mickelson, at his home in Gladesville on the lower north shore.

George took pride in his modest home. By mid-morning on the day of Caroline's visit, the table would always be set. He was well into his eighties but remained sprightly. The same could not be said for his second wife, Christina. Also in her eighties, she had suffered with chronic ill health for going on three years. George was attentive and he did his best, but with each passing week it became harder to manage his wife's care.

On this day, Wednesday, 1 October 1947, Caroline left her city flat in Haymarket at 10.30 a.m. She stopped at the local grocery and general goods store and came out with a small brown paper bag. She then walked to the bakery and bought a currant bun, then went further down the street to the fish and chip shop and placed an order. She timed the order precisely so she could collect it through the small tuckshop window at the front of the shop and jump straight onto the bus.

Once on the bus, Caroline carefully arranged the items in her string shopping bag. She removed her latest knitting project (a cardigan for her husband) and sat it in her lap. She unwrapped the brown paper bag, removed a small dark glass bottle and slipped it into her pocket. She returned her groceries to the string bag, placed the currant bun inside, and on top she laid the hot parcel of fish and chips. She made a couple of tiny tears in the newspaper wrapping so that the parcel might breathe and prevent the fried food within from turning soggy.

The bus passed through the working-class suburbs of Rozelle and Balmain. Situated on the appropriately named Iron Cove, it was a residential area forged by the blue-collar men and women who raised their children there. It would have been hard to find a more working-class area in Sydney at the time. Labourers and maritime workers lived in the area because it offered close proximity to employment: the docks, local factories and the White Bay Power Station. A coal mine had even occupied part of the area until the 1930s. Caroline knew this life first hand. She had been born in Balmain, had been raised here and married in the South Balmain District Registrar's office at just sixteen.

Heading north, the bus passed through Drummoyne. This too was an area where poorer families lived and worked, but the working class seemed a little less hard-edged here. The streets were wider and the scenes that rolled by the bus window were more suburban. The overcrowded and ramshackle workers' cottages which choked the narrow inner-city roads of Balmain and Rozelle began to disappear. The long strings of rundown tenements transformed into neatly parcelled homes, each on a separate patch of land.

The bus sped on, further northwards. As it approached the Parramatta River it slowed to a crawl. The crossing at the Gladesville Bridge was narrow, and on this day the traffic was so heavy the bus came to a stop. We cannot know what Caroline thought as she waited on the bus for the traffic to clear. What we do know is what she would have observed: the factory smoke of Balmain had dispersed and fresher air blew into the bus off the Parramatta River.

This was not the affluent north shore of Sydney but it certainly wasn't Balmain. When the snarl of cars eventually cleared and the bus lurched forward, Caroline noticed the pristine suburbia ahead. Although only about half an hour by bus, the trip from Haymarket to Gladesville took her from cramped and noisy lodgings in the busy city to a quiet and uncluttered suburban home.

She alighted at a stop on Pittwater Road, ready to complete the remainder of the journey to Gerrish Street on foot. She stopped briefly to re-balance the load in her string bag. A short woman, the weight of the groceries made the string bag stretch so much that it almost scraped on the ground. Caroline was known for wearing coat-styled dresses which buttoned all the way up the front and had patch pockets just large enough to carry a handkerchief, or perhaps a few boiled sweets. On this day, she felt the weight of the small glass bottle as it bounced freely in her pocket as she walked.

As soon as her father's home came into view she sensed trouble. Although it was only a little after midday, and the traffic jam had not delayed her much, George was already waiting outside, pacing back and forth.

George Mickelson had left the city of Bergen, Norway, as a young man, bound for America. Bergen was a picturesque town known for its neighbouring mountains and fjords, but in the mid-1800s this natural beauty offered little comfort to the locals. Like Ireland, Norway faced famine and widespread agricultural failure. Bergen was on the brink of economic collapse.

Confronted with overpopulation and starvation, George joined an exodus of farmers, seeking to emigrate to countries which offered better prospects. He settled in Hawaii for a short period, before heading to Australia. While he may have boarded the boat leaving Bergen as Gjert Mikkelson, when he disembarked in Sydney he had become George Mickelson. Like many migrants, he hid parts of his cultural identity so that he might be better accepted in his new home.

At some point on his journey across the world, George abandoned his plans to become a farmer. He worked for a period of time in the more lucrative position of merchant seaman, but also as a labourer and bricklayer when work at sea was not available. He was a strong man with a rugged, thickset build who had worked hard as a single parent of eight children: Mary, John, Caroline, Margaret, George, Annie, Emmanuel and Manoel (who had died in 1942). Caroline had been young when her mother died and George was the only parent she had ever known.

The Mickelson children described their father as a difficult man who believed the gruelling regimen of work life could be applied to home life as well. His children did not agree and his relationships with many of his offspring remained strained well into adulthood. Caroline was now almost sixty, but her father continued a strict authoritarian. She did not call him by the more relaxed and familiar 'Pop' or 'Dad' or 'Pa'. She didn't even refer to him as 'Father'. He was known by the honorific 'Grandfather'.

As Caroline approached his house, she could see her father's agitation. To others his behaviour might have seemed overbearing, but Caroline had been exposed to it her whole life, so she barely reacted. 'I would always try and get the fish hot so he could have his dinner straight away,' she would say. 'Grandfather expected me there at twelve and if I was not there at twelve – sometimes the bus got held up on the bridge – he would be going silly.'

The property at 12 Gerrish Street was bare: a neat suburban block with a plain brick oblong building, two simple windows facing the street, and a manicured lawn with no garden beds to clutter it. George Mickelson kept an ordered home and considered it essential to maintain routine.

Caroline may have at one time been intimidated by him, but she now had an influence over him that she hadn't when she was young. 'Grandfather,' she said steadily, 'I'm here now. Lunch is still hot.' But once his anger had boiled, it took some time for it to cool. Caroline showed patience. George was getting older. Although he was still sprightly compared to many men in their eighties, Caroline saw him struggle with his responsibilities in a way he hadn't before, particularly the needs of his chronically ill wife, Christina.

By October 1947, George had been her full-time carer for three solid years. Christina was diabetic and doctors had failed to develop an adequate treatment plan to manage her insulin. She had lost so much muscle mass and gained so much weight that she was unable to lift herself out of bed. Her diabetes followed many other health battles. She struggled with incontinence and George tried keeping a pot next to the bed, so she did not have to navigate the long walk to the toilet at night in the dark. But given her weight and her fatigue, she couldn't get out of bed anyway. So George rigged up a stretcher with two long poles and a length of canvas. He planned to roll Christina out of bed while he bore her weight on the makeshift stretcher. The contraption didn't work, however. The narrow bedroom only seemed to add to her mobility challenges. Just that year, George had bought her a wheelchair because walking had become so difficult.

Caroline had watched with concern as her father strived to deal with his wife's medical needs and dutifully visited every week to help. She made black tea, properly brewed, just as Christina liked it. She held the rim of the cup to her stepmother's lips and all but forced her to sip it. Caroline also bought groceries for them and helped her father prepare meals for the week. For the first time, George conceded some control and afforded Caroline a latitude he did not give to others. Their relationship slowly began to change. Caroline still spoke her mind reservedly, but more freely than she ever had before. She insisted that her father could not cope, and that the current living arrangements weren't good for him or Christina. She was blunt. 'You cannot handle her, she's too big for you.'

George moved his wife out of the marital bedroom and by that October, Christina was spending most of her time in an overstuffed lounge chair. At night, she even slept there. The family room now resembled a suite in a hospital ward, with Christina's many tonics, pills and liniments arranged neatly across the sideboard. George ensured The Bible was within reach. With the efficiency of a hospital, the practical now took precedence. A pot sat on the floor for her to toilet.

The chronic pain Christina had suffered for some time worsened. She also appeared to be losing her eyesight, and her hair. George was shocked that his wife's health was declining so quickly. A practical man known for his brutal realism, he was now seen as foolish because he seemed unwilling to accept the fact that he and his wife were old. As one close relative to the family noted, 'Christina is well into her eighties: what does he expect?'

Christina's diabetes was not new and everyone in the family understood the need for her to carefully manage her diet. Despite being told of this many times – and being very aware of her stepmother's medical condition – Caroline insisted on bringing desserts each week, saying she was simply 'spoiling' Christina. She also insisted on sharing how affronted she was when Christina did not eat the treats she provided. 'I always took a little plain cake or a bun loaf or something . . . And I always took sweets. I used to take a box of chocolates regularly and when I found out she gave it to her granddaughter,

I only took boiled lollies. I cannot afford chocolates for her to just give them away.'

Christina's illness had not only changed the relationship she had with her husband, but with other family members too. Unless family visited, she did not see them. It isolated her from her own biological daughter and granddaughter because Christina could not travel. While there were three other sisters in the family, all of whom lived close by, Caroline was the only one who seemed willing to spend time with her stepmother. Caroline's sisters described their father as proud and stubborn, and there was little point in arguing with him. As one sister noted, 'He's a very independent man. He wouldn't let anyone help because he insists on doing it all.'

While Caroline's relationship with her stepmother may have been described as close by some, it was perhaps better described as convenient. There's little evidence they actually liked each other, despite their spending so much time together. Though poor health now prevented Christina from leaving the house, this had not always been the case. Before Christina lost mobility, Caroline had accompanied her on weekly outings to the city. The pair caught the bus together and spent the day window-shopping and shuffling through arcades. In many ways they were well matched. Christina moved slowly and Caroline had bad ankles and tended to toddle. One incident seemed to capture the complex nature of their relationship. It was an anecdote that Caroline delighted in retelling.

Caroline had taken her stepmother to the grand department store in Haymarket – Mark Foy's. It was not their usual shopping haunt. They had visited because the lingerie and brassiere department offered an undergarment-fitting service. Christina wanted a corset.

In the 1940s, particularly among older women, the corset was considered the essential foundation garment of a wardrobe because it hid what were perceived to be physical defects. If breasts were too small, a corset could be fitted in a way that plumped them up; if a waist was too wide, the corset could be laced to narrow this too. Mark Foy's had a private fitting room with an expert retail consultant paid to advise customers on the most appropriate style of corset for them, taking into consideration the woman's vital measurements: weight in stones, waist and hips in inches, and overall body shape. Professional fitters instructed women on how best to squish, pinch and press perceived flaws into a bone-and-fabric torture device in order to create what was thought to be a more desirable silhouette.

With her significant weight gain, Christina found it difficult to find comfortable clothing and undergarments. After giving much consideration to a corset that she thought might do the job, she was ready to pay. But she was stopped abruptly by a saleswoman whose passive-aggressive attitude was veiled by a polite retail smile. Looking down her nose at Christina the saleswoman said, 'That will be no good to you,' and snatched the corset away. Caroline recounted the story, often. She peppered her account with commentaries of 'how awful' the woman had been that day and how 'it was such a terrible thing to say'. Yet Caroline always made sure she ended her story by repeating the saleswoman's cruel taunt, using her stepmother as the punchline.

There is no doubt that Caroline and Christina's relationship was defined by formality rather than closeness. Caroline was nine when her own mother died. Already thirty-nine when her father married Christina Louisa Adelaide Carr in Balmain in 1927, Caroline had lived a lifetime without a mother. While this was not statistically unusual for this period – as many children lost their parents at a young age – it seemed to define her life. Her grandmother visited a local spiritualist in Balmain for years, in the hope of receiving a message from her daughter on the other side. Caroline knew this because she was dragged to the clairvoyance sessions as well.

Like many teenagers, Caroline railed in her own way against her authoritarian father. But she didn't do anything illegal. Keen to be free of George's control but also conflicted about breaking his rules or curfew, she rebelled in the most socially acceptable way possible at the time: at the age of sixteen she asked for her father's permission to marry.

If Caroline had been searching for the very opposite of her father, she found it in Richard Grills. George was a tall, stern man with real strength in his hands from years of hard labour. Richard was little, in addition to being a little cross-eyed and a little soft around the middle. One of Caroline's sisters had married an engineer and owned a grand home nearby. Another was happily settled in more affluent North Sydney. In contrast, Caroline married a somewhat hapless financial manager and was still renting a flat in Goulburn Street.

Situated behind a shop, the Grills's home was in what was considered at the time to be an undesirable part of Sydney. It was not the first shop the Grills had lived behind. For a short while, at the beginning of the 1930s, they lived behind a shopfront on busy Chapel Street in Bankstown, south-west of the city. Richard leased the space with the intention of running his own business, City Price Radio. The shop dealt in everything from small Bakelite radios for the mantel through to large freestanding cabinets with decoratively carved walnut panels, designed to be beautiful showpieces. The venture failed almost as quickly as it began. As economic conditions tightened with the coming Depression, and families focused on necessities rather than luxuries, City Price Radio struggled to make any sales at all.

In the mid-1930s, Richard tried his hand at another business venture. Just to the west of the city in the suburb of Petersham, the family rented space behind a radio and amplifier store on Stanmore Road. Again, Richard's business failed. For over twenty years, the Grills found themselves trapped in a cycle. Leases ran out. The couple moved on. They lived on main roads and on traffic intersections with views of shopfront awnings and concrete. Household life for the Grills had been shaped by the rhythm of opening and closing hours of the pubs, banks, butchers, cobblers, hairdressers and grocers which surrounded them.

In the early 1940s, Caroline and Richard moved yet again, this time to the working-class and houseproud suburb of Matraville. For a short while they rented a brick bungalow on

Malabar Road. The house had been decked out with modern conveniences including a heater, a gas copper, and a new Roman bath with clawed feet and a spouted tap. The house was walking distance to the beach. Although modest, it was still the grandest home that Caroline had ever lived in. Unable to keep up with the rent, however, they did not stay long.

From Matraville, Caroline and Richard moved to Goulburn Street in Haymarket, another working-class neighbourhood. Haymarket was close to the wharves and the produce market and, like The Rocks, had never quite shaken off its dark history and association with the plagues at the turn of the century. Vessels from all over the world docked at Darling Harbour and were fumigated for pests. Any vermin that survived the poison, it was said, skittered out to find shelter in Redfern, Glebe and Haymarket. While these suburbs today may be highly desirable locations because of their proximity to the city, in the late 1940s they were far from respectable.

George felt protective towards Caroline in a way that he did not feel towards his other children. Her husband, Richard, had assumed many jobs in his life; apart from his failed radio businesses, he'd worked as a labourer and a clerk, and was now trying his hand as a real estate agent. However, none of it had adequately provided for Caroline. Her father, George, on the other hand, had emigrated, worked in what was reputed to be a brutally hard occupation, and had managed to raise his family and buy a home – much of it without the help of a spouse. George had also seen Caroline experience great tragedy and had been close to both of Caroline's sons who had died. It is possible George even believed the boys took after him more than Richard.

Caroline's son Bill died in 1940. A likable, popular and strapping young lad with an adventurous spirit, his death shocked everyone. He'd played fullback in a local soccer team, the Magpies, and by all accounts had been the star player. A motorcycle enthusiast, he had been riding from Marrickville to Mascot late one night when he struck a cow. With little street lighting, and still surrounded by farmlands, the beast had wandered into the roadway. Bounced from his bike, Bill fractured his skull as he hit the road. An ambulance rushed him to Marrickville Hospital, but he was dead on arrival. He was only twenty-eight, and had never married. Caroline, understandably, took her son's death hard.

She lost another son only two years later.

Also twenty-eight years old, Harold worked as a lifesaver at Maroubra Beach. One day, he bravely retrieved a drowned surfer. The next day, Harold became suddenly and dramatically ill. He was weak, feverish and confused. Interviewed at the time, his father said, 'He became sick the day after bringing in the body. He lost his usual hearty appetite . . . he seemed strange, sick and languid.'

Harold tried to go back to work, but his illness overtook him. He deteriorated rapidly. With a raging fever, he was sent to hospital. The doctor's diagnosis was typhoid fever. Medical experts suspected he had contracted the disease from handling the dead body, although the timeline for the disease did not add up. Doctors were shocked at the speed with which the man had become symptomatic, as typhoid usually had an incubation period much longer than a day or two. In the end, medical staff conjectured that Harold's close bodily contact with the deceased surfer had been coincidental. He had most likely contracted typhoid from his daily exposure to the raw effluent which washed into Maroubra Beach from a nearby sewer. Harold was young and strong, and his body fought hard for ten weeks in hospital before finally succumbing.

More than 4000 people attended his memorial. Affectionately known as Wally, his ashes were placed inside a casket, carried through a guard of honour of Maroubra surf men and put on a surfboat. On top rested a miniature life reel. For Harold's service, the life reel had been severed from the belt which typically harnessed the lifesaver to the shoreline. It was symbolic of a good man lost.

George Mickelson took the deaths of his two grandsons hard. They were strong, physical boys making their way in the world in a way that George understood. As a seafarer, he found Harold's funeral service particularly moving. Harold's ashes were scattered in the very same body of water that he had patrolled and loved.

•

In those early weeks of October 1947, when conversations between Caroline and her father turned to Christina's health, something in George finally surrendered. When Caroline persuaded her father to redraft his will and suggested Richard ought to help, George agreed. In her distinctively strange turn of phrase she told George, 'Grandfather, I'll bring Father to discuss it next week.' George simply nodded.

As they assembled in the front room of the Gladesville home, George looked at his ailing wife. Christina's day had been particularly hard: the pain in her legs and feet had been excruciating. George then looked at his ageing daughter and her ageing husband. They were nearing retirement age, and had nothing to show for it. George reflected on the vulnerability around him and decided to take action.

The will was signed by George and witnessed by Richard. Titled 'George Mickelson of 12 Gerrish Street Gladesville', it instructed the executor to give the house and all personal effects to Caroline Grills 'on trust that she will permit my wife Christina Mickelson to live and remain in the said property rent free during her lifetime and upon the death of the said Christina Mickelson then to the said Caroline Grills absolutely I give and bequeath the rest and residue of my estate to my said daughter Caroline Grills absolutely. Will signed and witnessed on 15 October 1947.'

George Mickelson's will was clear. In the event of his death, Christina would have the right to reside at 12 Gerrish Street for as long as she was alive. After she died, however, the balance of the inheritance would change. No part of George's estate would pass to Christina's biological daughter, nor her granddaughter, nor any of her children. George's will ensured that his inheritance remained within his biological family, and included some very specific provisions around this as well. His only asset – the home – would not be divided equally among his children in the manner of a normal will. Once Christina was gone, George's home would become Caroline's exclusively.

•

No arrangements had been made for them to stay over that night, but Caroline insisted she did not want her father left alone while Christina was so ill. George did not like the break from routine but, too exhausted to fight, he gave in and said Caroline and Richard could stay.

Richard and Caroline rolled bedding out across the carpet in the front room. Though her father and her stepmother were asleep, it was far from quiet in the home. Mindful of not waking them, Richard and Caroline whispered like children. Christina, slouched in her lounge chair in the next room, wheezed and whistled as she snored with the relentless chirrup of a cicada in the night. Every now and then, George's rolling snore echoed down the hall. When the house finally fell quiet, Caroline and Richard fell quiet too. Caroline did not go to sleep right away. Instead, she rolled onto her back and looked up dreamily. Though she could not see the night sky, the moonlight came through the curtains and cast dappled patterns around the room. The stippling on the ceiling glowed in the reflection of the moonlight and twinkled like constellations in a real night sky. As Caroline closed her eyes in the suburbs that night, she made a wish on an asbestos star.

•

When Christina's daughter, Alma, visited the following day, Caroline was still there. Alma noted that Caroline always seemed to be there of late and was shocked by what she saw. Her mother's health had deteriorated in only a matter of weeks. Christina was now bald, and had become so childlike and disagreeable that she was unable to wear a wig. Caroline had resorted to draping a scarf over Christina's head and knotting it babushka-style at the chin. The pins and needles in Christina's legs and feet now appeared to be unbearable. She was not coherent. Her thoughts were confused and non-sensical. Doctors attributed all of these symptoms to nerve damage caused by her diabetes.

Certain that her mother would die soon, Alma insisted that she needed to send for her daughter, Jean, who did not live in Sydney. Caroline's response was emphatic. Alma should not call Jean. Jean should not see Christina. 'Better to remember Grandma as she was, dear,' she said. Caroline patted her stepsister on the arm with the flat of her palm.

By mid-November, Christina could no longer eat or drink. George called the doctor, who called an ambulance. Lying in a hospital bed in St Margaret's in Gladesville, Christina was easily diagnosed by doctors. She was dying, and although the aggressiveness of her symptoms surprised them, the rapidity of her decline was attributed to the natural process of ageing.

On 29 November, Caroline and Richard drove up to Forster for a few days at the beach. It was three and a half hours north of Sydney, not that far away should they need to return quickly. Christina died the very next day. Within hours of her death, Dr Bulteau, a local GP who had been Christina's treating physician, signed the death certificate: she had died due to natural causes including chronic myocardial degeneration and senility.

Caroline and Richard returned to Sydney immediately. They did not bother going home, but drove straight to Gerrish Street to stay with George. Caroline dutifully assisted her father in clearing away all of Christina's medicines, pots and liniments, and wheelchair and stretcher. She sorted through her stepmother's clothing and personal effects and placed them neatly in a box for Alma.

In the early morning of Tuesday, 2 December 1947, George gathered his family together, including Caroline and Richard, at a small funeral home in Ryde. From there the family travelled to local Catholic cemetery Field of Mars to lay Christina to rest.

Black tea (1947)

Ingredients
Black tea leaves
Boiling water
Teapot
Strainer

Method

Place one teaspoon in the bottom of teapot for each person drinking. Put kettle on to boil. Wait until water achieves a rolling boil, as black tea needs a high heat to infuse. While vigorously boiling, pour over leaves in pot. Cover tea with lid, and a tea cosy, to keep warm while the leaves infuse with the water. Use strainer while pouring. Serve hot.

4

PORK ROAST

IN LATE DECEMBER 1947, CAROLINE GRILLS RECEIVED A LETTER. A woman by the name of Angelina Thomas, a good friend of Richard's late mother, Evelina, had written to ask for help. Caroline and Richard were close to Angelina, even though it had been years since Richard's parents had died.

Originally from England, Angelina had never married, nor had any children. She had worked her entire life at the leatherworks and had scrimped and saved every penny she earned. Just before she turned sixty, she withdrew her savings and bought a block of land and a one-room shack in Leura in the Blue Mountains, two hours' drive from the city. When she turned sixty she retired, left Sydney for good, and moved to the clean mountain air. It was a dream come true.

When Evelina finally made the long trip up to the mountains to visit her friend, she did not find a woman living her dream. Angelina had bought a substantial block of land, but the house was a broken-down shack with little more than a dirt floor. Richard's mother paid for Angelina to have a proper house built so her friend might enjoy a decent retirement. She refused any compensation for her extraordinary generosity. 'I don't want anything,' Evelina said. 'Just gift it to Dicky [Richard] in the will.' Angelina had never forgotten her friend's act of kindness and Richard was duly named as the sole heir of Angelina Thomas's estate.

Angelina had lived in Leura for twenty-seven years. But at the age of eighty-seven, she had finally begun to slow and the house and property were becoming too much for her. She was known locally by some as Mrs Thomas – and known by everyone as the tiny and very serious-looking spinster with thick glasses who could be seen regularly walking up and down the long hill to Leura, carrying her bags of groceries. Neighbours were friendly, but they had their own families to worry about. With no children of her own to care for her in her old age, Angelina relied heavily on Richard and Caroline Grills. Richard was the closest thing to a son she ever had.

The tone of the letter Angelina sent to Caroline just before Christmas 1947 was urgent. She'd been feeling poorly, she said. Her eyesight was failing. She had been feeling giddy. One day, while out in the yard, she'd had 'a turn'. One minute she'd been walking in the garden in the middle of the day, the next she'd woken up on the ground, the sun dimming in the sky. At some point she had passed out, but she had no memory of what had occurred. The Blue Mountains were known for their changeable weather. For a woman her age, a mishap like this could be dangerous. There was more. When walking home laden with groceries, she often felt dizzy and had to stop to catch her breath.

Angelina made some specific requests in her letter. It had been unseasonably cold: could you buy three more woollen singlets? I cannot source good pork up here for Christmas dinner: could you buy a roast in Sydney? I still have to cook my two puddings – one for Christmas Day and one for New Year's: could you buy the dried fruit and the flour? Caroline immediately began attending to the requests. Though she had her own family she might spend Christmas with, that year Angelina Thomas appeared to be Caroline's top priority.

In the years leading up to 1947, Richard and Caroline had been particularly attentive to Angelina's needs. For a long time she had lived independently, planting fruit trees, growing vegetables, and keeping chickens. On weekend visits, on more than one occasion, Richard and Caroline would stop by the animal produce market in Sydney, buy live fowl and drive them all the way up to the mountains in a cardboard box. For years, the couple had gone back and forth between Sydney and Leura. They had visited so often, part of the house had been furnished to accommodate them.

The relationship between Angelina and Richard resembled that of mother and son in other ways too. Just like a son, Richard endured the odd scolding. There was pruning to be done and the yard needed clearing, she said. Richard was plain lazy, she said. She complained to neighbours about how little Richard visited, or that when he finally did he just lay about on the lounge doing nothing. She quarrelled with Richard, though the greatest threat she seemed able to muster was, 'If things don't change, I will sell up and move back to England.' Caroline and Richard were quietly amused by the emptiness of this threat: Angelina's fear of travelling was so profound she couldn't even bring herself to get into a car.

The Grills arrived at Leura on Christmas Eve 1947. The first thing that Caroline did was use Angelina's phone to call her brother, John. 'Would you and Mary-Ann like to come up for Christmas? Angelina is all on her own.'

When neighbour Mrs Hurry saw the Grills's car in Angelina's driveway, she came over almost immediately to say hello. She told them that she'd noticed Angelina slowing down. She'd also noticed the unkempt garden and the unmown lawn. It was a jungle and the sheds had completely rotted away. The chickens were running amok.

For months Angelina had declined the neighbours' offers of help. 'The fowls will clear the weeds,' she said dismissively. 'Just let them loose, they'll clean up the yard.' But Angelina had exaggerated the landscaping and carpentry skills of her poultry. Some thirty fruit trees had overrun the garden. Blackberries had grown wild and were now spreading arachnid-like across the property, their long and spike-covered tendrils making part of the block impenetrable. The chicken coop had disintegrated and the birds now roosted in the low branches of the trees. They had destroyed what remained of the vegetable garden and laid eggs all over the yard. Like a local gang, they roamed the streets looking for other gardens to pillage and plunder. Mrs Hurry spoke to Angelina and saw her each week, but she seemed more concerned about the overgrown yard, and the rising rates of chicken street crime, than she did about her neighbour's health.

Mrs Helena Schonbeck, another neighbour, dropped in to wish the Grills a merry Christmas. Mrs Schonbeck also raised concerns about Angelina's health, and the dubious role she seemed to be playing in the local food chain. 'You see, where there are chickens, there's grain, and where there's grain, there's rats,' she said pointedly. Just to ensure that the Grills had not missed the point, she added, 'So if there's chickens, there's *always* rats.' She said Mrs Thomas refused to lay down poison, because she was 'worried about the fowls eating it'. Mrs Schonbeck advised Caroline that she had therefore no other option but to lay rat traps herself – under the house and around the garden.

Angelina had always been fiercely independent, but also fiercely difficult. She hated the city, she hated the car, and she didn't seem overly fond of people. All of this was making it hard to care for her as she aged.

•

In the small house in Leura, Angelina, Caroline, Richard, and Caroline's brother John and his wife, Mary-Ann, had

Christmas dinner together. Caroline prepared the meal. Richard carved the roast. Angelina supplied the pudding.

Angelina became very ill soon after. John and Mary-Ann returned to Sydney, but Caroline and Richard stayed on for a few days. Angelina was weak. She couldn't seem to get out of bed. She was nauseous and in pain. Despite this, Richard and Caroline eventually left for their flat in Haymarket on 4 January. Richard had to return to work.

They were not home very long when they received a telegram.

POSTMASTER'S GENERAL DEPARTMENT OF NSW
URGENT TELEGRAM
MR AND MRS GRILLS (STOP)
PLEASE COME URGENT (STOP)
MRS THOMAS ILL (STOP)

When Richard and Caroline arrived at Angelina's house a few hours later, Mrs Hurry was already there. Richard pulled up in the car outside, but didn't stay long; he dropped Caroline off and drove back to Sydney again.

Mrs Hurry had come in to check on Angelina after the Grills had left. She became scared when she saw how ill Angelina was. The woman was struggling to breathe. Her lips were dry and cracked and she seemed to have an unquenchable thirst. By the time Caroline arrived, Mrs Hurry was deeply distressed. 'What's wrong with her?' she asked Caroline.

'It's just old age, dear,' said Caroline with all the confidence of a diagnosing doctor. Mrs Hurry shook her head in disagreement but knew there was little point in arguing.

Angelina couldn't eat, although Mrs Hurry could get her to take a little coffee. Her eyesight was failing too. She seemed unable to tell the difference between night and day and had lost the power of speech. Whatever afflicted the woman now had a powerful and cruel hold on her. She was imprisoned within a body that could not move, eyes that could not see, and lips that could not speak.

Caroline called a Dr Alexander Allan from a list of phone numbers she found in the kitchen. Dr Allan was at the very end of his medical career, and his own eyesight and faculties were not what they once were. He viewed Angelina's failing health through the prism of his own experience and had come to the conclusion that poor mobility and declining health were inevitable. But when he knocked on the door of the little house on Lawson Street that day, he was taken aback at the sight of what he would later describe as a 'short and stout' woman who very forwardly and thoroughly reviewed Angelina's symptoms with him.

The doctor noted Angelina's cardiac degeneration over the years. He observed that her weak and irregular heartbeat could barely be heard through a stethoscope. She was eighty-seven years old, and this was all to be expected. He noted the impairment of the central nervous system, which he classified as peripheral neuritis. The problems with her eyesight were most likely due to the milky film of cataracts. Perhaps this had created disorientation and caused the weakness in her legs. In one of the most depressing and brutal reflections on growing old ever penned, Dr Allan's notes attributed Angelina's 'vomiting' and 'diarrhoea' to be simply 'symptoms of ageing'. He prescribed fresh air and sunshine and suggested they carry her outside to sit in the garden for a while each day, just as one might put a pot plant in the sunlight.

•

Richard returned later that week, sometime around 10 January. Angelina was still at home, but now in a coma-like state. After months of badgering about the disarray of the house and the terrible state of the garden, Caroline began sorting Angelina's clothes and clearing the rubbish that had been hoarded in the house. Richard macheted the garden.

On Thursday 15 January, Caroline knocked on the door of Mrs Jones, another next-door neighbour. Initially, Mrs Jones thought Caroline might have come over to ask for help, or perhaps even to tell her that Angelina had died. No, Angelina was alive and still gravely ill. Mrs Jones was shocked by the real reason for Caroline's visit.

'We are clearing out her things,' Caroline said. 'I thought you might like Angelina's dressing gown.' She passed it through the door and stood chatting on the doorstep for a few minutes. Always fond of sharing a story about family, Caroline told Mrs Jones that, 'Under her bed we found a box. It was alive with tiny mice. They had made a nest of her clothes. Imagine that.' Richard found some things too. With a chit signed and Angelina's passbook, he walked into the local bank and withdrew almost the entire balance of the account: thirty pounds. He left a pound, just enough to keep the account open.

On the morning of 17 January 1948, Angelina Thomas died, in bed, at her home in Leura. Mrs Hurry watched as the body was taken away. About half an hour later, she brought over a posy of flowers from her garden. She knocked lightly, and Caroline answered the door. She looked like someone who had been vigorously exercising. She and Richard were both red in the face and sweating. Mrs Hurry attempted to make her excuses but Caroline insisted she come in. In the middle of the room, they had already begun taking apart the large wooden bed frame that Angelina had died in that very morning.

Caroline sorted Angelina's clothes, keeping some for charity and giving some to the neighbours. She kept one smart day suit for Angelina Thomas to be buried in.

Festive pudding (double up to make two)

Ingredients
Half pound self-raising flour
2 teaspoons mixed spice
2 teaspoons nutmeg
2 teaspoons salt
Half pound breadcrumbs
1 pound margarine
3 pounds & 3 ounces mixed fruit

Half pound dates

2 pounds sugar

6 eggs

Half pint milk

5 oz rum

Half teaspoon gravy browning

1 teaspoon almond essence

Method

Mix flour, spices, salt and margarine in a bowl. Add fruit and rest of dry ingredients. Stir in eggs and milk, then add rum and essences. Wrap in cloth and knot at the top. Boil in pot on stove for seven to eight hours.

5

CRACKLING AT CHRISTMAS

On Wednesday, 3 December 1947, the NSW police advised Yvonne Butler that her husband would be released from gaol. He would not, however, be coming home – the authorities had taken Desmond's (alleged) threat of suicide seriously and had arranged alternate accommodation.

In New South Wales at the time it was illegal to commit or attempt to commit the act of suicide, or self-murder. Society's belief that suicide was morally wrong and a shameful anathema to natural human instincts ran deep. A suicidal gesture would remain a criminal act for the next forty years, and would not be legally decriminalised until 1983. In 1947, police had the discretion to detain individuals who had made threats of self-harm and either criminally charge them or refer them for psychiatric assessment. In Desmond's case they handed the matter over to medical experts. Doctors assessed him closely and decided his erratic behaviour warranted closer examination.

No longer considered a criminal, Desmond was admitted to the institution at the forefront of treatment for severe depressive and nervous disorders at the time – Broughton Hall at Callan Park Hospital in the inner-western suburb of Lilyfield. Though his status legally changed from prisoner to patient, he remained captive. Desmond Butler would not be permitted to leave.

It is hard to imagine what Desmond would have thought as he was put on a stretcher, loaded into the back of a medical transport and taken to Callan Park. The institution was only just outside the city centre, but it was designed to look and feel like somewhere far removed from city life. Surrounded by sixty hectares of green space and landscaped English gardens, the hospital was built on what had once been a gentleman's estate on a quiet bay alongside the Parramatta River. The road leading into the area known as Lilyfield, and then further down to the Callan Park estate, has been described by one writer as winding and serpentine. The trip by motor vehicle is certainly circuitous and slow. If Desmond was conscious, and not overwhelmed by pain, he would have had plenty of time to contemplate what awaited him as he made the twenty-minute journey from Darlinghurst. Having operated as an institution for the insane since the 1880s, Callan Park had earned a fearsome reputation.

The asylum itself was huge and island-like: a sprawling and imposing complex of dozens of blocks, pavilions, wings and wards, annexes, chapels, gates and towers surrounded by greenspace. It was like a moated castle. Fashioned from locally quarried sandstone, the main building had a distinctively colonial aesthetic and looked more like the penal settlement of Port Arthur in Tasmania than a hospital designed to deliver care.

Built using an architectural feature known as a 'ha-ha' wall, Callan Park was constructed to ensure unobstructed views of the natural environment and water. These were considered beneficial for rehabilitation. Walls were very definitely present, but only visible at the bottom of a ditch or a trench at the base of a hill. The ha-ha wall made the sandstone of Callan Park sit even more boldly on the landscape. It also made it almost impossible to escape. In essence, it was a beautifully landscaped prison complete with many of the tropes central to a modern-day horror movie: a secluded position with imposing iron gates; an oppressive stone mansion with high walls and dark secrets; and a house full of guests with mysterious pasts. The area on which Callan Park was located was even aptly named: the secluded bay was known as Iron Cove.

The 'otherness' of Callan Park would have been felt by residents at every level. The institution functioned much like a separate society, with its own rules, roles, politics and economy. Visitors could not enter or exit without permission. Patients were typically stripped of their civilian clothes on entry, and given smocks and pyjamas to wear. There were gardens to grow produce, tended by residents. Kitchens cooked food on site, served in dining halls run according to a strict schedule. Bedding, clothing and all linen were laundered on site. With its own power station, a large boiler room, and a tall flue which vented gas, the compound would have looked like a walled city – a community living off the grid. It did not even rely on Sydney for water. A tall Victorian-era Italianate water tower dominated the skyline and the institution was supplied by vast underground tanks. Even the drinking water would have tasted different.

Patient records and administrative documents remain sealed, so a detailed week-by-week account of Desmond Butler's stay in the institution is unavailable to us. Local stories and personal accounts written by patients and staff in the 1940s do exist, however, and these help to provide insight on what life inside the institution would have been like around the time of Desmond's arrival. What is known is that he was admitted to the part of Callan Park known as Broughton Hall and joined a group of men who had lived there almost all of their adult lives.

Outwardly at least, Desmond's condition resembled a nervous disorder, a condition with which Broughton Hall staff were well acquainted. The mobility of his lower limbs was affected. His legs shook uncontrollably and his steps were unsteady. In medical terminology, the affliction was called 'hysterical gait' and closely resembled the common ailment known as shell shock. Desmond's fellow patients were returned soldiers, most of whom had come home from

World War I suffering the effects of nerve damage and what is now called post-traumatic stress disorder. The Broughton Hall estate had been absorbed by Callan Park in the wake of World War I, when the hospital needed more room to accommodate the influx of patients with complex trauma needs. The men were offered the promise of rehabilitation. What they got instead was lifelong institutionalisation. For many, their trauma was found to be so acute and the methods of treatment so ineffective, they were deemed unfit to ever re-enter society.

How staff interacted with vulnerable patients was also problematic. Only the following year, a patient would die from injuries sustained while engaged in a struggle with attendants. The cruelty shown to 28-year-old ex-serviceman Leslie Winter had been so violent that chairs had been overturned, crockery smashed and clothing sent flying. Winter's bowel had been ruptured; he had been kicked and punched. The man had been subdued by two attendants, given a bath and put to bed. No doctor had been called. There was a last ditch attempt to save his life, but infection had well and truly set in before he was assessed by a medical expert. He died of peritonitis and abdominal haemorrhage twelve days after the incident. Winter's depositions, taken from his deathbed, were used to champion a public inquiry into allegations of cruelty within the institution. The man had been at Callan Park for only eighteen months, and had been a fellow inmate of Desmond's.

Reporter Victor Valentine investigated the abuse of Leslie Winter and his subsequent death, and published an exposé in *The Sun* newspaper. It was extensive and covered every aspect of the institution's operation, including staff shortages and overcrowding. That year a public inquiry was opened by the Public Service Board to investigate allegations that officers at Callan Park regularly abused patients and the living conditions were cruel and unsanitary.

The details of the allegations were horrifying. Buildings were reported to be rundown and dangerous. Servings of food were meagre. Pyjamas and night clothing were often not supplied and patients were left naked. They were required to work for long hours unprotected and barely dressed in the scorching Sydney sun. They were not issued socks or warm coats in winter. Patients who were skilled tradesmen were treated worse than prisoners and forced to work as many as sixty hours a week for a shilling. Some were ignored or were targeted and roughly treated because they were pegged as troublemakers. Those suffering sexual disorders were allowed to prey on other patients and there was little attempt to prevent the abuse.

Around the time of Desmond's admission, Callan Park held around 1800 male patients and hundreds of female patients. Reasonable ratios at the time deemed that this number required a team of sixty doctors, ninety nurses, fifteen social workers and five psychologists. In actual fact, there were only five doctors on the books (in reality, only three worked the wards), a single superintendent who was in the office and never on the floor, eighty nurses and 150 attendants who were usually untrained. There were no psychologists or social workers.

The descriptions of Callan Park available to us are conflicted, at best. Some describe conscientious medical teams, eager to offer what was considered to be the most humane ministration of mental health care available at the time. Others describe the outright cruelty of staff and/or indifference to the feelings of residents.

While treatment regimes varied from patient to patient, the hospital aimed to offer the full suite of therapies considered important in healing mental illness at the time: pharmaceutical drugs; medical treatments and surgical interventions; physical therapies (rehabilitative projects in the form of craft pursuits like weaving or woodwork); exercise routines; and talk therapy. Patients followed a routine of treatment, strictly set out by the medical staff. Many could walk the grounds and enjoy the gardens. But if deemed by the state to be dangerous, like Desmond, they were unable to leave until there was demonstrable improvement in their condition.

•

On the day after his admission, Desmond was assessed by Dr Kirkwood. After three days in Reception House, and a little to eat and drink, some of his symptoms seemed to ease. He was now able to hold a conversation. Dr Kirkwood sat down beside Desmond's bed and asked him not only about his physical symptoms, but also about his home life.

'Are you happy with your wife?'

In his distinctive and slow drawl, Desmond answered, 'We were. For a while.'

'So when did it begin to be unhappy?' asked Dr Kirkwood. His pen hovered just above the paper.

'I would say it changed sometime around March of this year. She accused me of being unfaithful. She said that I went out dancing too much. She said I neglected her.'

'Was it true?' asked Dr Kirkwood. It was important, the doctor felt, to understand whether the patient's account was a delusion or reality. He made a note to interview Mrs Butler as well.

Desmond sidestepped the question. He answered slowly, but lucidly. 'I would say the opposite is true. I had become very suspicious of her and how much time she spent away from home. It all made me feel very depressed.' By this time, and in the absence of any other explanation, Desmond had clearly begun to believe the only reason for his illness that had ever been offered to him. To use the terminology of 1947: he was mad.

The decision to place him in Broughton Hall is significant. Since World War I the facility had formed a critical role in providing repatriation care for some of the most seriously ill returned servicemen – those suffering from severe shell shock. In the late 1940s, Broughton Hall took in some of the most complex psychiatric cases in the state. While Yvonne may have struggled to attain a diagnosis for what ailed Desmond prior to his admission in October 1947, it is very clear that after he entered the institution he was deemed to be seriously psychologically ill. During one assessment, when Desmond was clearly having a very bad day, the attending physician described his condition in the most brutal terms. He reported that Desmond was so weak he couldn't walk, so sick he couldn't eat, and so confused he couldn't think. He wrote in his notes that, 'He is a man unable to give account of himself.'

By December 1947, rather than improving, Desmond's condition began to deteriorate again. He suffered a rigid paralysis in his legs. Walking was now out of the question and he was confined to bed, or rolled around in a wheelchair. His hair – once a thick, dark mane of which he had been very proud – fell out in large chunks.

When Dr Kirkwood spoke to Yvonne, she objected strongly to what Desmond had claimed. 'He accuses me of going out all the time, but I am only going to get the doctor for him!' The doctor stopped questioning her when she began to cry.

As Christmas approached, Podgey, Ronnie and Yvonne visited Desmond in Callan Park. Whether they travelled together is not known. There is no evidence that Yvonne visited very much, if at all, after Christmas. What is known is that visitors were encouraged, although the Deputy Inspector General of Mental Hospitals of NSW decreed that no outsiders were permitted to enter any mental hospitals in New South Wales on Christmas Day. Boxing Day was deemed the official day of Christmas celebration.

Visits from wives, particularly in cases like Desmond's, were not always viewed as positive. Wives were often seen as conflicted, and perceived as unable to objectively assist with a patient's rehabilitation. Women were thought to be beholden to the desires of their husbands, and in suicidal cases this presented doctors with a challenge.

A few years before Desmond's arrival, Catherine Mary Thompson, a housewife from Paddington, had come to visit her husband, Horacek. He was found shortly after on the sandstone verandah of the main building looking out over the glorious gardens, with a bullet in his skull. Catherine claimed she had not shot her husband, but admitted bringing a gun into the facility, hidden in her handbag. She also claimed that it was her husband who had begged her to bring in any kind of weapon she could find. He suggested a razor and poison too – anything that might end his life. She further claimed that it was her husband who had instructed her on how to saw and file down the barrel and butt of a pea rifle so that it might be easier to conceal. On the day of her visit, she said, 'I handed him the gun and a bullet. When the attendant walked inside he put the bullet in the gun, put the gun to his temple and pulled the trigger.'

But the gun misfired. Not closely monitored by staff, Thompson had time to make another attempt. Mrs Thompson said, 'Don't try to save him, doctor. You know he's incurable.'

•

Two men in particular took a direct hand in Desmond's treatment: Drs Kirkwood and Wechsler. Dr Kirkwood had studied medicine at the University of Sydney, worked in a practice at Gladesville, and had served as a major during World War I in Egypt, Gallipoli, Turkey and France. He had just taken up the position of Deputy Medical Superintendent at Callan Park. He was a man who had seen a lot of action, including a lot of frontline medical emergencies. He had operated the field ambulance and tended severely wounded men at the casualty clearing stations. When serving on the frontline it was rumoured that while dodging heavy shelling, Dr Kirkwood had heroically worked ninety hours straight to save lives. He had seen men suffer the very worst. He had seen men die.

Upon examining Desmond on 4 December, he wrote, 'very sick man. Inflammation of the upper respiratory passages, great muscular weakness. Skin was dry and scaly. It was dry and peeling – desquamating. Eyes were inflamed. Tongue was dirty . . . He was emotional, in a popular sense, hysterical. Very depressed. Very difficult to talk to, because he was flying from thing to thing. Couldn't concentrate. No evidence of delusions or hallucinations . . . Hair falling out. Scalp dry . . . Very hard to tell which was hysteria and which was due to physical causes. But I thought he was suffering from depression and recognised he was toxic.'

But as to the cause of Desmond's affliction, Dr Kirkwood was less certain. 'He was unable to walk but whether due to hysterical exaggeration or real peripheral neuritis – I couldn't say.' At one point in his notes Dr Kirkwood wrote, 'he is putting on an act'. Unfortunately for Desmond, his speech impediment would have made it even more difficult for him to articulate what he was experiencing. It is possible that doctors may have assessed his cognitive function to be lower than it actually was.

The Resident Medical Officer at Broughton Hall, Dr Zacharias Wechsler, also personally oversaw Desmond's treatment. Born in Poland and trained in psychiatry at the University of Zurich, Dr Wechsler had worked extensively in prestigious psychiatric care institutions in Switzerland. The war ended his career in Europe when he fled Poland and wound up in Western Australia, becoming Acting Medical Superintendent of Heathcote Hospital.

Dr Wechsler had been an aspiring business student before transferring to medicine. He maintained an eye to economy throughout his career as both practising physician and medical administrator. With the influx of war veterans, Dr Wechsler (in medical partnership with a colleague called Dr Frank Prendergast) treated hundreds of veterans at the facility at Heathcote Hospital. It was in Western Australia that he refined the rehabilitative and therapeutic treatment regime for nervous disorders which he would apply to Desmond.

The regime was otherwise known as electroconvulsive therapy, or ECT.

Desmond Butler received medical care at a time when there was a lot of enthusiasm for the use of seizure-based treatments. Dr Wechsler was a leader in this field and the practice had a long and controversial history. Camphor oil (an extract from the wood of the camphor laurel tree) had been force-fed to those suffering schizophrenia as early as the 1600s. A poison, it caused convulsions which were believed to change brain function because connections were severed and forced to re-form. The practice persisted for hundreds of years and there are reports of camphor oil solutions being injected into schizophrenic patients as late as the 1930s. By the 1940s camphor oil was replaced with a synthetic chemical preparation called Metrazol (Cardiazol).

While ECT remains a controversial treatment to this day, in the 1940s there were far fewer controls in place to regulate its use. The therapy aimed to induce a convulsion and deliberately prompt confusion in the patient by applying a charge of electricity to the brain. It was cheaper than sourcing natural oils or synthetic preparations, easier to administer, and deemed to be safer because technicians could control the dosage administered. Desmond did not receive just one treatment of ECT, but many. The Callan Park administration's enthusiasm for the treatment was only exposed because of a case that occurred just before Desmond's admission.

On 17 July 1946, Dorothy Nellie Graham was diagnosed with 'nervous collapse' and admitted to Callan Park for treatment. Three weeks later she was dead. Her husband blamed the ECT she received. At the inquest, the Coroner sidestepped the issue and focused on Nellie's underlying condition. The Coroner found that she had died from exhaustion, following acute mental confusion. The medical care team in charge of her case defended their approach, saying that there had been more than 9000 cases of ECT administered at Broughton Hall without a single documented medical misadventure.

Desmond's treatment had been deemed safe after extensive testing, which spanned scientific research across many continents. Italian neurologist Dr Ugo Cerletti had developed the technique in 1938, after seeing electrocution used by a local butcher to anaesthetise pigs. He observed that the animals convulsed, then became quiet and subdued. The technique was soon adopted by Australian physicians who developed their own instrument and voltage. The method of electrodes on the head had been determined to be safe after early unsuccessful experiments on dogs which involved placing electrodes in the rectum. The electrical current had passed through the heart, and this had led to death. Placing the electrodes on the head seemed to resolve the issue of unnecessary jolts to the heart. Dr Wechsler also demonstrated that ECT could produce solid economic benefits. Of the 200 veterans who had been treated, all but one had been able to leave the hospital and return to the community. By the time Desmond arrived, the benefits of ECT were believed to be proven and doctors committed to it with conviction.

•

For Christmas 1947, the hospital held musical concerts and the residents sang carols. Christmas dinner was poultry, pork and pudding. The Red Cross organised festive hampers and each resident was given a bottle of beer. Desmond received many gifts, including his first dosage of ECT.

Sometime after the festivities were over, a nurse arrived at his ward. Two orderlies lifted him onto a gurney, looped a lash around his waist and wheeled him down a long corridor, across a hall, through a door and outside. The musty odour to which he had become accustomed disappeared and he smelled the green of the outdoors. When the summer sunlight bathed his face in yellow gold and warmed his cheek, he opened his eyes, just for a moment. Through the trees he saw the water glittering in the basin of Iron Cove. In a nearby building, just out of his line of sight, he heard a piano playing. The gurney bounced and jerked on a loose stone along the outdoor path. An orderly placed a hand on Desmond's chest, like he was a breakable load being steadied during transportation. He closed his eyes again.

They rolled him up a ramp and into another building which felt wide and open. The smell of the outdoors immediately died away. His nostrils filled with chemicals again, and even behind closed lids he could feel the light had turned from gold to white. A squeaky filing cabinet drawer was opened somewhere.

Down the end of the corridor, the gurney turned sharply left and entered a very small and windowless room. The chatter of patients and the clatter of equipment receded into the distance. Orderlies lifted Desmond off the gurney and onto a long examination table. He was in pain, but he was lucid enough to scan the room which seemed crowded. Two doctors and two nurses hovered nearby. A tall freestanding lamp sat in one corner, its arm floating awkwardly in midair. A wide shelf was stacked with medical trays of sutures, syringes, dressings and folded towels. On an oblong table there was a large decorative wooden box with several big dials and numbers on the console. Plugged into the wall, it looked like a polished and ornate walnut radio cabinet.

One of the doctors present wore a stethoscope around his neck, and appeared to be the junior of the two. The other held a clipboard and a pencil and remained in the corner of the room with an air of superiority. The junior doctor moved forward to examine Desmond. He touched and squeezed, prodded and poked. He pushed his fingers into Desmond's mouth and pressed down on his tongue. He leaned into Desmond's chest, and listened to the rhythm inside him. A nurse stood over Desmond, her hands suspended in the air with what looked to be a long thin, catheter tube, thick and round at one end. The length of the tube was curled around her fingers. A second nurse moved forward with a tube of salve. The senior doctor assumed the stance of a conductor. He peered over his glasses, his pencil held like a baton, ready to direct the ensemble of medical musicians.

A nurse squeezed some clear liquid onto the tips of her fingers and smeared it with great care into Desmond's temples. She then dipped a swab into another small bowl and streaked something sandy and grainy across his head. The other nurse uncoiled the long rubber tube, plugged one end into the wooden radio console, then attached the other end, with a small round disc, to Desmond's temple. She adjusted a strap which tightened around his skull. The disc felt hard and cold. From a nearby tray, the nurse took a long rounded stick, with small holes in it like a woodwind instrument, and held it up to Desmond's mouth. Then she prised open his lips and slid the instrument inside. Desmond could taste rubber.

The junior doctor assumed his position at the big walnut radio. Everyone in the room seemed to hold their breath as the senior doctor, who had not moved from his position, now rocked back on his heels. He raised his pencil, just like a baton, tapped it, then waved it swiftly and purposefully in the air.

The junior doctor turned the dial.

For a split second, Desmond wondered why he couldn't hear the music. He knew the big walnut radio was on. But it was silent. Then the air inside the room began to crackle with the crunchy sound of an electrical current. Somewhere Desmond heard the sweep of a jazz brush beat on a snare drum. He felt something surge within him, like the low, dark rhythm of a double bass. He felt his body stiffen. His back arched. His chest bounced up. His arms swung back. His fingers twisted. He shook. He shuddered.

The machine crackled again. Suddenly, the room filled with bright searing light, before it fell dark. Desmond realised where the music had gone. He couldn't see the big band playing, but he knew they were there because he could feel them. He couldn't hear the music, but it didn't matter. He no longer needed the sound, because it was already moving within him. He could feel it beating inside his head. It throbbed in his heart and it bounced through his bones. And when this happened, he could not resist the urge to dance.

His body rolled to the beat. With feet bent and toes pointed, his legs jangled. With muscle memory he remembered the movements. He no longer needed to hear the melody, because music was in his blood. Desmond was doing the jitterbug once again.

Roast pork (1947)

Ingredients
1 joint pork (rib, loin or shoulder pieces are all suitable for roasting)
Salad oil
Salt
Extra fat and baking tray

Method
Preheat oven to 350°F. Melt about an inch of fat in the bottom of a baking tray. Place raw piece of pork in baking pan, uncovered with the fat side up. Rub the top with salad oil and plenty of salt. Allow half an hour cooking for each pound of meat. Serve when crackling is crispy.

6

HEAD CHEESE

Angelina Thomas was buried in January 1948. Richard Grills was both the executor of her estate and the sole beneficiary. He organised a funeral service and paid for a single plot in Katoomba Cemetery in the Blue Mountains. As she was in her eighties, many of the people Angelina had known during her life (including Richard's mother) had already passed away. It was a small memorial. A few neighbours attended. Caroline's brother John and his wife, Mary-Ann, came, but left shortly afterwards. John had not been feeling well since Christmas, and seemed to have a constantly upset stomach.

The finalisation of Angelina's estate was straightforward. Richard now owned her house, but he and Caroline had no plans to move to the Blue Mountains. Angelina's property in Leura was broken down and small and a hundred kilometres from the city. Nevertheless, for the first time in their lives and on the cusp of retirement, Richard and Caroline Grills had become homeowners.

Caroline and Richard had faced significant emotional upheaval since November, with the deaths of both Caroline's stepmother and Angelina. By late January, however, life began to return to normal. Richard went back to his job as a real estate agent. Business seemed to be picking up and he engaged his married sister Eveline Lundberg as an assistant. She came into the office a few days a week to help with filing and paperwork.

Richard and Caroline continued living at their flat in Goulburn Street, Haymarket. Caroline resumed her busy schedule of social engagements. She helped out with a local charity for the elderly in Balmain. She met for social card games with friends. And just as she had before her step-mother's death, she continued her weekly trips to Gladesville to see her father. Though life seemed to settle back into an easy and predictable rhythm, this was not to last.

On Tuesday, 30 March 1948, Caroline and Richard received a call. George had taken a tumble. It was bad, the hospital said. Now ninety years old, and still fiercely independent, he had attempted to board a moving tram at Pyrmont. While there is no exact account of what happened before the incident – he may have misjudged the speed of the tram, or the distance he would need to leap safely inside; the tram driver may have been speeding – what occurred after the accident is clear: George fell and was taken to hospital with a broken leg.

There is no doubt that a terrible accident had occurred, and that George's condition worsened significantly after he went into hospital. He developed pneumonia and was dead ten days later. Although there were several things that interested the Coroner – George's health had declined rapidly and unexpectedly; he died in a hospital; and he'd been involved in a transport accident on a major public road – the state did not need to look for other reasons why the ninety-year-old man had died. On 30 April, the City Coroner ruled that George Mickelson had died of hypostatic pneumonia following a fractured thigh, which had resulted from a fall when trying to board a moving tram at Pyrmont on 30 March 1948.

George Mickelson had lived in Australia for sixty years. Even without the neighbours and local Balmain peninsula families, the size of his own family – he and his first wife, Mary, had eight children – ensured a big memorial. The service, however, was economical and modest. Performed by an ordained Salvation Army minister, it had a quasi-military atmosphere, which seemed fitting given George's desire for order and structure. The will identified Caroline Grills as the sole beneficiary of his estate.

Just as he had with Christina and Angelina's deaths, Richard Grills played a key role in bringing about a swift finalisation of the estate. He organised the memorial service, acted as informant for the death certificate, and was executor. The affairs were sorted so quickly that in less than a year Caroline and Richard were living at 12 Gerrish Street, Gladesville.

At that point Caroline's life changed almost overnight. She did not drive, so had not ventured to North Sydney and its surrounds all that much. Her new home in Gladesville gave her access to previously unexplored parts of Sydney, and offered closer proximity to her family. Caroline's sisters lived only a short distance away; however, any plans she might have had to heal wounds of the past were quickly abandoned. Her sisters were not having a bar of it. Caroline's inheritance of the entire Mickelson estate did nothing to improve the already strained relations between them. Instead, Caroline spent time with John and Mary-Ann, who lived in Ryde, less than half an hour's walk away from Caroline and Richard's new home. John had been a hardworking man like his father and was looking forward to a well-earned retirement.

It was not to be.

Rather than enjoying his twilight years, he was sick all the time. Mary-Ann feared it was an ulcer, but John was a stoic man and refused to see a doctor.

Mary-Ann was only a few years younger than Caroline and in many ways the two women had lived parallel lives. Both had strong marriages to men they loved: Mary-Ann had been married to John for over thirty years, Caroline to Richard closer to forty. Both had lost children and both had lived through two world wars, the Depression and the Spanish Flu. Each of these events had created immense social and economic change, and had produced shifts in the pattern of living for many women in the north-western suburbs of Sydney. Many neighbours and friends had moved into the labour force to undertake paid work. Caroline and Mary-Ann were among a cohort of women who had observed first-wave feminism at a distance. They had been a little too young to be stirred by the suffragette movement that led to the vote for women, and had been too old to capitalise on the paid work opportunities afforded to women during World War II. Their relationship appears to be one forged from shared understandings about the world, and conservative values about family and marriage and home. There is no real evidence they liked each other. Mary-Ann's health was poor and she found walking a challenge, so instead she and Caroline organised a regular, weekly outing: an afternoon matinee in town. In seemed to suit both well. At the cinema, they didn't have to speak.

It was the heyday of classic American film noir and crime thrillers were the most popular. Postwar Hollywood produced hundreds of films which played irreverently with gender roles. During the war, women entered the workforce in huge numbers but the postwar period saw rapid displacement of women from paid work and the dilution of the independence that they'd experienced earning their own incomes. By 1948 many had returned to dependence and domesticity. Film noir represented an ideal way to subconsciously explore feelings of repression by offering the opportunity to delight in the fantasy of revenge. Although these films featured Americans and American stories, they were immensely popular with Australian audiences.

As gender studies essayist and American feminist scholar Heather Fireman notes, film noir in the postwar era presented us with images and narratives of women who were cynical and anxious, but also playful and provocative. Women pursued men's goals for power and for money, but they did so through exploitation of their sexuality and psychological manipulation. Movies in the postwar period did more than any other form of mass media to reinforce the idea that women had unique capacities to deceive, and that any woman could use perceptions of them as weak and diminutive to their advantage.

By June 1948, the pattern of a weekly get-together between Mary-Ann and Caroline was well established. The pair saw a succession of films that each dealt with remarkably narrow and similar themes. And they were not alone. While their husbands were at work, many women crowded into cinemas to watch a young Lucille Ball in the crime drama *Lured* (1947). In *The Suspect* (1944), heart-throb Charles Laughton is accused of murdering his wife using drops from a bottle of the painkiller and deadly poison anodyne. In *Possessed* (1947) Joan Crawford plays a woman who coldly commits murder in secret, but is ultimately driven mad by guilt. In *A Woman's Vengeance* (1948), starring Charles Boyer and Jessica Tandy, a husband is trapped in a bitter marriage and acts as carer to his invalid wife. While she is terminally ill, she is still characterised as demanding and needy. When the wife is poisoned, a complex plot ensues in search of the killer – who turns out to be not the husband, but a woman.

In many of these stories, murder is commonplace but rarely seen. Bodies are found, discovered; violence is ever present, but it is brought about quietly and stealthily. Dark shadows across the silver screen provide a sense of menace on which the viewer cannot ever quite fix. No one is who they present themselves to be.

Academic critiques of gender roles in film noir note that the role of the woman is typically characterised in one of two ways – the 'fatal woman' or the 'fatal wife'. Men, on the other hand, have agency. They exact strategy and although they may do so with cruelty, they act with purpose. Men are ruled by power and conquest. In contrast, the fatal women are ruled by desperation and madness. They are driven to murder because of wounds of the heart that cannot heal. Women wait. They are patient. Then they plot.

•

John's health worsened first, Mary-Ann's shortly after. John's symptoms started around Christmas, and although they were persistent, they waxed and waned in intensity until June, when his condition suddenly deteriorated. He began vomiting and there was no respite from the nausea. When Mary-Ann looked in the sick bucket by his bed, the contents of John's stomach resembled coffee grounds. When he went to the toilet, the bowl was full of blood. Frightened, Mary-Ann called a doctor. She also called her daughters. John's condition went downhill at a pace that left everyone stunned. Before they even had time to acknowledge what was happening, he was dead.

It was only at the autopsy that the doctors found an answer. The cause of death was determined to be haemorrhage from gastric ulcer. Much like today, gastric ulcers were fairly common, but in an era without sophisticated body scanning technology, they were hard to diagnose. Doctors conjectured that John had been sick for some time, and it was unlikely the tragedy could have been avoided. Which all sounded plausible, until Mary-Ann also fell gravely ill. Gastric ulcers were not contagious, and the similarity of symptoms had doctors scratching their heads.

Gladys, Mary-Ann's daughter, distinctly remembered her mother being sick around the same time as her father. She also remembered her mother still feeling unwell at her father's cremation. However, it was difficult to tell if Mary-Ann's physical condition that day was due to illness or grief. Her other daughter, Jean, recalled that her mother's symptoms emerged a little later, in August, at her birthday party. Mary-Ann had pains in her shoulders and legs, lost control of her bowels and was unable to move for long periods of time.

Jean also remembered that their Aunty Caroline had brought a dish for the party that turned her stomach – a jellied meat concoction made with offal known as brawn, or 'head cheese'. Made traditionally, the dish took a long time to prepare because the meat needed to boil down sufficiently to soften and activate the gelatine. With the advent of pressure cookers, however, home cooks could prepare dishes like brawn with ease. As Caroline set out her dish, she noticed with pride that the chunks of meat were beautifully suspended in the translucent jelly, as if floating. In Caroline's mind it was a triumph: a dish so pretty it resembled a square window of stained glass.

The dish made Jean and Gladys queasy. They were younger and from a different generation of women eager to embrace the freedom of a postwar era of cooking which did not involve rationing and substitution, mock meats and economical cooking. The sisters looked at the grey squares, dotted with pink chunks of mystery meat, and could barely hide their disgust.

Years later, Caroline still talked about how humiliated she had felt when the girls had judged her.

There was no doubt that Mary-Ann was grief-stricken over the death of her husband but, as the months wore on, other symptoms began to emerge. She began to experience pins and needles in her hands and fingers. Her mobility and balance were affected. She was stiff and had pains in her shoulders and legs. The symptoms never seemed to go away, and had begun to impact Mary-Ann's quality of life. She decided to move in with her daughter, Jean.

Doctors could offer no other explanation for Mary-Ann's condition than a diagnosis of diabetes. Within months, Mary-Ann began to lose her hair. Jean bought her a wig. Her condition declined rapidly, and Jean and Gladys huddled close to each other fearing that their mother was about to die in a tragically similar way to their father. Though the idea that Caroline might have played a part had not occurred to them, both daughters remembered Caroline's behaviour around this time, particularly her attempts to sabotage their mother's diet.

Family had been given strict instructions – no cakes or desserts (no sugar) – but Caroline continued to bring sweets, and lots of them. Jean remembered Caroline cajoling and bullying her mother to eat. Caroline fed Mary-Ann acid drops (a kind of sour, hard candy), crystallised ginger, chocolates and biscuits. On one occasion, Caroline took a chocolate out of a mixed tray assortment and with defiance in her eyes stared Jean down. 'One won't hurt her,' she said, and with an intimacy that disturbed everyone who saw it, pushed the sweet right into Mary-Ann's mouth. By this point Mary-Ann was so ill, not only did she not resist, she barely seemed to notice.

Gladys recalled that the night before her mother went into hospital, Caroline barely left Mary-Ann's bedside. Caroline leaned in quietly to Gladys and Jean and said with a coldness that disturbed them both, 'If I were you, I would get money out of the bank. I've just seen your mother's jaw drop and she won't last much longer than a fortnight.'

Caroline's predictions proved to be chillingly accurate. Mary-Ann died within the fortnight. Gladys and Jean did not for a moment suspect Caroline was involved, but their aunt's behaviour was very troubling. At best, Caroline's acidic remarks showed insensitivity at a time when people were vulnerable and grieving. At worst, she had been downright macabre.

•

Once again, Richard Grills assumed the role of executor for the estate. He helped Gladys and Jean organise the funeral, make the arrangements and liaise with the lawyers. Caroline helped sort out the house, pawing through John and Mary-Ann's possessions, including her dresses and intimate undergarments, shoes, gloves, hats and jewellery. Gladys and Jean resented Caroline for the way she coldly sorted items into piles 'for charity' or to 'give away', but they felt powerless to object. Richard was doing so much for them; Gladys and Jean felt they had little option but to tolerate Caroline's abrasive and pushy behaviour. Neither Caroline, nor Richard, would financially benefit from the deaths of John and Mary-Ann Mickelson, so their involvement was perceived by all to be selfless.

In two short years, Caroline Grills had lost her stepmother, a close family friend and her father. By April 1948, she had attended three funerals in less than six months. The death of her brother in June 1948 made the count four in eight months. With the death of Mary-Ann in February 1949, the count would rise to five in sixteen months. During that time, Caroline and Richard had acquired two houses, one in Leura and one in Gladesville.

John had been Caroline's closest relative, and the last connection she had to her birth family. His death did not precipitate any healing in the relationship between Caroline and her other siblings. Instead, Caroline simply got on with her life. She did so by turning her attention to Richard's family, drawing closer to Richard's sister Eveline and her husband, John Lundberg.

Brawn ('head cheese') in a pressure cooker (1949)

Ingredients

About 3 pounds of any meat (gravy beef, sheep shanks, pig trotters,
    pig cheeks, tongue, mutton flaps)

2 teaspoons salt

Pinch cayenne

Quarter teaspoon nutmeg

2 dessertspoons gelatine (if not making your own). Ask butcher for
    knuckle bones, as these can also be ideal if wanting to make
    own gelatine.

Dash Worcestershire sauce

Small spoon of Bonox

Method

Place meat (including bone) in a large cooker. If using a pot on the
stovetop, boil bones for 3–4 hours with salt. If using a pressure cooker,
cook for approximately three-quarters of an hour. Remove meat from
liquid and separate into small pieces. Pour stock into a basin. Leave
this until the fat sets on top, and then skim it off.

Put two cups of the stock into a pan, add a little Bonox and
bring to boil. Add prepared pieces of meat. Pour mixture into a wet
mould or meatloaf tin. Make sure pieces of meat are spread across
the mix, so they will be suspended in the jelly when set. Place a
weighted plate on top to press into the mould. Put in refrigerator
to set and cool. For presentation, turn out as a jellied loaf on top
of lettuce leaves.

Acid drops (1948)

Ingredients
1 pound sugar
1 cup water
1 teaspoon lemon essence
Quarter cup tartaric acid

Method
Place sugar and water in a pan on the stovetop and bring to boil. Heat until it snaps like glass. Add lemon essence and tartaric acid. Combine well and turn mix out onto board and cut into small bullets, flattened out into a lolly shape with the finger.

7

CURRY AND BOILED VEGETABLES

BACK AT CALLAN PARK, DOCTORS BEGAN TO SEE SLIGHT IMPROVE-ments in Desmond Butler's condition. His appetite returned. His hair began to grow back. Though he still couldn't walk, he could sit for longer periods without support. His arms had regained some of their prior strength and he could lift himself in and out of a chair as well. Doctors attributed his improvement entirely to their therapeutic regime of ECT.

Patients at Callan Park were encouraged to engage in activities that would help them in the outside world. Women worked on handicraft projects – knitting and crochet, artificial flowers and quilting – while men were encouraged to learn a trade. It was thought that the quiet meditation associated with manual work calmed the agitated mind and that developing proficiency in a craft helped build self-esteem and confidence.

It was an ethos that had underpinned the approach at Callan Park since its nineteenth century beginnings. 'Moral therapy' was also perceived to be critical to recovery, as a connection to animals and nature, land and honest work were all considered vital to one's spiritual and psychological wellbeing. Gardening and animal husbandry were seen as particularly sanative. Men were encouraged to, and did, engage in very traditionally male-dominated activities. This served the economic interests of Callan Park as well.

By the time of Desmond's admission, the institution was facing some very public criticism over its 'dilapidated' buildings. The upkeep and repair of such a large facility was significant and maintaining a supply of cheap labour was essential. Desmond and his fellow patients were encouraged to learn skills like tiling, masonry or brickwork, basic carpentry or cabinet making.

Though there were many rehabilitative programs he might have participated in, he instead picked something rather unlikely. His manual dexterity had returned to a point where he could hold things between his fingers. He could rotate objects in his hands, and pass things between them now without dropping them. The project that Desmond selected was small and delicate. Though his work was clumsy and rough he had enough precision to make a very simple child's toy – a wooden peg doll.

Commonly known as a Dutch doll, the toys have a long history in the Germanic countries dating back to the seventeenth century. By the mid-twentieth century in Australia, however, Dutch dolls were seen as quaint European peasant artefacts because they were cheap to make, and every component could be fashioned by hand. Made of wood, sometimes with the assistance of a lathe, Dutch dolls have small bodies, and legs and arms which swing freely on rods sunk into the body. If the joints are loose enough, the doll can even be made to bounce on a board, with its legs jangling in movements not unlike a jitterbug.

Desmond approached his Dutch doll project with great care. He used a small saw and cut into a block of soft wood. He carved a torso, estimating it to be just about the right size to fit in the hand of a small child. He sanded the torso to give the body a more feminine shape. Holes were drilled around the level of the hips, so that legs might be fitted, and at the shoulder points, so that arms might be attached. Long gangly legs swung freely on peg-like hinges and dangled down from the compact body.

There is no doubt the project would have been healing. Like the doll, Desmond had felt motionless and inanimate – his legs a twisted jangle of bones and joints. But now, with his own determination, he was bringing the doll to life. Its hinged construction meant it could sit upright, if propped carefully. Desmond, too, could sit again, if the position of his body was just so. He turned the doll over in his hands, sandpapering its rough edges. As a final touch he painted the doll's face with red lips, dark eyebrows and lashes, and a spot of healthy pink for the cheeks. With each stroke of dark paint on the doll's wooden skull, his own black crown of hair, of which he had once been so proud, slowly began to return.

Desmond worked lovingly on his Dutch doll for weeks. Like a talisman, it represented something important to him, and for reasons that were not entirely clear to staff at the hospital at the time. When the toy was finally finished, he wrapped it in an oil cloth and placed it with the few meagre personal possessions he had been permitted to keep when he was first admitted to Callan Park.

•

By the end of June 1948, after more than six months' treatment, the doctors were satisfied with the progress they had made and no doubt congratulated themselves on their medical skill. They had mentally rehabilitated a man who had been defined as suicidal upon entry. Desmond Butler was now deemed legally 'sane' and the doctors at Callan Park telephoned Yvonne to let her know the good news.

Given a range of ailments continued to trouble him – some paralysis in his legs, pharyngitis (an inflamed throat and mouth) and chronic pain – he was transferred from the specialised mental health care facility at Callan Park to Royal Prince Alfred Hospital for further treatment. It was walking distance to the Butler home, if he'd been able to walk.

At RPA some of Desmond's symptoms improved, but not others. Ronnie and Podgey came to visit, as did Yvonne. 'I thought he improved while at hospital,' Podgey said. 'He seemed to have a better attitude, and I took that as an indication he was feeling better.' He recalled Desmond telling him, 'I am getting better, Podge. I'm looking forward to seeing the kids again. Won't be long now before I'm dancing again.'

While at RPA, his pharyngitis eased, but doctors still recorded that the pins and needles in his feet, along with his stomach and back trouble, never really went away. Unable to offer any explanation for these ongoing symptoms, the hospital explored further. Medical experts eventually conjectured he was suffering some form of toxicity.

When Desmond had originally presented at a Sydney hospital in late 1947, staff had been told that he was a suicide risk because he had threatened to take poison. When RPA staff revisited the idea that poison might have played a role in his condition more than six months later, they did so with an entirely different scenario in mind.

At some point after his admission to RPA, a doctor interviewed him extensively about his life. What was his diet like? Was he married? What was his home life like? What did he do for work? When Desmond said that he was a cleaner and had only been in the job for a few months before becoming ill, it piqued the doctor's interest. In September 1947, Desmond had begun working at Grace Bros. A month later he was sick.

The doctor asked Desmond about his typical work day. He described his regime and the cleaning fluids he used – soaps and disinfectants, bleaches and solvents. This led doctors to consider alternative explanations for his illness. Desmond had been asked before about his exposure to poisons, but he had been confused and distressed when he was first admitted to hospital. This time he was more lucid and his responses were more coherent. 'Yes, I work with poisons. Two at least,' he said.

It was Desmond's job to kill vermin and prevent infestations – in order to do this, he needed to understand what his pests liked to eat. Boracic acid could kill ants, but it was sour, so Desmond stirred the acid into a sugar and water solution and left shallow bowls of it where the tiny black specks had been seen marching single file through cracks in the walls and floor. To kill cockroaches, he used flour or cocoa (if it was available). The dense and dusty texture of common wheat flour and powdered chocolate helped to mask the bitter taste of borax. Although both boracic acid and borax were toxic to humans, they caused skin complaints more than anything else. Doctors discounted them as possible causes for Desmond's complex set of health conditions.

Desmond had responsibility for killing rodents at his workplace too. Mice generally preferred to eat whole cereal, so Desmond had soaked wheat in a liquid arsenic mixture until the grains bloated. He then left dishes of the wet mash in the darkened department store building, waiting for the nightly visitations by the vermin. But after decades of infestation in Sydney, rats had become shrewder. They avoided strychnine syrup because it was bitter. A mainstay poison since the plague, it was rumoured that many rats had become immune to it. And arsenic was no longer as effective as it once had been. Instead of strychnine or arsenic, Desmond's employer had supplied an alternative – phosphorus. Commercially packaged in paste form, it was Desmond's job to smear it onto fruit peelings and scraps of meat and leave it in the ceilings and the sub-floor.

It was common knowledge that the poisons Desmond worked with were toxic to humans, and if ingested could induce nausea and a range of other unpleasant symptoms. Desmond knew the risks, he said, but had taken precautions. Doctors considered the possibilities: perhaps he had absorbed the poison through the skin or inadvertently wiped it into his mouth or nose. Despite his protests, doctors at RPA took samples anyway: blood, urine and hair. They tested for the presence of cyanide, strychnine, arsenic, lead and phosphorus – all of which came back negative. Poison was discounted as a possible explanation for Desmond's condition in July 1948.

He remained at RPA for two weeks under observation. On 16 July, the registrar confirmed the prior assessment – 'no longer certifiably insane'. With no further answers available, Dr Goldie, Assistant Clinical Superintendent at the hospital at the time, discharged him. Desmond was still not a physically well man, but there was nothing more the hospital could do.

•

The doctors spoke frankly to Yvonne, telling her he'd be released into her care on 21 July, but that he still struggled to eat normal food, suffered immense pain, and couldn't walk on his own. The symptoms of peripheral neuritis hadn't really improved. Yvonne faced a sobering reality. The husband with whom she'd had a tempestuous relationship before he became ill was now coming home and would need round-the-clock care. We cannot know what she thought or felt privately; only what the neighbours observed.

Edith Roache lived at 43 Ferndale Street, just a few doors away from the Butlers. The day before Desmond's release, she'd been standing at the small section of broken wall outside her terrace talking to Mrs Withers when both women heard the Butlers' front door slam. A moment later, Yvonne barrelled out of the house and headed up the street.

While hundreds of families lived in the long rows of very compacted terraces which lined the streets of South Newtown, Ferndale itself remained quiet because it was not a thoroughfare. Beyond the corner of Ferndale and Margaret lay the main high streets of Enmore Road and King Street, and bustling Newtown train station. Beyond this was the hospital, the university grounds and Victoria Park, and the large Grace Bros. department store at Broadway. If one kept walking, the city was not far beyond that. Edith had become something of a street sentry on Ferndale Street as her terrace was positioned near the crossroad. She was older, her family had lived in the area for years and she had lived in the very same terrace for twenty of them. If you lived in Ferndale Street, and you wanted to get anywhere worth going, you passed Edith's front door.

Most pedestrians avoided the bumpy footpath and strode up the centre of Ferndale Street, confident they would not have to worry about traffic. And this is precisely what Yvonne did too. With brisk steps her heels clicked on up the road, and she shimmied with enough speed for her heavy faux-fur coat to billow a little. Despite being well acquainted with both of her neighbours, Yvonne gave every signal she did not want to talk. She looked flustered: her cheeks were flushed red, and fury radiated off her. Her eyes remained fixed on the intersection ahead.

Edith Roache boldly stepped in front of Yvonne as she tried to rush past. 'What's wrong, Bonnie?' she asked. Yvonne attempted to keep walking, but Edith wouldn't have it. The older woman held her hands up in the air, her arms extended, palms open, in the way one might when seeking to show reassurance to someone poised on the brink of a cliff edge. 'Bonnie?' she said again.

With one hand, Yvonne dabbed the corners of her eyes, curled her neck down and turned her face evasively away. Within the other hand she grasped a small overnight case. 'They're sending Dessie home,' she said in a high-pitched tone. 'I don't want him. They can take him back!'

Mrs Withers chimed in immediately. 'Oh, don't do that! Get the poor fellow on his feet first!'

'I'm not going to have him,' Yvonne replied. 'I'm not going to look after him. I don't want him.'

Mrs Withers didn't know what to say. Edith, however, did, and couldn't hide her disgust. She stared the young woman down. 'Gee, you're awful, Bonnie,' she said. Edith had seen Herbert Wood, the old pensioner, hanging around Ferndale Street. Edith and Mrs Withers had even gossiped about it on more than one occasion.

Emboldened by Edith's words, Mrs Withers turned to her neighbour and weighed in again. 'Dago Joe [their name for the dark-complexioned Herbert Wood] is always hanging around.' From her house, she'd seen him. 'He watched and waited to ensure that Desmond wasn't home. I know for a fact he sneaks in her back gate.'

At this, Yvonne pushed past the two women, picked up as much speed as her heels would permit, turned the corner and was gone.

•

Yvonne wasn't home the next day when the ambulance pulled into Ferndale Street. It crept past Edith Roache's house at number 43 in the distinctive way vehicles do when cruising to read house numbers. Further down the street, Phyllis Stewart noted the slow crawl of the approaching van as well. Both women observed silently from their different vantage points: Edith from her front porch; Phyllis from the rear of her property.

An ambulance attendant banged loudly on the Butlers' front door for what seemed like a very long time. When it was clear no one was home, the man walked down the side passage, right along the fence line, looking for the back door. He knocked loudly. When no one answered again, he returned to the vehicle. Phyllis now moved to the front of her house to listen more carefully. One of the attendants swung open the back of the van, and both men hopped out in the midst of a heated discussion about what they should do next. They agreed they could not drive the patient back to hospital because he had been formally discharged. At the same time, they were unwilling to leave him on a stretcher like a milk bottle on the front step. One of the attendants came up with a solution: break into the Butler home. Almost immediately, the same attendant returned to the rear of the Butler residence.

Moments later, the front door swung open, unlocked from the inside. 'I jimmied the latch on the back window. It was loose,' Phyllis heard one attendant say to the other. 'He's not a cooperative man,' said the other attendant. 'He's in a bad state for someone coming out of hospital . . . he wasn't able to walk,' said the first. Despite their reservations, the two men followed the orders given to them by more senior medical staff: take Desmond Butler home.

They carried Desmond in through the narrow doorway of the house on a stretcher and upstairs to the main bedroom, then lifted him into his marital bed. When Phyllis and Edith heard the ambulance drive back up Ferndale Street a short time later, they privately reassured themselves that Desmond was home safely.

•

Later that day, Edith Roache was surprised to hear a soft knock at her front door. When she opened it, a little girl was standing on her porch. 'The man from down the road said to give this to you,' the girl said, handing Edith a scrap of paper. For a moment she thought the child might be playing a trick, until she saw the words written in wonky scrawl: 'Can you come see me?' Next to it was simply the letter 'D'. Edith immediately set off in the direction of the Butler house.

When she arrived she was greeted with a scene that broke her heart. Desmond was sitting outside on the front porch. In the tumble of things tipped over, it was clear that he had managed to drag himself out there but been unable to do much else.

The Butlers kept a small table setting outside. Edith had memories of Desmond seated in exactly this spot. He had played cards with friends here, drunk liquor, talked work at the end of the day. The man she now saw bore almost no resemblance to the Desmond she had known. The garden bed outside was dead. No one had tended it for a long time. The old faded furniture was flaking paint. The chairs were overturned. Desmond sat in a wobbly outdoor chair, slumped like a marionette with no puppeteer. He was broken, framed by the backdrop of his broken-down home.

His attempts to retain the street-smart swagger that had defined him struck Edith as terribly sad. His striped and stained pyjamas hung slackly on his wasted frame. He had managed to balance a felt hat atop his head, tipped at an angle. Although he was slightly hunched over, and his wrist and hand were claw-like, Edith could see he had something grasped tightly within his fist.

She was speechless but she needn't have worried. After months in the hospital and the long absence away from friends and family, Desmond was eager to talk. He raised his fist in the air, and from it swung a jangle of wooden legs and arms. It was the Dutch doll he had worked so carefully to make at Callan Park. He slurred his words. Though he'd always drawled, and at times Edith had dismissed him as one fond of drink, she was sure he wasn't drunk now. 'I wanted to show you the doll I made; it's for Ellen,' he said with some excitement.

Ellen was a baby, Desmond's youngest, and his only daughter. The wooden toy he held in his hands was anything but pretty, and it didn't look suitable for a child that young. Edith admired the spindly legs and tapped the arms to see how freely they swung from their hinges. The doll shook unnervingly in the man's unsteady grasp. He smiled weakly and sadly for the longest time, before he let the stiffness of his arm drop, and the doll fell into a heap in his lap.

'Vonnie said I'm not to see her,' he said. Edith was confused for a moment, thinking that Desmond was somehow referring to the doll. Then she realised, with horror, that Desmond was talking about his daughter. 'Yvonne told her she's not to call me Daddy, she said that.' Then he fell quiet again.

Edith held back tears. She swept the doll out of Desmond's hand. 'She's just beautiful, Des,' she said. 'Beautiful.'

•

The next day, Yvonne came home and from the outside, at least, some normality appeared to return to the Butler household. She was seen leaving, and then returning with groceries. The sound of conversation could be heard. She was also seen running errands. One of those errands took her to Callan Park. The day after Desmond was discharged, she bowled up to the front desk and insisted on speaking to the most senior doctor on staff, Dr Kirkwood.

'I cannot manage him,' she told Dr Kirkwood, begging him to readmit Desmond on the grounds that he had not been cured. 'Broughton Hall has to take him in . . . I want a solution.'

Dr Kirkwood refused. 'Mrs Butler, the legal position is that your husband has been discharged. The patient is no longer certifiable. We have no authority in the matter at all . . . and no responsibility either. He is a free citizen and will remain so until he is recertified under the *Lunacy Act*, of course. You are a very brave woman in a difficult situation.' He then sent her on her way.

•

The following week, Phyllis heard a loud scraping, like a spade when it rasps and scratches, with the ringing of angry metal dragged across concrete. She tried to ignore it, but the noise was relentless, and loud. She went outside to investigate. The sound seemed to be coming from the very earth below, and she bent down and peered through the fence palings into the Butlers' property. When she saw the flash of striped pyjamas, she knew it was Desmond. Kneeling down, she watched carefully through the narrow slit of the fence. All was quiet for a moment. Then the noise resumed.

Phyllis had seen Desmond struggle before, but it was now even more pitiful. He couldn't use his legs, so he had folded them up onto a washboard and was attempting to use it like a toboggan. The scraping was the sound he made as he wrenched himself along the concrete path beside the house. Phyllis watched in stunned silence. Without wheels or any kind of traction, Desmond's washboard toboggan was failing miserably. For a moment she wondered why he persisted, until she realised where he was trying to go. He grunted and wheezed, and cried in frustration as he struggled to make it to the outhouse in time.

Though she wanted to help, the indignity of what she had witnessed stopped her. Desmond was a proud man, and had once been a strong man, and she knew how embarrassed he would be if she should reveal that she had seen him. Although she was less than a metre away, she slid back from the fence line without making a sound. Shaken, she went inside. She would wait for a more opportune time to say hello.

By that afternoon, Desmond had made his way around to the front porch and was clearly visible from the street. Phyllis took this as a signal that he wanted company. If she had not known for certain that it was Desmond, she would not have believed it. He was hunched, like a frail old man. His hands looked crippled and curled as if in pain. With a needle in one hand and a long coil of raffia in the other, he was attempting to stitch a table mat. But even this task seemed beyond him. He struggled in frustration. Even from the street, Phyllis could see dribble pouring from the corner of his mouth.

•

Podgey dropped in to see Desmond each day. He brought playing cards and booze, although Desmond struggled to even hold a hand. Instead they talked. On occasions, Desmond became so overwhelmed by sharp shooting pains in his legs that Podgey simply couldn't stand it. Any awkwardness the men felt about touching vanished. With his meaty hands, made strong by loading crates and ice, Podgey grabbed Desmond's spindly legs and swung them onto his lap, gently massaging his calves and feet.

But the suffering continued. As the week wore on, more and more of the street became aware of Desmond's declining health. Not a night passed without him crying out from the house at number 57. While neighbours saw Yvonne come and go, she never seemed to be there at night. The children had been moved to Yvonne's mother's house. This left Desmond alone much of the time, and neighbours had little choice but to notice. Desmond seemed to scream most when he was alone.

One particular night, a noise emanated from the Butler residence that disturbed Phyllis and Ronnie more than anything else they had ever heard before. Desmond did not cry out for help, nor did he rage, nor yell in fury. Instead, he beat on the floor. He thumped on the wall. Whether it was Morse code or not, his neighbours could not tell. Ronnie heard it and immediately went next door. He stayed with Desmond all night, just sitting quietly beside him in bed.

As time passed, the situation only got worse. Early one morning, neighbours were woken to the sound of a primal scream of pain. There were no words and the cries were so guttural it was hard to be sure they were human. They woke many people in homes surrounding the Butlers' including Roy and Phyllis and Ronnie next door. The Backhouses across the street were also jerked from sleep. The neighbours rushed out the front door, following the direction of the noise, and arrived outside the house on Ferndale Street, each with a small hand-held torch. They shuddered. For a house that had been filled with the sound of chatter and betting, laughter and the sound of the wireless, there was now something positively dark about number 57. There was no light on inside, the front door was wide open, and they all stared into the darkened hallway. In the shadows a man was screaming, just out of sight. The smell of urine and faeces wafted out into the street.

Desmond was alone. Yellowish-brown stains adorned one wall of his bedroom. The neighbours did what they could to settle him, but it was undignified to see a man behave in this way. When he fell asleep, they returned to their respective homes, shaking their heads in disbelief. They remained sceptical about his illness.

Phyllis was furious with Yvonne for failing to care for her own husband. She kept watch on the Butler home, and waited for Yvonne's return. At the first sound of a heel on concrete next door, she raced outside. Sure enough, it was Yvonne, entering from the back of the property and walking along the side path. Phyllis ran out the back of her own terrace and called boldly to Yvonne from over the fence.

'Vonnie!' she barked. 'Dessie was calling us all night! He seemed to be in pain.' She wanted to prick Yvonne's conscience and make her realise that the man needed attention. 'We had to go into him,' she said in desperation.

Yvonne started crying. 'I couldn't stay with him. I was frightened. Dessie might go at my throat with a knife. I cooked him a curry but he threw it at the wall. He can't even sip from a cup now. I have to feed him his Bonox from a spoon otherwise he won't have it.'

'Dessie wouldn't harm a fly!' Phyllis said. 'And he wouldn't hurt you, Yvonne. He hasn't got the strength to hurt anyone.'

•

Podgey's daily visits continued. While he had always stopped by after work, he now began coming after he finished his milk run, usually between 7 and 9 a.m. Then in the afternoon he would walk the dogs past the house at number 57. Conscious that his friend needed rest, he didn't knock, but would call out from the street. 'Are you there, Des?' Most days a meek 'Yes, Podge' wafted out. Podgey tied the dogs to the fence and would go in and spend half an hour with his friend. Podgey suspected that Yvonne was no longer living there, but she seemed to be coming and going regularly so he took comfort in the fact that at least Desmond was being fed, if not looked after in other ways.

Another night, the Backhouses followed the sound of weeping to the front door of the Butlers' home. They called out to the pitch-black house. Desmond didn't have the strength to reach up and flick on a light switch. This night frightened them. Like an increasing number of people in Ferndale Street, they saw just how desperate he'd become. When the sun went down, he sat alone in the dark with his thoughts. Lillian and Patrick Backhouse regularly heard him weeping. When they could stand it no more, Lillian sent Patrick to get a torch and go over there. The couple sat with Desmond. 'I'm frightened,' was all Desmond said. In the dark, and alone, Lillian and Patrick were frightened too. Unable to think of anything else to do, Patrick went home and came back with a bottle of brandy. They poured Desmond a few hard slugs, put the glass to his lips carefully, then left.

•

Yvonne made arrangements for a local physician, Dr Keith King, to visit. She asked him to support her husband's readmission to hospital. Dr King assessed Desmond on 22, 26 and 27 July and found that the man was clearly ill, but he could provide no clear reason as to the cause. Dr King's first description of Desmond was grim. 'He is suffering from peripheral neuritis. There is complete loss of hair, diminished eyesight and hearing. He has difficulty with speech. He is bedridden and incapable of getting out of bed unaided. He has lost the use of his hands and it is difficult for him to move his body. His condition appears to be one of utter helplessness.'

Edith found an old wheelchair, in the hope this might offer Desmond some mobility and a little more dignity. Within a fortnight, his legs had become almost completely paralysed. On one occasion, he managed to shuffle himself into the street in the wheelchair. He also successfully managed to get himself about halfway up the road by creeping the chair along a centimetre at a time, but became snagged on a bump in the footpath. Too weak to move, he sat marooned on his little metal island of wheels. When Edith came out into the street, she found Desmond weeping like a child. She felt compassion, but she was also embarrassed. Doctors could not and would not confirm that his pain had any real physical source. Word spread: it was all in the man's head.

One day, Edith invited Desmond over for lunch. She came around to his house, and then pushed him in the wheelchair up the street. As it was too wide to fit inside the narrow doorway of her home, she set up a small table outside and parked him on the front porch, trying to make the most of the warm winter sun. It was more cheerful to sit outside in the sunlight and fresh air, she said. Edith served curried eggs. Desmond said all he could stomach was boiled vegetables, so she cooked those as well. They talked about his health. He even managed a joke. 'I know you're always laughing, Edie. If I show you something do you promise not to laugh?' He lifted up the trouser of his pyjama legs and revealed what was underneath. The flesh was hanging off the bone, his skin sagging like a deflated balloon. Edith gasped. He then dipped his head so his hat fell to the ground. With great effort, he lifted his arm and dragged his hand across his scalp. His head was shiny and smooth and the remaining hair was so loose it simply rolled off his head into the palm of his hand. Edith gasped again. Desmond had a wide, sick grin across his face and a large hairy ball of black in his open palm.

'My God, you asked me not to laugh. You've made me cry now,' she said. Then they both started crying. Edith put her arm around Desmond's shoulder and leaned across him in the wheelchair. His was thin and brittle and she felt his skull against her chest.

As the afternoon wore on, Desmond grew concerned that he'd been away too long. 'Take me home before she gets there, Edie,' he said. 'But I've had a lovely day. Thank you.'

•

The Stewarts called a doctor next. They'd heard Desmond cry. This time it had been so loud and long and mournful it seemed inhuman. The man was so weak he could barely sit upright. He was bald and stooped and his body shook. He seemed to be blind as well. Dr King did not know why the man's condition had deteriorated so quickly, but he knew that he was looking at someone who was dying.

Phyllis watched as the ambulance took Desmond to hospital. He had always been very careful with grooming and proud of his thick black hair. This vanity did not go away. As he was leaving, and completely unaware of how pathetic he seemed, Phyllis saw him self-consciously stroking the few strands of hair that were left, combing them down with great care. She looked away and began crying.

In hospital, the doctor noted Desmond's physical condition upon arrival. 'He is incapable of doing very much . . . a protoplasmic mass . . . in the nature of a jellyfish.' Unsure what to do with the man, but acknowledging that he was not in a fit state to go home, they referred him back to Callan Park. On 28 July, duty of care for Desmond Butler passed back to Dr Wechsler at Broughton Hall.

Twenty-four hours later, he was dead.

When Podgey found out from the police what had happened, he went directly to Roy and Phyllis and Ronnie. Heartbroken, the friends huddled together in the kitchen, waiting for Yvonne to come home. As she unlocked the back gate, and proceeded towards the door, Phyllis called out loudly, with the shrill tone of someone strangled with emotion and grief, 'Mrs Butler! Did you know Dessie passed away last night? The police have been here.'

Yvonne paused. She was standing under the lean-to of the wash house. She called out, 'What?!' and then dropped like a stone, her legs collapsing beneath her. The group ran with haste next door. Podgey swept Yvonne up off the ground. Ronnie jimmied the latch on the Butlers' back door so that Podgey could bring Yvonne in. They laid her on the kitchen floor. Phyllis got her a glass of water. Podgey fanned her face.

•

On a table in the morgue, the medical examiners conducted an autopsy on Desmond Butler, finding that something had eaten away at the body of the man. The legs that had been tanned and lean were now thin and pasty. The arms which had been muscular and toned were now skinny and bony. In eight months, whatever ailed Desmond had taken his luscious crop of hair as well. The doctors had never seen anything like it, and had no explanation for what had happened.

Desmond George Butler was just thirty years old when it was determined by medical examiner, Dr Stratford Sheldon, that he had died of natural causes: a heart attack. Doctors suspected that his heart trouble was simply another manifestation of his madness. He had been such a nervous wreck, doctors also suggested he had compulsively torn his own hair out.

At his burial at Rookwood Cemetery in July 1948, the neighbourhood of Ferndale Street closed ranks, and refused to speak ill of the dead, at least openly. In an effort to leave the family and the man himself with some dignity, the cause of his death was sidestepped. It was thought that Desmond had gone mad, and in 1948 this was a humiliating way to die. He had not stoically shown strength, only fragility and neurosis. He was weak and everyone knew it. Though Yvonne had argued he was dangerous, no one had believed her. They did, however, think he was mad. And because he was mad, you couldn't believe a word that he said. The many doctors who had assessed him during his time in hospital all seemed to agree on one thing: Desmond Butler had stressed himself to death.

Curried eggs and boiled vegetables (1948)

Ingredients

4 hardboiled eggs, shells removed

1 cup milk

1 dessertspoon flour

1 dessertspoon butter

2 teaspoons curry powder

1 onion, finely diced

1 sour apple, finely diced

Method

Cook apple and onion together in a little water on the stovetop and set aside when soft. Using butter, flour and milk make a white sauce. Melt butter in a saucepan over a low heat, then add flour. Mix to make a thick paste. Slowly add milk, making sure to mix to prevent lumps forming. When a sauce is formed, add curry powder and mix. Add cooked apple and onion to the curry sauce. Then float whole boiled eggs (without shell) in sauce and reduce to a very low heat until warmed through.

Serve with boiled vegetables.

8

SPLIT PEAS

ON A SPRING EVENING IN 1951, BERTRAM HENRY FLETCHER prepared to go out. It was a cool night so he pulled on his worsted woollen trousers with the very deep pockets, and slipped into his warm sportscoat. He slammed the front door of his home in Alexandria and headed on foot towards the inner-city suburb of Erskineville, about twenty minutes away. It was late, and the suburb had fallen quiet as residents settled in for the night. Bertram passed row after row of terraces as he walked. Most were dark: only a few windows glowed with lamplight. Here and there, a dog barked at the sound of his footfall.

In his deep-grey herringbone sportscoat he blended into the shadows and crossed a lightless park unseen. Accustomed to navigating in the dark, he moved expertly through the streets.

He flew up Knight Street as if drawn to the fluorescent light which beamed out through the high louvres of the warehouse. As he skirted the long brick wall he looked left and right. Hand to mouth, Bertram inhaled deeply from the tiny nub of a cigarette wedged in his fingers. He approached a small door, curled his still-smoking fist and knocked quietly, twice.

The door opened, just a sliver. A thin column of light shone into the dark alley, bouncing off the garbage cans stacked in a row. Their metal lids momentarily gleamed gold like giant pennies, and the greasy puddles of petrol in the roadway reflected rainbow-coloured slicks. Bertram fumbled in his pocket, pulled out a quid and held it up so it was visible. The door opened, just long enough for him to slip inside.

The warehouse was crowded with several hundred men and quite a few women. It was hot and stuffy, and Bertram immediately regretted the choice of his warm sportscoat. A large sheet of metal had been propped against the one low window, and a man remained guard at the door, using the mail flap as a peephole. A large square of red carpet had been rolled out, muffling the sound of leather shoes and boots and heels on the concrete floor. An older man in a sharp suit, the ringleader, stepped forward and raised his hand in the air to attract the attention of all assembled. The crowd gathered more closely together in a circle.

The ringleader called out in hushed tones. 'The rules tonight, gentlemen, are sudden death!' And with that, another man, alone in the centre of the ring, placed three pennies on a long wooden paddle. The crowd now jostled, as punters began digging into their pockets, drawing out money and negotiating wagers. It remained very quiet in the warehouse but a sense of tension was building as the punters hurried to lay their money down. The ringleader called out in a whisper-shout, 'Come in, spinner!' just loud enough for everyone to hear. The man in the centre of the ring – the spinner – bent his knees and flipped the long wooden paddle into the air over his head. Three pennies took flight and rotated freely before they hit the carpet with a dull thud. Wins and losses were felt simultaneously across the room. It was over in seconds.

Illegal gambling was rampant in Sydney at the time, and there was a criminal racket to tempt every demographic. Changes to gaming laws in the late 1930s had sought to confine betting to racecourses, but attempts to stamp out illegal gambling appeared to have only driven it further underground. SP (starting price) bookmaking on the greyhounds and the horses was popular among men, particularly young men.

Illegal 'two-up' games had become a problem in the inner city, and it was not just men who turned up to play. Nicknamed 'two-up schools', they had sprung up in Paddington, Erskineville, Surry Hills and Redfern. One game had even been uncovered in a home on Ferndale Street in Newtown. It was easy to see why it had become a gambling craze in the postwar era: the game was logistically very easy to set up and popular with ex-soldiers. Only pennies, a paddle and punters were needed. The two-up games which operated in the inner city at the time were usually a rapid-fire variant of the game known as 'sudden death'.

Wins and losses in two-up are determined by throwing doubles – either two heads or two tails. In a regular two-up game, not every throw will yield a double. In sudden death two-up, three coins are tossed on every throw. This ensures no time wasting with re-throws because with every single flip at least one person gets lucky. Like hundreds of other locals who entered the Erskineville warehouse that night, Bertram Fletcher was hoping it was going to be his night. Yvonne Butler was at the very same warehouse on the very same night for the very same reason. Now a widow for over three years, she too was looking for a lucky break.

The war had been good to Yvonne, the most stable years she had ever known. Her job as a box maker had been steady and she had managed to hang onto it even though employers often preferred single women. With an income and with Desmond in prison, it was the most financial independence she'd ever had.

After the war was over, box manufacturers adapted to the changed demands for their product. Many local factories continued to employ women in 'light factory work' and in the canteens. But some contracted and changed their hiring practices, seeking to employ 'girls and women', but only if 'aged 15 to 25 years'. They were cheaper (their rates of pay were lower than men) and females at this age were less likely to be married and have children. Older women were considered a riskier proposition from an employer's standpoint.

Women with families were viewed as less committed to their jobs and less reliable – at least, according to the logic of the day. The desire for part-time work expressed by some women also created employer push-back. As J H Holman, General Manager of Butterfield and Lewis (printers and cardboard box makers, and one of Yvonne's previous employers), noted, 'We have never employed part-time workers and we don't intend to start. They cause too much disorganisation and jealousy.' In 1947 Yvonne turned twenty-five and was considered to be an 'older' woman. Any career she had was over.

For four years Yvonne worked part time – hosting in cafés, making sandwiches, and clearing tables – but none of these jobs lasted. The rosters were irregular and she did not make enough to feed two children and maintain a home. Yvonne was also unskilled. The certainty of her work in the box factory had ended with the war. After the war, with many returned soldiers needing work, the labour market had returned to the custom and practice of hiring men over women. Yvonne was struggling to get by.

She complained to her neighbours that Desmond had no life insurance. He'd blown all her savings, she said. She'd had to borrow ten pounds to pay for his funeral and it had taken her months to repay the loan.

Yvonne's mother, Dottie, tried to help her daughter in her own way, though this assistance did not always resemble the maternal support that social mores of the time might have deemed appropriate. Dottie showed little interest in helping Yvonne by looking after her grandchildren, although she had allowed Yvonne to stay at her house. She wouldn't help Yvonne pay bills, but she did buy her a flashy new sofa. She didn't prepare meals or do laundry, instead she helped Yvonne dye her hair. Yvonne's hair has been variously described as fiery auburn, sultry dark brown, and bold blonde. Dottie took pride in the results she had achieved with her own hair – a cropped and brassy platinum bob.

For a woman in Yvonne's situation in 1951 – with two children and nearing thirty – remarrying was about the only way to achieve economic security. But Yvonne was hesitant to repeat the mistakes of the past. Since Desmond's death she had received one marriage proposal, but rejected it. Mr Wood, the widower from Annandale who had taken a keen interest in her while she was married to Desmond, continued to pursue her. He took her to the pictures, to dances and on day trips to a house he owned in the Blue Mountains. Wood was at Yvonne's place a lot as well. Neighbours noticed, and asked about their relationship. Both denied it was anything other than platonic. Wood's explanation never changed: he had been hanging wallpaper at Yvonne's for over three years.

Though his name was Herbert Wood, everyone in the neighbourhood knew him as 'Dago Joe'. His dark complexion made him look 'continental', some said, and in the late 1940s this was racist code for 'foreigner', and more specifically 'a dark Italian'. Wood waited what he believed to be a respectful period for Yvonne to publicly mourn her husband, then made his move. On 1 January 1951 he proposed.

Yvonne did not mince her words. 'I can't see you anymore,' she said. 'It's time for me to look for a job and I need an eligible husband to marry.'

Wood was undeterred. 'But you could marry me, Yvonne. We already get on so well.'

'No.' In an awkward attempt to soften the blow, she added, 'I would marry you. If you were a much younger man, I would. But it would only be a repetition in a year or two of what I have already gone through.'

Yvonne had been widowed once and had no intention of that happening again.

•

We cannot know what words were exchanged between Yvonne and Bertram Henry Fletcher on the night they met at the two-up game, though we do know what they saw. Bertram looked and dressed sharp. Known locally as 'Bluey', he had wide, fleshy lips which he pulled into a smile that was so big and full, it created playful dimples. He was clean shaven, with slicked-back auburn-red hair and a lean and strong body. In his dark-grey herringbone sportscoat with grey flannels, he gave the appearance of a man who was pretty happy with how he had turned out. Yvonne took great pains with her appearance, too, and in her beloved faux-fur coat she was hard to miss. She used make-up to accentuate her features: her eyebrows were lined pencil thin, her lips were heart shaped and painted a sultry red.

Both were prepared to take risks to get ahead. Both had chanced arrest to attend an underground two-up game. Both were barely thirty years old and had already lived a lifetime of trouble by the time they met.

Bertram had failed as both a husband and a soldier. He had served during World War II as part of the CMF (Citizen Military Forces), but the reputation of these soldiers in the area was poor indeed. The AIF (Australian Imperial Force) was made up of volunteers who had signed up indefinitely and could be sent literally anywhere in the world. The local CMF comprised many who had enlisted to undertake home defence, because they had been compelled to. Bertram had walked down to sign up at the local enlistment office in Forest Lodge. The rivalry between the AIF and CMF was legendary and it had been to the CMF's detriment.

Members of the CMF could be transferred to the AIF, but many were not. The CMF recruits were classified and treated differently within the armed forces and it led to a wider perception of these enlisted men as non-soldiers. Ridiculed as 'chocos' (short for soldiers made of chocolate, who pranced about looking good in uniform but melted under pressure), Bertram's service record was not the kind that earned him respect in the community.

Both Yvonne and Bertram had also experienced catastrophic failures in their relationships. Bertram married Hazel Walker in 1946, but the marriage had not lasted five years and they were divorced barely a month before he met Yvonne. Yvonne had been a widow for over three years, and it was rare to find someone local who had not heard of the scandalous Butler relationship and the marriage of a Newtown girl to a man from Melbourne who had gone mad.

Yvonne and Bertram went to the warehouse two-up game in 1951 as alike as two peas in a pod. In that smoke-filled room, the man cloaked in grey herringbone saw the woman draped in leopard print, and they recognised something familiar in the other – like littermates reunited. By 1950s standards Bertram and Yvonne were no longer young, but they were still young enough to want more from life than what had been handed to them. On 17 November 1951, Bertram Fletcher and Yvonne Butler (née Bogan) were married in a local church in Newtown. They had known each other less than eight weeks.

By all accounts, the marriage soured almost immediately. If Yvonne had assumed that Bertram would swoop in to parent her two children, she was sorely mistaken. Bertram cared nothing for Ray and Ellen. Yvonne knew this because Bertram told her so. He verbally abused the children and said they were as worthless as their dead father.

Tensions in the marriage escalated. Rows were heard coming from the Fletcher home. Bertram withheld money. He lost money at the races. He drank. He began to beat Yvonne. He also beat Ray. According to Yvonne, the boy endured some savage hidings. He was only eight years old at the time.

Even though Bertram was physically abusive towards Yvonne and her son, she still did not initially consider divorce as an option. For a start, divorce was not straightforward:

there were many steps involved and it took a long time, some-times years. In the 1950s, a circuitous legal process had to play out in court, and was resolved only after a judge had assessed who was to blame for the marriage failure. The *Family Law Act* of 1975, which introduced 'no-fault' divorce, was more than twenty years away. In 1952, a divorce on the grounds of abuse was hard to prove. To achieve a legal separation Yvonne would need many things: evidence of ill treatment, determination, and something even harder to get – enough money to pay a lawyer. In order to legally dissolve a marriage, even an unhappy one, a petitioner needed to accuse and lay blame, and had to be prepared to lay their own life bare in court as well. Unless Yvonne reported her husband for assault, evidence of ill treatment did not exist.

Yvonne's reluctance to divorce was about more than the legal hurdles. The terminology used in the mid-twentieth century to describe divorce was derisive and judgemental. In an article printed in *The Sun* newspaper, an editorial summa-rised the societal perceptions surrounding the dissolution of a marriage. 'It is impossible to pick up any child delinquency treatise without seeing pointed references to the factor of the "broken home" as the outstanding causation of the problem child. A parent who fails to consider that before contem-plating divorce or separation is simply refusing to do his or her job.' There is no doubt that Yvonne felt doubly conflicted about the notion of divorce. She worried about the impact it might have on her children. She knew first hand what it was like to carry the social stigma associated with being a child of divorce – because she was one. Yvonne had come from what was described at the time as a broken home, and when it broke, the noise of its demolition had been heard across Sydney.

When Dottie and Harry Bogan divorced in 1927, it made headlines. At the time, divorce proceedings were covered extensively by court reporters. Newspapers regularly published updates of divorce matters just as they did with birth, marriage and funeral notices. These updates routinely included orders of decrees 'nisi' and 'absolute'; the reasons for a divorce being obtained; and a recount of the accusation and defence made by the petitioner and respondent. Many petitioned for divorce on the grounds of desertion. For women, desertion was relatively easy to prove because economic security usually came from a husband's income. When a husband absconded, and failed to financially provide, women could claim destitution because the labour market at the time offered limited opportunities for them to earn a living and provide for themselves. Desertion was not, however, a factor in the Bogan divorce. Their marital differences were about sex.

Discussion of sexual intercourse in the divorce court was not unusual. Husbands and wives often raised issues of sexual discord and judges ordered the restitution of conjugal rights to aggrieved parties in the belief this would 'save' a marriage. Even by 1920s standards, however, the Bogan divorce was a scandalous one.

Harold Bogan did not petition for divorce because Dottie was uninterested in sex. He had found the opposite to be true.

Dottie sought sex, a lot of it, and Harold's main objection seemed to be it wasn't occurring with him.

In the matter of *Bogan v Bogan* in the Supreme Court of NSW, Dottie's infidelities became a matter of public record. Her adultery with her lover, Alfred (West aka Westweller), was transcribed in forensic detail. Journalists printed news of the infidelities in *The Sydney Morning Herald* and *The Sun*: in November and December 1927 for the granting of the decree nisi, and in 1933 for the granting of the decree absolute. The legal proceedings reported how Dottie had conducted her affair and it changed the way that family, friends and neighbours viewed the Bogans forever. The Bogan residence was no longer just a regular two-storey terrace, identical to the thousands of others like it in the Newtown and Erskineville areas, but a site where forbidden carnal desires had been fulfilled. Family and friends could read, in detail, how Harold had come home after a day's work to rest in his family room, only to find Alfred nested in the love seat he had bought for himself.

Though the divorce was granted, the trouble did not end there. Harry left the inner city and went to live in Parramatta with a new partner. He did not take his children with him. Dottie remained in the family home, but she did not keep the children either. Yvonne and her siblings were separated and sent to live with other family members. At just six years old, the divorce of Yvonne's parents had not just dissolved their marriage but led to the dissolution of her entire family.

For Yvonne, there was more confusion to come. After their harrowing and humiliating divorce, less than five years later Dottie and Harry reconciled. Not only were they living together again – now as divorced husband and wife – but they had returned to the same place where it had all ended so badly. Although her parents were seeking to rebuild their family and pick up where they left off, they did not see fit to include Yvonne in these plans. Yvonne was raised by others and her early childhood experiences would have left her with one clear and resounding perception – divorce was catastrophic, and there was no healing from it.

Now, barely thirty years of age, Yvonne had gone even further backwards. Her life with Desmond had been difficult, and unhappy, but she had not lived in fear. Four years later she found herself living in terror, in a terrace which bore a striking resemblance to the broken home of her own childhood. Yvonne faced a tough choice. Leaving represented risks, but so too did staying.

It was only after Bertram punched her in the face, with a key between his fingers, that new feelings stirred within Yvonne. For the very first time in her life, she began to seriously consider divorce. She spoke to Edith Roache, and to the Stewarts who lived next door, but not her mother. She even spoke to Florrie, Bertram's sister. After one particularly vicious beating, she turned up at Florrie's house nursing a bruised face and a black eye. Yvonne told Florrie, 'I'm walking up to Newtown police station.' And she did. But it was the weekend and police were reluctant to press charges. They actively discouraged women from filing assault charges against their husbands, and did not always believe that violence within a marriage was a problem, as some defined it as discipline. Yvonne pressed the issue and showed the police her many bruises but the officer at the front desk told her to come back on Monday when more duty staff were on shift. They could help her take out a summons for an assault.

It is unclear why Yvonne approached someone in her husband's own family about the problems in her marriage. Perhaps she felt that although Florrie was Bertram's sister, she was still a reasonable person who would give her a fair hearing. Or perhaps it was a sign of how unpredictable and violent Bertram had become. Perhaps Yvonne believed that Florrie, as a woman, would sympathise. And for a moment, on Saturday, Florrie did seem to see how difficult Yvonne's situation was. This perception changed, however, the moment that Florrie spoke to Bertram's father, Henry. By the time Monday rolled around, Henry had talked Yvonne out of pressing charges against his son.

Yvonne experienced what many victims of domestic violence knew to be a major barrier to disclosure: family loyalty. Experts in the field of domestic violence argue that loyalty remains a complex barrier to many victims speaking out, even to this day. Some victims feel loyal to partners, despite suffering years of abuse. Victims also fear the wrath of in-laws, as old family loyalties align to silence the victim and preserve the respectability of the family name.

The arguments in the Fletcher household continued. Bertram complained about the cost of running the house. Neighbours noticed that Yvonne and Bertram were barely seen together anymore. Bertram stayed out, and came home late. The children stayed away from their own home, often for long periods. Yvonne did her best to keep them out of Bertram's sight.

While sitting at the breakfast table one morning, the very same table she had shared with Desmond, Yvonne spoke to Bertram about the problems with the house. It was now summer and the rats were breeding.

'You have cleaning products and poison at work, don't you, Bertie?'

'Yeah, why?'

'Can you bring home some rat poison? The rats around here have got terrible. I've spotted a great big one I want to get rid of. I'm frightened of it, Bertie.'

Bertram brought a bottle of Thall-Rat home the following day, dropped it onto some wet bread, lay it in a saucer and placed it in a dark place – under the house.

•

The arguments escalated in the lead-up to Christmas. The screaming was so loud, it carried into Ferndale Street.

'You know what they say about you, Von? They reckon you killed Dessie because you were a terrible wife!'

'Don't be ridiculous, Bertie!'

On another occasion, neighbours heard wailing in the night. They recognised the scream as Yvonne's because they had heard it before. Then a dark female silhouette was seen in the street, shepherding two smaller figures into a terrace two doors down from number 57. As she ran, the neighbour heard Yvonne yell clearly, 'Don't let him kill my children! Please!'

On yet another occasion, Phyllis saw Yvonne in an absolutely shocking state. Yvonne claimed Bertram had punched her so hard she had needed a blood transfusion. As a boxer, he knew how to punch hard.

When the Fletcher household fell silent again, neighbours disregarded what they had seen. When neighbours saw the house fall into a kind of normal rhythm, they dismissed any notion of danger. Smells of home-cooked meals still wafted into the street. Bertram still left for work each day just like every other man in the neighbourhood. He was moody, Yvonne said. The neighbours thought little more about it.

Yvonne continued to cook for Bertram, and the convenience afforded by kitchen appliances of the time assisted her ability to do so. Bertram didn't eat at home with the family, but he always had breakfast before he left for work. With the convenience of an automatic pop-up toaster, Yvonne prepared a breakfast very common for working-class families because it was cheap – toast with butter and jam. Tinned jam was an affordable luxury. Toasters were not only labour saving but popular with budget-conscious families as they ensured that an entire loaf of bread was eaten, even if stale. Toasters also reduced wastage. Bertram had no objection to the purchase of a toaster.

Yvonne also made lunch for Bertram every day. Sometimes it was a sandwich wrapped in a sheet of newspaper, but most often it was a thermos of soup. Yvonne capitalised on the opportunities presented to her – a market flooded with postwar consumer durables. The manufacture of the portable pint aluminium-and-glass thermos had been important during the war because it permitted the storage and transportation of food stuffs without spoilage. In the late 1940s, astute manufacturers turned their attention to a new market: working families. Lunch pails and thermos bottles were sold in their thousands. Yvonne bought one for Bertram. She cooked soup in the evening – split pea and ham or vegetable – then reheated it in the morning and put it into his thermos so it would stay hot until his lunch break.

Lionel Morgan, a work mate who shared a roster with Bertram, noticed the change in him first. He noticed because he felt that Bertram was bludging, and it was Lionel who was picking up the slack. Bertram had worked in nearby Alexandria for fourteen years as a bottle sorter at Butler and Norman glass merchants. He picked the faulty bottles from the good ones as they came off the production line. Lionel watched Bertram eat his soup from his aluminium thermos, and not long after he would see his colleague sneak off.

'Lionel, I gotta go lie down. Can you keep an eye out for the boss?'

Lionel had heard the request more than once and was annoyed. 'Married life doesn't agree with you, mate,' he said. 'You used to be a good worker.'

'I just feel sick, mate, I gotta go lie down for a bit.'

•

On 7 February 1952, Edith Roache heard a soft knock on her door. She assumed it was a neighbour, come to share the big news that had just broken – King George VI had died. At the time, Australia maintained a colonial mindset and still looked to England as the mother country. Edith had already heard the news on the radio, and expected Mrs Withers was knocking on the door to tell her about it.

The last person Edith expected to see was Yvonne. The two women were not really friends, but neither could they be called enemies. They had lived in the same street for seven years, and both knew the importance of remaining on good terms with neighbours. Edith was not just startled that Yvonne was there on her front doorstep, she was shocked at the state she was in. Yvonne had a huge sticking plaster across her forehead, which did little to cover the bruising. Her hair, usually meticulously styled in glossy pin curls, looked a wreck. She held both her hands up to her face. Scrunched in one hand was a handkerchief, soaked in blood. She was unsteady and with her busted face she looked to Mrs Roache like someone who had gone three rounds. It was clear whose face had hit the canvas.

'Von! What's wrong? You look terrible!' she said. Edith had heard the arguments in the Fletcher household but didn't know about the violence. Still, she didn't believe the situation warranted any kind of neighbourly intervention. Marriages were private matters between husbands and wives, and no one else's business.

'We've had another row,' Yvonne said. 'He hit me over the head. He's split it open, I think.' Yvonne peeled away the handkerchief to reveal a jagged cut in her face.

'Von, this can't go on. You have to come to some kind of agreement and part, because if you keep on like this it's only a matter of time before one of you will land a fatal blow. You'll be charged with murder.'

'Oh, don't say that,' was all Yvonne said.

•

About a month later, on Saturday 8 March, Bertram turned up at Florrie's place unexpectedly. She lived in Newtown, but further north in Susan Street, just near Royal Prince Alfred Hospital.

'I don't know what's wrong with me, Florrie. I've got a funny feeling like pins and needles in my feet.' Bertram moaned in pain as he said it. He banged his feet on the floor, as if desperately trying to wake them up and jolt some feeling back into them.

Florrie brought her brother in and helped him put his feet up. She made him a cup of tea.

'I know you're not well, Bertie, but you don't seem very happy either,' she said.

'It's her. We had another real big argument last night.' Bertram told Florrie they had argued about poison. 'I think she's trying to kill me. The neighbours now all think she killed Dessie Butler.'

'You can't be serious, Bertie.'

'You don't think she would?'

Flo sipped her tea.

'I tell you how silly she is, Flo,' Bertram went on. 'She says she has a glass with my fingerprints on it with orange juice and poison in it.' It was proof, perhaps, that if Bertram was poisoned, he had done it himself. 'She even asked me to bring home another bottle of rat poison. She said, "I'll drink it to prove it – I didn't kill you."'

'Bertie, if you really think that, you have to go to the police.'

Bertram didn't stay long. Florrie was worried, but not overly. Her brother's new relationship was stormy, but she did not believe there was much to be concerned about, and certainly not enough to change her plans. She left home about 11 a.m. to spend the day at the racecourse.

Early on Sunday morning, less than twenty-fours later, Florrie's phone rang. It was RPA. Bertram had been admitted. A nurse spoke with a sense of panic in her voice. 'I recommend you come urgently,' she said.

When Florrie got to the ward, Bertram was in an absolute panic. 'Flo, they are trying to send me home! My legs are gone!'

Florrie argued with the hospital staff, advocating on Bertram's behalf. 'There is something seriously wrong. My brother is a healthy man. He barely smokes and he rarely drinks. He's a sportsman. He boxes. You need to get to the bottom of this.'

They discharged him anyway. Bertram wrapped his arm around Florrie's shoulder, and she took most of his weight as she walked him home to her place so she could nurse him. She didn't think he should be left alone.

By Tuesday, his condition had worsened. Florrie called Dr George McDonald Thomson and asked him to make a house call. The suddenness of Bertram's illness disturbed the doctor. He was vomiting violently and regularly. Dr Thomson ordered Bertram back to hospital. He also started talking to Bertram's family. He believed that Bertram was suffering the effects of metallic poisoning. He had seen it before.

Florrie asked Dr Thomson directly, 'Could the poison have been given to him?'

'It could be given, just like rat poison.'

In that moment, Bertie's words returned to her. 'I may as well tell you. I've been told that my brother's wife's first husband died like that.'

But she did not entirely believe the outrageous thing that her brother claimed. Later, during a moment of calm, they discussed it again.

'You don't think she would toast that bread and give it to me on that, do you, Flo?'

'I do not think she would do that, Bertie.'

'It looks as though I was the rat. All I want is a hole to crawl into and die.'

'You don't think she would poison you, do you, Bertie, really?'

'I think she would do anything, Flo, if she thought she could get away with it.'

•

Bertram's father, Henry, came to the hospital, demanding to know what was going on. He did not entirely believe that Yvonne would do what Bertie claimed. He also knew his son could be pretty wild and reckless. 'Did you take anything to make yourself sick?' He looked at his son sternly. 'Did you take poison or anything like that? They are asking questions, Bertie, they are better off knowing if you have.'

'Pop, no. That is one thing I would not do. If I had I would have made a good job of it and not been suffering like this.'

Henry looked for a long time at Bertram, prostrate in bed. Until very recently, his son had been a strong man with a good boxing stance who wasn't afraid of a fight. Now, he barely recognised him: he whined, his mouth was covered in sores, and he was unable to stand. Henry sought out a doctor and told him his son wasn't like this before he married Yvonne. Authorities were alerted to the possibility that Bertram Fletcher was being poisoned not because of crack police work, but because he told them so.

Dr George McDonald Thomson and Dr John Ernest Goldie, senior staffer and Clinical Superintendent of RPA, concurred. Bertram was suffering from peripheral neuritis, and the cause was most likely poisoning. There was just one problem – which poison?

Doctors knew that heavy metal poisoning caused hair loss and gastric symptoms. Those poisoned with arsenic often smell of garlic; those poisoned by vacor smell of peanuts; and those who have taken cyanide smell of bitter almonds. Bertram's symptoms did not fit the known profile of poisons.

Dr Goldie ordered the tests for arsenic and lead immediately, but both came back negative. Bertram had mentioned Thall-Rat and the doctors considered the possibility of thallium, and how they should test for it. They did not know, however, how quickly they were running out of time.

On 23 March 1952, Henry went to see his son, who was now in a terrible state. 'I'm crook. I'm dying,' was all he could say.

He died later that very same day, at 4.45 p.m. He had remained remarkably lucid till the end, and had told everyone who he thought was responsible. Still, in accordance with protocol, the hospital released his body to Yvonne, his next of kin, who brought him home and laid him out in the front sitting room so that friends and family might say their final farewells.

•

Bertram Henry Fletcher's funeral procession left from number 57 and travelled down Ferndale Street. Neighbours assembled in front of their own homes – at their gates, or in their yards – forming a silent guard of honour.

Mrs Withers called out, 'Look! Mrs Roache! It's Dago Joe!' Herbert Wood, the elderly widower who had been seen with Yvonne around the time of Desmond's death, had come.

It stuck in Edith Roache's craw and she did not hide it. He was leaning against an electricity pole and waved at Yvonne. Watching from her yard, Edith gasped at the disgraceful shamelessness of it all. She shook her head as the cortege crawled slowly past.

Yvonne waved back.

Split pea soup (1952)

Ingredients
1 cup diced split peas
2 and a half quarts cold water
2 cups milk
Half pound pickled pork
1 onion
3 tablespoons butter
3 tablespoons flour
Salt and pepper
Teaspoon Worcestershire sauce
Milk, as needed

Method
Soak peas in water for several hours. Drain. Add cold water, pork and onion. Simmer for 3–4 hours until mixture is soft enough to rub through a sieve. In another saucepan, make a roux with the butter and flour. Add roux, salt and pepper, and Worcestershire sauce to the pea and ham mixture. Dilute or thicken with milk to taste.

9

STOMACH, HEART, LUNG, LIVER AND KIDNEYS

HENRY FLETCHER AND HIS DAUGHTER FLORRIE CONTACTED THE police and shared their suspicions regarding Bertram's death. They talked about Yvonne, and about the rumours circulating around the death of her first husband, Desmond. The matter was referred to the Criminal Investigation Branch (CIB): the unit within the NSW police force responsible for solving serious crimes like murder.

Superintendent James Wiley, chief of the CIB, was sceptical. A narrow-faced man with an aquiline profile, Wiley was known for his measured and controlled judgements. By 1952, he had worked on countless murder cases and his experience was virtually unmatched in the department at the time. He had cut his teeth on some of the toughest cases in Sydney, including the murders of Bessie O'Connor and Iris Marriott in 1932. He had smashed drug rings – the 1930s equivalent of meth labs – by raiding illegal pharmaceutical manufacturers. He had exposed counterfeit money rings. Early in his career, he had even been shot in the face while chasing two armed robbers. He had lived to tell the tale, but his mouth had been permanently marked with a bullet-shaped dent in his top lip.

Wiley was seasoned, cautious, and had good instincts. He knew that building a successful murder case relied on some key pieces of evidence, and with Fletcher's death some of these elements were missing. Bertram Fletcher had fallen ill and died; the fact that doctors couldn't diagnose his illness was not overwhelming evidence of anything nefarious as far as Wiley was concerned. Henry Fletcher presented as an angry father with a deep dislike for the woman his son had married, but this did not make her a murderer. An accusation alone was not enough. An investigation could not progress without good reason.

Wiley's concerns were well founded. Unexplained deaths which suggested poison might have played a role were among the most difficult cases for police to navigate. Intentional poisoning remained a tricky thing to prove: suicide was always a possibility and accidental exposure to the toxin had to be ruled out as a cause of death as well. The science often confounded the investigating officers. Many struggled to comprehend laboratory and pathology reports, because the baseline level of scientific knowledge among officers was so low. The science surrounding the study of poisons was also continually changing: the data needed to understand acute toxicity was developing, but slowly.

As chief of the CIB, Wiley was required to report publicly on the performance of his department. He remained keenly aware of the need to maintain high clearance rates for serious crimes like murder, because it was a metric closely scrutinised by both the government and the press. The reputation of the police force relied on the preservation of law and order, and this meant ensuring murder investigations progressed to trial. A high rate of unsolved murders reflected very poorly on the department.

Taking on a case like Fletcher's – one with so many uncertainties – was not something that a savvy police superintendent would do lightly. A criminal act like murder required police to gather evidence on two elements: presence of a guilty mind (mens rea) and guilty conduct (actus reus). Wiley carefully considered the legal findings relating to the death of Desmond Butler. The matter had already been thoroughly investigated by the medical examiner back in 1948 and nothing suspicious had been recorded at the time. How can guilt be proved when it is not even clear that a murder has been committed?

Within two weeks of Henry Fletcher's call to the police department, startling new developments began to unfold. The doctors at RPA who had assessed Bertram Fletcher, and then helplessly watched him die, were also beginning to ask some very serious questions. How had a young and healthy man who presented at their hospital with no signs of chronic disease died so suddenly? The doctors refused to sign a death certificate.

Dr Stratford Sheldon and Dr Percy, the government medical officers responsible for undertaking autopsies, were called in. Neither could identify a cause of death. They removed Bertram's stomach, heart, lung, liver and kidneys, and snipped hair and fingernail clippings before the body was released to Yvonne. It took more than two weeks for the laboratory tests to be completed. No cyanide. No arsenic. No lead. But the tests did confirm the presence of 0.2 milligrams of a heavy metal per 100 grams of the samples of organic material gathered from Bertram's body. The metal was called thallium.

Once thallium had been identified, some questions surrounding his death began to be answered. It was not found in Bertram Fletcher's hair, nor in his fingernails – as might be the case in someone who had experienced metallic poisoning over a prolonged period. In Bertram's case, it appeared he had ingested large doses. After it is swallowed, thallium has the potential to travel to many sites across the body, concentrating quickly when large quantities are taken over a short period. Thallium had compromised Bertram's entire cardiovascular system. It had poisoned his heart.

By the end of March 1952, it was clear that further exploration of Bertram Fletcher's death was necessary. With the information supplied by the toxicology reports, Superintendent Wiley now knew what had killed Bertram. What they needed to find out was how the thallium had been ingested, and who was responsible.

Wiley assigned the investigation to Detective Sergeant Donald George Fergusson and Detective Constable Frederick Claude Krahe. Fergusson, who would lead the investigation, was born in 1912. Krahe was born in 1919. Both were country boys, but from very different families – Fergusson was from Newcastle, Krahe from Kyogle, a tiny town in the far north of New South Wales just near the Queensland border. Together, however, they would form a powerful partnership.

At the time of his recruitment, Krahe had been one of many young men in the town of Kyogle looking to improve his station. The Krahes were a family of factory hands, clerks and blacksmiths, many of whom had suffered during the tough economic period of the 1930s. With limited job opportunities in the town at the time, and few career options in an economy that was only just starting to emerge from the impacts of the Depression, Krahe picked the police force. One account of his life states that he was one of seventeen local boys to sign up on April Fool's Day 1937. As Tony Reeves, investigative journalist, notes, 'No one in the same intake would make such a name, or as unsavoury a reputation for himself as Fred Krahe.'

By the late 1940s, the career achievements of Detective Constable Krahe and Detective Sergeant Fergusson had been slow to accumulate. For Fergusson it was break and enters, burglary investigations, and collaring those involved in punch-ups in swish city restaurants. None of Fergusson's early policing efforts had been very distinguished. Fergusson had even faced the humiliation of being tricked by criminals. In a 1948 case, he had raided homes in pursuit of escaped prisoners. It was a mad scramble of an operation, and Fergusson had been fooled completely: every tip-off about the locations in which the escapees were hiding had been false.

Still, he had risen through the ranks, his position propelled by two vital factors – family and fraternity. Donald was the only son of high-profile police superintendent George Gilbert Fergusson, and both men were deeply committed to a secret fraternity. Dr Richard Evans, lecturer in criminology at Deakin University, notes that advancement in the NSW police force has historically been aided by one's religious affiliation. The Fergussons were Freemasons. Donald Fergusson had risen quickly through the ranks, and so had his father, aided by the affiliation with another high-profile Freemason – Commissioner William John Mackay. Investigative journalist Evan Whitton, who has written extensively on the underbelly of NSW policing, argues that Fergusson was a dedicated member of the guild and especially dutiful in the memorising and recitation of the liturgies, rituals and ceremonial protocols.

There is no doubt that Fergusson enjoyed perks that other officers did not. His role as a police officer had even got him to the Olympics. As a young man, he'd been a keen sportsman. He played football and ran track and field, but had not excelled. In 1936 he went to the Olympics as a rower, as part of a police team that his father promoted and managed.

George Fergusson was an ambitious man. In 1936 he announced that the NSW police would be sending their own rowing team to the Berlin games. While there was nothing that prevented police officers from competing as individuals, it was highly unusual for the police to enter their own 'branded' team. Stranger still, the police decided to do so without any funding from the official body – the Australian Olympic Committee – which seemed to tolerate more than outright endorse the contingent. Constable Donald Fergusson was picked for the Australian Olympic NSW Police Men's Eight, managed by his father, Inspector George Fergusson. The NSW Police Federation funded the trip, with every police officer in New South Wales levied two shillings from their pay to cover the costly international travel.

George Fergusson's arrogance did not stop there. Throughout the training regime and official engagements, he seemed determined to stir the pot. While the rest of the athletes always sported the official Olympic uniform – deep green blazers with gold piping and the Australian coat of arms – the Men's Eight were often seen publicly wearing full police uniform. Of the thirty-three Olympic athletes to compete for Australia that year, it must have been strange indeed to see the rowing team in full blue regalia with 'NSW Police' emblazoned across specially made hats and jackets. George Fergusson went along as the team's unofficial manager, paid for courtesy of the NSW Police Federation as well. For Fergusson, Olympic participation seemed to be about police patriotism more than anything else.

Once in Berlin, the NSW police team's performance confirmed why the Olympic Committee had had their reservations. The rowers did not even get past the qualifying rounds. Their failure did not deter George Fergusson from glorying in the fact that his son had made it to the Olympics. It didn't seem to matter to him that nepotism, not merit, had got him there. The Fergusson residence in Rose Bay, the place that Donald's mother and father proudly called home for many years, was named 'Rowlands'.

Detective Constable Krahe might not have had family connections in the force, but his advancement was greatly assisted by his close association with Fergusson. By 1952 Krahe was a high-profile officer in the homicide squad, with a reputation as a fearsome, determined man. There was little that seemed to rattle him. Krahe got outcomes. He had a habit of eliciting typed and signed confessions behind closed doors, which were then wholly denied after the fact. In one of the first cases of its kind, Krahe had managed to secure a conviction in a murder where there had been no body, and the case had been built entirely on circumstantial evidence. There is no doubt that Krahe took personal pride in the psychological victory of mentally conquering a suspect. He had a reputation for hard and violent interrogations.

The formation of the alliance between Fergusson and Krahe occured at an auspicious time in the era of policing in New South Wales. Both officers were eager to get ahead, and both knew that career progression was as much about image as it was about accomplishment. By 1952, both men had advanced to higher-status investigative roles. Outwardly, at least, both were of good character. Both were married, raising families in Sydney's eastern suburbs. Donald George Fergusson married Sylvia Pearl Doring from 'Sylvania' in Bendemeer, an area just outside of Tamworth known for its respectable agricultural and pastoral families. Krahe was married to Phyllis Gladys Roache, a respectable Church of England girl. In the police force, maintaining a reputation of good character was vital. The very public disgrace of an officer in the 1940s had proven this beyond doubt.

As head of the CIB's homicide squad, Detective Sergeant Thomas Walter McRae had been a kingpin. His career highs had included the successful capture and conviction of infamous eastern suburbs killer Eric Craig throughout 1932 and 1933. In 1934, McRae had been pivotal in the investigation of the famous 'pyjama girl' found dumped in a culvert in Albury. Even though his efforts had failed to discover the identity of the victim, this didn't hurt his career progression. Indeed, none of the professional wins or losses would be the deciding factor in McRae's career trajectory.

In November 1940, someone tipped off police that McRae had been seen meeting with a woman, on a regular basis, in a local hotel. The woman was married, and so was McRae – but not to each other. A hearing was held, witnesses came forward, and McRae was dismissed for committing an immoral act unbecoming of a police officer: adultery. He mounted an appeal, and many rumours surrounded the validity of the claims made against him, but the accusation alone was enough for him to lose everything: his job in the CIB, his career in the NSW police force, and his thirty years of accumulated service pension.

Fergusson and Krahe knew how to benefit from the culture of policing created by Commissioner William John Mackay. In the histories written of NSW policing, there are few accounts that praise Mackay's leadership. Many accounts identify the 1930s as an important antecedent period to the generations of corruption that would follow. Under Mackay's stewardship, cadets were encouraged to consider an area of specialisation, and were required to acquire skills.

In Mackay's words, police were not people but 'crime-hunting machines', and this required skill sets. Mackay specialised the police force by aligning officers not just around skills but interests, all under the guise of more scientific policing. The notion of scientific evidence had begun to penetrate policing in both the United States and England in this period, and Mackay was eager to adopt techniques that would lift conviction rates. He took several overseas research tours to gather insights on how a workable model might be introduced here. Surveillance techniques were refined, but so too were suspect identification, interviewing, interrogation and the techniques used to gather eyewitness testimony. Under Mackay, the investigative work was compartmentalised into specialists who knew gambling, sly grog, forgery and prostitution.

On one hand, it might be argued that this approach encouraged the police force to expand a diverse suite of skills and aptitudes. Cadets were required to study Pittman shorthand, were encouraged to enrol in law degrees, and to consider a specialisation. Fergusson took a course in handwriting analysis at Nottingham Police Laboratories. Krahe was not book smart and showed no inclination for science, but described himself as an expert stenographer.

On the other hand, historians and commentators argue this operational model of policing encouraged corruption as officers claimed dominion over areas of vice, with little transparency of their undertakings. The specialisations were mobile, exercised a high degree of autonomy and reported directly to the most senior staff at headquarters. David Dixon has written of the role that corrupt police played in expansion of the illegal gambling sector in particular, describing the CIB as an organisational structure with many faults. The culture created by William John Mackay between 1935 and 1948 aided the advancement of men like Fergusson and Krahe.

•

Fergusson was not an intimidating man. He was pale haired and pale eyed, and had no gift for repartee. In an interview in the 1960s, a journalist cheekily described the bureaucracy of NSW police operations as being 'like Kafka'. Fergusson replied stony faced and without a hint of irony, 'I don't know Kafka', like he was a fellow police officer whom Fergusson had never met.

Media reports written after the 1950s retrospectively claim that Fergusson's contemporaries were wary of him and perceived him as odd. Inside jokes described him as warped and lampooned him for his morbid fascination for cases involving corpses. While this is difficult to confirm, it is corroborated to some degree by Fergusson's own words. In interviews with the press, he said on more than one occasion that he 'helped out with an exhumation'.

In contrast to Fergusson's reputation as limp and strange, Detective Constable Krahe was seen as scary. A physically capable man, his hair was dark, as were his eyes. His broad face squared off sharply, making his profile unusually flat, like a besser block with box-like eyes. His wide mouth, with its turned corners, earned him the nickname 'Froggy'. A heavy smoker, he was rarely seen without a cigarette balanced between his fingers, often leaving a trail of ash behind him as he walked through the CIB. When teamed with Fergusson, who had significant political influence within the department, they were regarded as a formidable pair. Commentators agree on one other defining characteristic: they were both corrupt to the core.

10

INGREDIENTS

FERGUSSON ASSUMED RESPONSIBILITY FOR THE INVESTIGATION
of Yvonne Fletcher and carefully considered the ingredients
necessary to move the case forward. With chemists discovering
poison in Bertram Fletcher's body, Fergusson also turned to
science to more closely explore the case of Desmond Butler.

At the time, NSW police had access to one of the most
sophisticated and well-equipped laboratories in the state. In
the inter-war years, both federal and state governments relied
heavily on the insights that scientists could provide. The CSIR
(a precursor to the CSIRO) had expanded significantly in the
period 1930–50, as Australia sharpened its capabilities for
agricultural production and preservation of foodstuffs. At
the state level, the NSW government supported these efforts

by funding a laboratory capable of studying the safety of food for sale.

Although often referred to in the singular, in reality the 'Government Analyst' was not one person but many. Located at 93 Macquarie Street, it was a branch of the health department with its own testing laboratory and a large team of highly qualified scientists trained in medicine, pathology and chemistry. The facility was run by Dr H B Taylor, who, with a team of staff, had maintained an impressive output and shown a capacity for very careful laboratory work.

In 1936, Thomas Alan McDonald was one of two analysts appointed 'within the meaning and for the purposes of the *Pure Food Act* 1908'. The Act was introduced to ensure the wholesomeness of food and the purity of drugs so that the state had recourse to remove from sale things they deemed dangerous or injurious to health, and to prevent food contamination. To achieve this, the state needed analysts with sufficient technical skill to carry out the tests and sufficient eloquence to prepare statements that could support prosecutions in court.

McDonald's work during the war had focused on food labelling and fraud. With shortages of many ingredients, fraud had become common. Raspberry jam was found to be made of apple pulp and apricot jam was found to have no apricots in it at all. Since the war, the workload of the Office of the Government Analyst had grown significantly, with much attention placed on contamination. In 1951 alone, the lab had tested some 30 000 samples, with 17 000 of these gathered from dairy products. Everyday food and drink items such as milk, soft drink and tinned/canned goods could be tested in the government labs to ensure they were unadulterated and safe for public consumption. In a single year 8000 samples of meat were tested.

By the early 1950s, the skill of the Office of the Government Analyst had grown, as they were given more exposure to new fields and they employed more and more staff. They had been asked to investigate everything from drinking water to bath water, from insect-infested Easter eggs to contaminated canned fruit. The Government Analyst was also responsible for routine checks of everything from ink and paint to grease, soap and disinfectant. Occupational diseases also fell within the remit of the Analyst, and 366 tests had been used to exhibit a link between work and illness.

By the 1950s, police too had begun to acknowledge the capacity of the laboratory to assist in building an evidence base for many different kinds of cases. In 1951 alone, the police department had called on the Government Analyst to examine 280 exhibits, and the Coroner had requested an assessment of 716 exhibits. Scientists could test hair, nails, blood, skin, teeth and organs. But since the 1930s the Government Analyst's office had continually proven their capability to adapt to the changing needs of the police force, and were constantly searching for avenues of science to explore to support criminal investigations. Science expanded the reach of policing in the identification of suspects and it allowed prosecutors to sustain increasingly complex and compelling lines of argument when those suspects were brought to court. In the years leading up to the Fletcher case, the Government Analyst had done groundbreaking work.

In the 1940s, robbery in Sydney was a big problem. The economy was under pressure, and the belt-tightening required to sustain Australia's contribution to the war effort meant leaner times for many. Theft, particularly commercial theft of unattended warehouses and banks, was rife. In one case, a large-scale robbery had left a business substantially out of pocket, yet all police could find when they examined the scene was a busted safe, blown to pieces with a high-powered charge. A possible suspect was located but a search of his premises yielded no safe-cracking tools, nor any stolen property or cash. Police took what they could, amounting to little more than the suspect's suit, which was very clearly unwashed and dusty. Scientists determined that the dust matched the rare sedimentary rock which had been used to line the safe during the manufacturing process. Prosecutors were able to link the suspect to the robbery because the safe was rare, imported from England. The suspect was convicted because he had never left Australia, so could never have been exposed to the dust in any other way, and because he chose to wear a man's suit with cuffed pants. The cuff had formed the perfect gutter to collect and hold the dust. Cases like this had proven the value of science to policing, as it appeared that a suspect's property had the potential to be harvested for incriminating evidence.

When Thomas Alan McDonald was given responsibility for the Fletcher analysis, his first task was to understand the ingredient he was dealing with. McDonald knew of thallium, but only vaguely. In the 1950s it was still considered a relatively recent discovery (its existence noted for the first time only in 1861). McDonald, like many scientists at the time, would have had little exposure to it during the course of his career.

Thallium is a natural element which sits near mercury and lead on the periodic table, and although found in many locations across the planet, it is usually only present in minute amounts. It does not exist in a free-form state in the earth's crust like gold, silver or copper. The impacts of thallium on the human body are cumulative. If poisoning is acute, the victim might feel sick almost immediately. But if a small dosage is administered, the victim may feel nothing at all to begin with. If dosages continue to be given, a wide range of symptoms can emerge including delusion, extreme fatigue, respiratory difficulties, heart problems, nerve pain, hair loss and blindness. McDonald knew enough about thallium to know that, like any heavy metal, the impact on the body could be slow.

In the early 1940s, thallium was not routinely tested for. The fact that doctors and laboratory analysts struggled to initially identify thallium poisoning is not surprising. Even today experts acknowledge that it's hard to detect. Because of its powerful systemic effects, inaccurate diagnoses are common. Thallium victims have been mistaken for alcoholics and epileptics, those suffering depression and brain tumours.

Doctors have also suspected typhus when thallium poisoning was the real cause.

Thallium tricks the body into thinking it is potassium. It blocks the nerve impulses and metabolic processes that need potassium to function. After it's been ingested, thallium combines with the sulphide groups of amino acids. The proteins are ruptured and the result is an unstoppable chain reaction. The cell dies. Nerve cells are particularly affected. For some, thallium poisoning resembles the flu which progresses to bronchopneumonia. For others, thallium creates a major disruption to the nervous system.

McDonald began researching thallium in order to understand its effects on the body. Meanwhile, Fergusson and Krahe quickly, and quietly, got to work. They knew about Fletcher's death, and knew what had killed him. They now needed to know about his life.

•

To build a murder case against Yvonne Fletcher, police had to find a motive. To do this, they attempted to understand her mindset, particularly her attitude towards marriage. Fergusson reconsidered the comment made about Yvonne by her in-laws that 'her first husband died this way too'. Had Bertram Fletcher died so quickly because Yvonne knew how to kill him? Fergusson wanted to know more about the death, and life, of Desmond Butler. But there were obstacles. Butler's death had not been recorded as suspicious and if police wanted to challenge this, they needed to reverse the findings.

They made an application to court to exhume Butler's body. They then drafted a list of people they believed would be important. They spoke to the greengrocer and the general storekeeper where Yvonne bought her groceries, and to the hairdressers and housewives, textile workers, collar makers and tailoresses who lived in her neighbourhood. Co-workers who knew the Fletchers were happy to talk. The ice-men, milk men, firemen and delivery men talked about their comings and goings to the Fletcher household as well. The taxi drivers and ambulance drivers who had carried her husband when he could no longer walk also had their own stories to tell. While 57 Ferndale Street formed the epicentre of the investigation, with police interest radiating out to anyone nearby, not a single detective nor constable ever visited to conduct the interviews. All of the witness statements were collected at CIB headquarters, with the exception of those conducted in Melbourne, where Fergusson and Krahe travelled to speak to members of Butler's family.

The detectives asked open-ended questions: What kind of woman was Yvonne? What did they know about her husband Bertram? And Desmond? What had they seen and heard? Because none of the interviews were conducted in the neigh-bourhood, and no one visited a witness in or near Ferndale Street, Yvonne remained unaware of the interest the police were now taking in her and how eager people were to know more about her.

Mrs Edith Roache, the neighbour at number 43 who had made Desmond lunch and looked pitifully at his Dutch doll, was eager to share her reminiscences of the turbulent lives of the Butlers, then Fletchers, on Ferndale Street. Lionel Butler, who had accompanied Desmond to the dance all those years before, said he liked Yvonne, but that the marriage was not a happy one. He offered up his recollections of staying with his brother in Sydney. 'Yvonne had a boyfriend,' he said. 'Desmond had to mind the children when she went out.' And Mrs Withers described the heated arguments she had heard. 'He [Bertram] tried to give her [Yvonne] eight pounds instead of the usual ten. She refused to take it and she threw it back at him.' Mrs Withers also said she'd seen Yvonne waving at 'Dago Joe' on the day of Bertram's funeral.

Police now saw Yvonne as the kind of woman who would smile and wave at her husband's funeral. Mrs Withers also shared stories of Wood's numerous clandestine visits. He and Yvonne had been seen together in Newtown and in Glebe: Yvonne in her bright lipstick and her faux fur on the arm of the widowed Wood in his faded but respectable coat. He had been a modest, hardworking man, and he now seemed eager to shower attention and gifts on Yvonne. Mrs Withers also noted that while the neighbourhood had a nickname for Herbert, so too did Yvonne. She had heard Yvonne call him 'Dadda' and at other times 'Daddy'. The detectives interpreted the story in the very way that Mrs Withers had intended. Wood was no father figure to Yvonne. If he was a daddy, he was the kind who gave sugar.

Mrs Phyllis Stewart, at number 59, described the strange goings-on in the Butler home, telling police how Desmond used a washboard as a toboggan to drag himself across the yard to get to the outhouse, and that his bedroom wall was smeared with faeces.

When it came to interviewing the doctors, local GP Dr King spoke about how puzzling Desmond's condition had been, Yvonne's distress, and the challenges she'd faced in completing the necessary paperwork for Desmond to be eligible to draw an invalid pension. Dr Kirkwood from Callan Park remembered the severity and complexity of Desmond's illness, and Yvonne's pleas for help to readmit her husband to their facility. Doctors from RPA were simultaneously interviewed about their experiences in treating Desmond and then Bertram. Much later on, when Fergusson was asked to reflect on the process, he said his recollections were hazy: he couldn't remember the sequence of interviewees nor how many there had been in total because so many had occurred in such a short period of time.

When Desmond Butler had presented at hospital in late 1947, his symptoms had confounded medical experts. Dr King, Dr Goldie (at RPA) and the doctors of Broughton Hall all concurred that Butler suffered from peripheral neuritis. While the cause of his condition remained unknown, the symptoms were attributed to a systemic failure in which the 'nervous system failed to pass impulses through the heart'. When no physical source could be identified, the doctors also concurred that the cause was psychological – mental anguish, despair and nervous tension. But four years had now passed since Desmond's death, and medical practitioners had begun to see patients who'd been exposed to thallium. Accidental poisonings had presented to hospital and attempted suicides with thallium had been referred to Callan Park. Thallium poisonings left distinctive traces – hair loss, pins and needles, nerve pain, impaired vision, severe gastric upset, and madness. It was anecdotal and not embodied in manuals or in esteemed journals, but in four years word had begun to spread.

Gordon Bruce Wooster, the superintendent of Callan Park, said he had treated several suicidal patients for thallium poisoning since Desmond Butler, and now knew more about the poison. The patients had all admitted to having eaten Thall-Rat. It had not made medical staff revise Desmond's case, however, because they simply assumed that his mental illness had led to a suicide attempt.

Two critical witnesses had not made statements: Desmond's good friends, Podgey and Ronnie. Many of the other interviewees were women and were able to attend the CIB headquarters because they weren't working. Perhaps Podgey and Ronnie were too busy. Or perhaps they just didn't want to be interviewed by the police. They'd been very close to both Desmond and Yvonne and they may have felt an enduring loyalty to her even after Desmond was gone. Ronnie still lived next door, and it is known that Podgey still visited Yvonne even after she married Bertram.

With the vast amount of interview material, Fergusson and Krahe believed they had a robust case against Yvonne Fletcher and an application was prepared for the Coroners Court. Mr Forrests, City Coroner, reviewed the case the morning of 17 April 1952. By the afternoon he issued permission for the police to gather the necessary evidence to more closely explore the death of Desmond Butler.

Just before nightfall on Thursday, 17 April 1952, Detective Sergeant Fergusson stood at a gravesite in Sydney's largest necropolis, Rookwood Cemetery. He was not alone. Detective Constable Krahe was by his side, as was a small team of analysts. The undertaker who had buried Butler was also there to confirm that this was indeed the right coffin.

Although parts of Rookwood Cemetery were beautiful, in 1952 this section of the site was bare. There were no decorated mausoleums, no garden beds, and few headstones to offer comfort to mourners. Instead, the soil was cut in patches: a patchwork of common people affordably laid to rest beneath unadorned mounds of earth.

The officers watched the gravediggers as they pitched their shovels into the firm crust of the earth. As twilight approached, storm clouds swept in from the coast. It began raining. The pitter-patter formed a polka-dot pattern across the felt of Fergusson's fedora. This part of Rookwood was rocky and the entire graveyard was strewn with tiny grey pebbles. As the rain began to fall harder against the stony ground, the tiny pieces of flint seemed to twinkle and glow, like fragments of carbon scattered across a night sky.

Desmond Butler's casket was lifted from the ground. Having been buried for close to four years, decomposition was well progressed but not complete. Though the grave had been sealed, and the bones remained intact, the summer rains so common in Sydney had flooded the area then drained in the drier months. The bones had floated up, drifted and dispersed, then sunk again out of place. As the analyst noted at the time, 'The material was quite unidentifiable . . . I could not say I could identify the particular organs in a particular anatomical feature.'

The analyst gathering the material from the grave resembled a cook in the kitchen, measuring ingredients. With an empty heavy glass jar in hand he scooped into the coffin and lifted out a rounded pile of something soft and wet and rancid. Like plunging a cup into a flour bin, he scraped the top of the scoop with a palette knife to knock the excess away. What he now held in his hand was a neat and full cup of what looked like soft pale-coloured suet. He repeated this process several times, separating the samples and labelling them carefully: one cup of tissue and fluid; one cup of fluid from the posterior of the body; one cup of coffin trimmings; one cup of earth from the sides of the coffin; one cup of earth beneath the coffin; one cup of water from the open grave. The samples were sent to the Office of the Government Analyst and allocated to Thomas Alan McDonald. Police needed answers to two questions: Was thallium present? And, if so, was it present in lethal quantities?

McDonald examined 9.5 pounds of tissue from Desmond Butler's coffin. It took weeks of testing but he eventually found one-third of a grain of thallium salts in the slurry that remained of the man. It was not much, but McDonald also noted that the grave had flooded, that sediment had moved.

He provided a report to Fergusson and on the basis of this evidence the State Full Court quashed the Coroner's finding of 1948 that Butler had died of natural causes. Fergusson and Krahe had achieved their first victory – the opportunity to try Butler's death as a murder was now back in play.

In June 1952, a City Coroner committed Yvonne for trial for the murder of Bertram. The following day, the state reopened the death of her first husband, Desmond Butler, with a new inquest. It was held, but it was a formality. Everyone knew what the outcome would be: Desmond had died of thallium poisoning.

When it came to the second question of how much thallium was lethal, the answer was not straightforward. McDonald turned to medical journals and sought the counsel of colleagues – no one seemed willing to state definitively what they believed a lethal threshold for thallium might be. There was simply no body of medical literature as yet to support a firm answer.

While McDonald continued testing the remains of Desmond Butler in the laboratory, Fergusson and Krahe pursued tasks which fell within the more traditional purview of detectives.

Thallium was rare, and really only existed in one commercial preparation in Australia at the time. The raw material – thallium salts – was sourced from Germany and imported by pharmaceutical company Sayers, Allport. At a small factory in the suburb of Enfield in Sydney, thallium salts were mixed into a water-based solution. Bottled in tiny glass vials, four different sizes were available to cater to a range of consumer needs. To deal with a small household pest problem, the smallest vial was sufficient: 1 ounce (about two tablespoons in liquid volume) containing approximately ten grains of thallium salts. There were also 2-ounce and 4-ounce bottles available but these were generally marketed for larger-scale vermin problems in businesses and warehouse spaces. The 16-ounce (just under half a litre in metric) was available for farmers dealing with pests of plague proportions. In Australia, the product was branded 'Thall-Rat'.

McDonald ordered bottles of Thall-Rat directly from Sayers, Allport to assist him with his research. The first thing he noted was the affordability of the product. It was priced around two shillings and three pence for a 1-ounce bottle – which was about the same price as a jar of coffee at the time. Retailers also used the 'super-size' selling model – double the amount for only a fraction more. For a 2-ounce bottle the cost was three shillings and nine pence. The manufacturers claimed thallium had advantages over other widely available poisons, because it was palatable for those pests that shunned conventional baits. In the United States, the burrowing of prairie dogs and ground squirrels made them an ongoing threat to agriculture, yet the animals refused to eat the strychnine baits which had proved effective in killing other rodents. The tasteless and odourless thallium made it a unique offering. In Sydney, rats had a reputation for being among the most finicky of vermin. Thall-Rat provided a way to bait anything so it could become instantly delicious – and deadly.

McDonald made his first important discovery: he found the percentage of sulphate in each bottle to be approximately 2.5 per cent. A 2-ounce bottle therefore contained about twenty grains of thallium. His second major discovery came after the bottles arrived and had been sitting on his desk for a few days. The bottles were clearly labelled 'poison' and a blue vegetable dye had been added as a precautionary measure. The manufacturers claimed this reduced the risk of accidental poisoning. After the solution settles, however, the colour fades: the blue dye separates and sits as sediment in the bottom of the bottle. With a shake, Thall-Rat regains its blue colour but if the dye sits at the bottom undisturbed, the solution remains clear. Sales of Thall-Rat had been slow. Sayers, Allport indicated that the product sometimes sat on grocery store shelves for months before it was sold. With this discovery, police now had an explanation. Thall-Rat could be added to anything, and it was tasteless, odourless and practically colourless. If deliberately poisoned, a victim would have no idea they were consuming something so lethal.

McDonald then made his third major discovery. He was not in front of a microscope, nor holding a test tube or a Petri dish in his hand, but a file. In the filing cabinets of the Analyst's office, he uncovered a case that was startingly similar, and had puzzled investigators in precisely the same way as the deaths of Fletcher and Butler.

Six years earlier, a Coroner had called for laboratory testing when a boy had died mysteriously in Maitland. Toxic levels of a substance had been found in his body, most certainly causing death. So little had been known about the drug used, published articles about the event misreported it. In August 1946, *The Sun* misreported that William Allan Cunningham Brocksopp had died of 'phallium' poisoning. The file led to a Coroner's inquest. McDonald read it in detail, and what he found was surprising. There was no discussion of rat poison whatsoever.

On 17 July 1946, three-and-a-half-year-old William Allan Cunningham Brocksopp died in Maitland Hospital after being prescribed thallium acetate for an aggressive case of ring-worm. Radiation was usually prescribed because exposure to X-ray made the hair fall out. Once bald, a topical cream could be applied to the scalp and the location of the ringworm.

Dr Arnold, a skin specialist of some experience at Bank Chambers in Newcastle, was reluctant to recommend X-rays for such a young child. Children wriggled, he said, and this compromised the effectiveness of the X-ray. The machines were also expensive to run, and Mrs Brocksopp would have to take her son to the hospital for treatment. Instead, Dr Arnold suggested an easy solution: a relatively unknown drug called thallium, which he reserved especially for children. It was a cheaper and quicker way to attain the same result: a completely bald child.

Dr Arnold prescribed a mixture to be given orally, at home, with William's dinner. Within a few weeks, the little boy would be completely bald and his mother could then easily apply the ointment directly to the site of the ringworm infes-tation. As instructed, Mrs Brocksopp gave her son a dose of thallium after dinner that night. William became dreadfully ill, immediately. He was weak and fatigued and could barely stand. He was cursed with an unquenchable thirst. His lips, eyelids and feet became swollen.

The next morning, Mrs Brocksopp rang the skin clinic. Dr Arnold was not available, but a nurse reassured the worried mother. The clinic had used thallium for over twenty years and there was nothing to be concerned about. Any symptoms would pass in a few days. Mrs Brocksopp listened to the advice. But William's symptoms did not ease, they got worse. Two days later, she rushed her son to hospital. Admitted to emergency on 13 July 1946, he died four days later.

At the post-mortem, William's organs were removed and examined, just as Bertram Fletcher's had been, and were found to be riddled with thallium acetate. What was also clear was how much the boy had suffered before he died. His stomach was perforated and gangrenous. Still, medical experts could not agree on the official cause of death and, much like the doctors who had pondered Bertram Fletcher's death, they refused to sign a death certificate.

Two theories emerged. One attending medical expert, Dr Youll, suggested death was due to encephalitis. The boy had been camping the previous Sunday and had most likely contracted a germ there, he said. A government medical expert, J J Hollywood, also weighed in. Thallium was a common treatment for skin disorders among children. William's case was an aberration, he said, and most likely to be a rare individual allergic reaction.

The debate among medical practitioners continued for another two months, in part due to the varying levels of knowledge about thallium across the medical profession. The matter was referred to the Coroner and a finding was handed down. The drug had been properly administered, the Coroner said. He went further to say that many still used thallium medically in the treatment of ringworm, so there was no evidence which enabled him to say what had caused the death. He returned an open verdict.

•

McDonald's discoveries did not end with Brocksopp. He continued to dig – this time in overseas medical journals and case studies. To his amazement, he had no trouble sourcing material to prove that thallium was deadly to humans, not just vermin. Most concerning of all was how long the problems with thallium had been documented. What he found was shocking.

While thallium was used in private practice in Australia, it was not particularly well known beyond these settings. It was used more extensively overseas to treat ringworm in children living in institutional settings. The fact that thallium could cause immense pain and death in humans was well documented. While the results were published in high-profile medical journals, those who exhibited strong symptoms were dismissed as aberrations. Most studies focused on children and dismissed the risks. In an orphanage in the town of Carmarthenshire in south Wales and in one particularly alarming case in an institution in Granada, Spain, many children had died. The symptoms before death included swollen feet, excess sensitivity to pain, mental confusion and rapid hair loss. Still, the confidence in thallium as an effective medical treatment was not shaken. It could not be thallium, it was argued, it had to be medical error. In Spain, an investigation was conducted, and the scales were found to be broken; the dosage administered had been wrong.

In the United States, experiments with thallium had extended to the beauty industry, but had ended abruptly. As early as the 1930s, the Bureau of Investigation of the American Medical Association had recommended that thallium not be used in any products that might be exposed to human contact.

Government policies on thallium had formed in other places in the world, but regulation was not uniform and even within a single legal jurisdiction there were inconsistencies. In the United States, thallium had been commercially marketed as a poison for rats and ground squirrels, but as early as 1931 it was found that it posed a significant contamination risk to the broader community. After its examination, the United States Department of Agriculture issued its official statement on thallium: 'a cumulative poison of high toxicity ... without taste, smell, or other warning property. It should not be recommended to the public as a rodent poison.'

Entrepreneurs in other industries were not so easily deterred.

In the 1920s, women's fashion underwent some radical shifts. The growing popularity of the sleeveless bodice and the knee-length skirt meant that women were exposing more skin than ever before. In turn, the beauty industry began to explore new ways to market powders and creams which claimed to hide blemishes and enhance the pallor of the skin. Creams designed to lighten body hair or remove it entirely also flooded the market. What consumers did not know at the time was that the thallium deemed too dangerous for rats was now the major ingredient in a new depilatory cream for women called Koremlu.

The manufacturer claimed that women need only apply the cream to their upper lip, or their armpit, and the hair would simply disappear. And in a sense it was true. The only trouble was that it disappeared not because the hair follicle detached, but because the optic nerve did. Women could no longer see their facial hair because Koremlu had sent them blind. In addition to the vision problems, hundreds of women suffered gastric upsets, aches and pains in the lower limbs, excruciating nerve pain and madness. Koremlu was taken off the market. More stringent controls over the contents of beauty products followed.

In Australia, the regulatory approach to both poisons control and therapeutic goods in the early twentieth century might be best described as lax. As early as the 1920s, researchers knew that thallium exposure could lead to pins and needles, paralysis, gastric dysfunction and mental illness. Still, its therapeutic benefits were seen to outweigh any risks.

In a paper examining the history of therapeutic goods regulation in Australia, the Attorney-General's Department notes of the decade preceding the introduction of thallium: 'During this period there was an increasing number of proprietary medicines appearing on an unregulated market, with many products regarded as "quack" medicines with amazing therapeutic claims.' While many areas of policy experienced an extension of Commonwealth powers during the war, this was not the case with the management of medicines or the wide range of products that fell under therapeutic products. Individual states continued to handle their own legislation in the areas of health management and poisons control, and the Commonwealth had little involvement in quality control. As one review of the legislative history in this field notes: 'The wartime and immediate post-war priorities did not include active control of therapeutic substances.'

About the same time Americans were pulling products containing thallium off the shelves, Australians had decided to introduce it as a rat poison widely available for commercial sale.

For McDonald, the analyst studying the effects of thallium, the revelations were profound. In the case of Koremlu, it was not just the blindness of the victims that interested him but the slew of horrible symptoms that preceded it.

The Cleveland woman who initiated the court action in the United States had used Koremlu for weeks. She'd been young and fit prior to the medical emergency that struck her down. She reported suffering pins and needles in her feet, followed by excruciating pain in her lower legs and toes. In the three weeks leading up to her admission to hospital she'd felt dizzy, with blurry vision, and the pain in her legs had become so severe that even 'the pressure of the bed clothes caused pain'. The medical response had been slow, and bore an uncanny resemblance to that which Desmond Butler had experienced. When the Cleveland woman saw her doctor, her tendency to cry easily was dismissed and she was diagnosed as having a 'nervous disposition'. This misdiagnosis persisted for five months until a diagnosis of 'arthritis' was made. No one was convinced by this either.

When the woman presented at a local health clinic in excruciating pain and suffering intermittent bouts of gastric, a new team of doctors began assessing her, fascinated by her unusual combination of symptoms. Then, another woman presented with similar symptoms. A pattern began to emerge. Twenty-eight years old and single, she was in the prime age group for hysteria. However, she also had other disturbing symptoms. She had used Koremlu too, but only on her top lip. When she presented for medical help she was, inexplicably, almost completely bald. In both cases, the strange symptoms had only emerged after the women began using the new depilatory cream. As soon as the story broke, more and more people began to come forward. They too had suffered symptoms which doctors had dismissed. Legal action against the company ensued. After a prolonged case, the company was ordered to pay well over two million dollars in compensation to consumers who had been injured by their product.

McDonald now had a compelling story to share with the detectives. Thallium was highly dangerous to humans, that much was clear. While many of the case studies had not dealt with grown men, the experiments of thallium-laced products with women and children highlighted the dangers. Thallium was deadly, and the dosage that could kill or maim someone could be quite low. McDonald estimated that about half a teaspoon could kill a grown man. A single bottle could kill up to forty, depending on their body weight.

•

After two months of preparation, including the gathering of witness statements, countless laboratory tests and the collation of a sizeable body of scientific research, Fergusson and Krahe finally went to meet the woman at the centre of all their work. Police policy at the time required a female police officer to be in attendance when a case involved a female suspect. In accordance with this protocol, policewoman Margaret Fisher accompanied the two detectives. As the dark blue police vehicle cruised down Ferndale Street, two suit-shaped fedora-topped silhouettes could be seen in the front seats. Fisher, a wavy outline of hair beneath a half-cup hat, peered out through the back window. The vehicle cruised past the terraces, checking the house numbers in a slow and ominous countdown to number 57. Up to this point the two detectives had gone to great lengths to remain clandestine, but today the police Hudson, with its distinctive bubble-shaped fenders and bonnet, announced its presence with a noisy squeak of the brakes as it pulled up outside the Fletcher home. Both front doors opened at exactly the same time, but as Fisher reached for the door lever Fergusson leaned over the seat and spoke. 'Wait here for the moment. We'll get you if we need you.'

At 9.30 a.m. on 19 May 1952, the detectives knocked on Yvonne Fletcher's front door. The distinctive bark of a small dog could be heard inside. 'We're the police!' Krahe yelled.

Yvonne swung open the door. 'Yes, I've been expecting you. I suppose it's about my husband?' A small, scruffy brown dog bounced up and down.

Neither officer felt inclined to answer Yvonne's question. 'Would it be convenient for you to come to the CIB with us? We'd like to have a talk to you.'

'Yes. Could you wait until I change my clothes?' Yvonne opened the door wide and led the two detectives into the house. Fergusson and Krahe waited in the small sitting room at the front, while Yvonne headed upstairs. Strangely, the dog did not follow her but instead sat in the sitting room and watched the officers with a steely glare.

Yvonne emerged minutes later fully dressed: a smart day suit, hair now curled neatly under a half-cup hat and a short-handled handbag hanging in the crook of her arm. 'I'll just put the pup out,' she said, then clapped her hands. She nudged the animal outside with her pointed toe and shut the door. She turned to the detectives behind her and said, 'I'm ready.'

As they left, Yvonne spotted Podgey in the street. It was just after breakfast and he was taking his greyhounds out for their regular morning run, just as he had done when

Desmond had been alive. Podgey slowed then stopped as he neared Yvonne's terrace. Flanked by the two suited men, she slammed her front door. Podgey furrowed his brow, sensing the seriousness of the moment. 'How are you, Bon?' he called out, hesitantly. The two detectives continued on with their business as if Podgey wasn't even there.

'All right, Podge,' Yvonne said, laughing nervously. 'I'm being arrested.'

The detectives led Yvonne to the waiting car. Podgey hovered nearby, unable to look away. Yvonne caught hold of her coat hem daintily, bent her head and folded herself into the back seat of the police car. One of Podgey's greyhounds, catching the scent of something familiar at number 57, tugged hard on the lead, lurched towards the mailbox, and led Podgey up the garden path. The lead pulled tight in his hand. Podgey watched in silence as the police car pulled away. The dog bowed low to the ground, arched its thin back, curled its tail high in the air, and began sniffing frantically at the door of the now empty house.

11

GRILLING

When they arrived at CIB headquarters, Miss Fisher led Yvonne into a small, bare room with a table and four chairs. Fergusson ran the interview and was responsible for asking all the questions. Krahe assumed the role of stenographer and took the only record of the interview in shorthand. Miss Fisher sat with Yvonne, although there is no record of her saying much, other than asking Yvonne if she needed a toilet break, or a cup of tea and biscuits.

The police had conducted weeks of interviewing and hundreds of pages of testimony had already been gathered from family and neighbours and medical staff. In many ways the heavy lifting was over, as all of these interviews would be used to establish that Yvonne was both capable and motivated to kill her two husbands. But there was still one interview that could either make or break the case.

At 9.50 a.m. Fergusson began. 'An analyst's report has revealed that thallium was present in the body of your first husband.'

'You mean my second husband?' asked Yvonne.

'No. I mean Butler.'

'It could not have been. You don't mean to say I murdered two husbands. I had plenty of reason to murder the second, but not the first.'

'So can you explain how two husbands have died from thallium poisoning?' asked Fergusson.

'No. My second husband must have known what killed my first husband and he poisoned himself to get me into trouble.'

'How is that possible? The Coroner found the first husband died from natural causes. The thallium has only been found after the exhumation which took place after your second husband's death.'

'My second husband used to say to me that I had killed my first husband.'

Fergusson continued to interrogate Yvonne about both deaths, flicking back and forth between the present (1952) and the past (1947–48). Hours passed. He could not get Yvonne to admit to anything. Fergusson pressed: 'Could you suggest anyone in a position to poison your husbands?'

Yvonne replied, 'You can talk to me for hours. I will not say it.'

In the late afternoon, Fergusson stood up. He did not ask Yvonne to rise. 'It has been established that your first husband, Desmond George Butler, died by thallium poisoning and your second husband, Bertram Henry Fletcher, also died from thallium poisoning. That, together with other enquiries that Detective Krahe and I have made into their deaths, and the answers that you have given to certain questions here today, lead to the conclusion that you were responsible for their deaths, and therefore we intend to charge you with the murder of Desmond George Butler and Bertram Henry Fletcher.'

Yvonne began crying. 'It looks black. It will just have to be black. Jesus will look after me. Everybody thinks I am a murderer.'

When the interview finally concluded, the two men got to work in isolation. Using Krahe's shorthand notes and a typewriter, they compiled the typed transcripts of all the statements. Yvonne did not admit, at any point during the interview, that she had poisoned her husbands.

Nevertheless, on 20 May 1952, she was formally charged at the Central Court of Petty Sessions and referred for trial.

•

The legal integrity of the interrogation that Fergusson and Krahe had conducted was called into question from the very beginning of the trial. For three days, with the jury dismissed, the prosecution, defence and the judge debated the legal issues regarding the admissibility of Yvonne's interview. Yvonne's defence team attempted to have much of her interrogation struck from the record. Although the defence lost this battle, the judge sent an early warning to the police about their approach.

'There is an omnibus question. The police should understand perfectly well that, to make an omnibus statement of a large number of facts and then await a general answer, is an improper mode of interrogation, and it had better be stopped. It is a tendency that appears to be developing more and more in police interrogations and I hope that the police will desist from it. The proper way to question a person whom the person intends to arrest or have arrested, is to place one fact before the person and get an answer to that fact, and not to combine a large number of facts and wait for a general answer.'

As the trial progressed, however, the fact that officers had blurred interview questions and moved back and forth between the two deaths fell away. At the end of the trial, the judge's criticism of the police work had eased. He could see the value in a largely circumstantial case, particularly given the complicated nature of the murders being committed. Circumstantial evidence, he said, had an important role to play in proving death by poison. In a lengthy statement, Justice Kinsella all but endorsed the detectives' approach and effectively legitimised the technique of interviewing about multiple murders at one time.

'In the case such as the present one, where the death being investigated has been caused by a subtle and little-known poison so that the investigation cannot be focused upon any particular acts or series of acts, or at any particular point of time, inquiries can rarely be of the nature to be confined with any precise limits, it is almost inevitably that they should range over a large number of subjects. They involve discussions with many people and may have very many aspects.'

Science had established that Desmond and Bertram were poisoned. There were only three ways in which it could have occurred, the judge said: intentional poisoning; accidental poisoning; or suicide. Neither Bertram nor Desmond had shown any suicidal tendencies. There was no manner in which accidental poisoning might have occurred, since neither man was regularly exposed to thallium during the course of their work life or home life. That meant they had been given thallium in their food. There was only one way this could have occurred: wives cooked for husbands and therefore must have administered the poison. Yvonne had many motives. She had marital trouble with both husbands. The prosecution did not need to prove which days she had poisoned and in what quantities. It was not an important detail.

It took three and a half hours for the jury to deliver a guilty verdict.

'You have had a fair trial and a patient and careful consideration of the evidence by the jury,' Justice Kinsella told Yvonne. 'If the conviction had been in respect of your second husband, possibly some palliation of your crime might have been found, for the evidence showed you suffered greatly at his hands. In respect of your first husband, there is no evidence at all of that nature. The crime of murder is a terrible one, and when the killing is by means of an insidious poison, secretly administered within the family circle to an unsuspecting victim, which destroyed him mentally and physically, while permitting him to linger for months in wretched agony, then the crime is a horrible one.' For this reason, the judge indicated he would formally recommend to the NSW government the sale of thallium be banned.

Justice Kinsella expressed no doubt about Yvonne's guilt. But he also recognised that this complex murder case, in which poisoning had been used as the weapon, presented the legal system with a challenge. He maintained that police should have the latitude to interview widely, with many witnesses, because maintaining this right helped to get to the truth. He also noted that Yvonne's failure to admit her crime did not dilute the ability of the prosecution to mount a convincing case regarding her guilt.

While being led back to a holding cell for the evening, Yvonne did not admit guilt, nor did she ask to speak to anyone. Instead, she asked the officer, 'Can you get me the papers to see what they are writing about me?'

Yvonne's life had been laid bare for the whole world to enjoy, and none of it was flattering. Newspaper journalists reflected on the factors that had led to the formation of deadly intent: infidelity, marital conflict, a deranged and self-serving woman, and the underlying capacity for women to deceive. But there was one article that hypothesised what factors had created the preconditions for what would unfold so disastrously in Yvonne's life.

Dottie Bogan was not interviewed by the police at any time during their investigation. But Yvonne Fletcher's story was big news: the first ever thallium murder case in Australian history. It's no surprise journalists travelled to Newtown and tracked down the murderer's mother for an interview. Never one to shy away from the spotlight, Dottie agreed to meet them in Yvonne's now empty home.

During criminal trials, particularly high-stakes trials like murder, close family members typically rally around the defendant, eager to publicly display their loyalty. Dottie did not defend her daughter in the way a protective mother might. Instead, she displayed a hard-edged pragmatism about how sour some marriages can turn. 'I don't want anybody's sympathy,' she said. 'I'm sure she's innocent. But if she did it, she deserves all she gets.'

12

POTATO AND BACON PIE

With Yvonne Fletcher's case concluded, Fergusson and Krahe turned their attention to other matters: a city robbery; a break and enter; a poisoning found to be the result of contaminated sediment in a bottle of beer. For a few weeks it felt like a hiatus for the two detectives.

In late July 1952, a long-distance call came through to the CIB from the central west of New South Wales. A Detective Killen from the small town of Cowra, about four hours west of Sydney, was calling for help. Killen wasn't actually from Cowra, but from a bigger regional town about a hundred kilometres away called Parkes. Given Cowra's size, he had been the only available resource the police department was willing to send there.

Killen told the two city detectives a 25-year-old man named Allan Williams had died of a mysterious illness at Cowra Hospital on 20 July and doctors were refusing to sign a death certificate. Initially, at least, senior police had not believed that a criminal act had been committed. Killen was sent to sort it out, but no one really expected it to be murder. When he got there, the case quickly became far more complicated. Locals were saying Allan had been poisoned.

For Inspector James Wiley, the head of the CIB, the decision of who to send to help Killen was easy. Fergusson and Krahe, the 'CIB poison experts', drove the four hours west to Cowra and arrived at the local regional hospital sometime in the last week of July.

They immediately began building a picture of Allan Williams's life – his family, his home, his workplace. It transpired Allan worked as a truck driver and was engaged to a local girl, nineteen-year-old Fay Norton. He was living at Fay's home – a small farm situated in a village called Noonbinna, on Cowra's outskirts. It was a tiny place, numbering only a few hundred people, and almost everyone knew each other, or knew of each other. The Nortons, Allan's soon-to-be in-laws, had quite a reputation in the village and one family member in particular – Ruby May Norton – had managed to alienate almost everyone.

Ruby was fifty years old, married, and had two grown daughters – Gwen and Fay. Gwen was in her early twenties and married to a local man, George Worth, while Fay was betrothed to Allan. They all lived together in the homestead at Noonbinna. And if these living arrangements were not cosy enough, Allan and George worked together too, at Waugoola Shire Council.

Ruby Norton cooked, cleaned, cared for children and worked outdoors on the farm. A country woman with a heavy-set jaw and large, round glasses which seemed to have an uncannily powerful ability to be able to magnify the faults in others, she was not well liked. For when not farming or cooking or cleaning, she was judging. While her future son-in-law did not appear to have enemies – indeed, Fergusson and Krahe found a town in mourning for a young man considered a local hero – the same could not be said for Ruby. That's where the detectives focused their attention.

Less than a month before, Cowra had faced a catastrophic flood. The army had been called in to evacuate, but the raging waters that swept through the town's main street had simply been too fast and too strong. Gangs of men tried to build levees, but they had little impact. A bus filled with passengers had been swept away. Some locals clung to treetops for hours awaiting rescue, while others floated capsized boats to rooftops praying that help might come. Allan had swum deep river crossings and waded waist high in putrid flood waters, to save lives using his council truck and his tools, which he refashioned into frontline rescue equipment. Two men who had been trapped in a tree and had almost died due to the rapidly rising water levels owed their lives to Allan's bravery.

Meanwhile, at Cowra Hospital, George Worth had been admitted with very similar symptoms to Allan's. He had pains in his legs and feet. He was nauseous and vomiting violently. The similarities did not end there: George worked with Allan and was married to Ruby's eldest. As matriarch in a country household, Ruby did most of the cooking. She prepared the lunches for the working men, including her husband, Allan and George.

Police insisted that samples be taken from George Worth, including his nail clippings and hair, faeces, urine and vomit. It took more than two weeks for the samples to be sent to Sydney and for the testing to be completed. This did not stop Fergusson and Krahe from assuming that someone within the Norton home was responsible for poisoning the men.

According to George, Fergusson insisted he make a statement. When he refused, Fergusson pushed, convincing Worth that it was in his best interests to do all he could to stop someone who had clearly proven themselves to be highly dangerous. 'Allan's dead,' Fergusson said. 'You are also going to die.' When George tried to stand his ground, Fergusson feigned resignation. 'I imagine it will be pretty cold out there with Allan.'

Doctors sent Allan's samples for toxicology testing at the Office of the Government Analyst. While waiting to see if he'd been dosed with thallium salts, the two detectives set about investigating the Noonbinna community. Very quickly, they decided Ruby Norton was their prime suspect.

Just as they had in Yvonne's case, Fergusson and Krahe then turned their attention to those neighbours closest to the Norton home. The Nortons shared a back fence with the Sinclairs, but they were more than just neighbours: Mrs Elizabeth Sinclair and Mrs Ruby Norton were sisters. Unlike the terraces of Newtown where neighbours shared walls, the Noonbinna properties were vast, yet the reach of neighbours into each other's lives still seemed to be significant. Elizabeth said that Ruby had come to her for rat poison. Her request had been casual, like a neighbour asking to borrow a cup of sugar. Elizabeth's claims did not stop there. She said that Ruby had said outright that she planned to kill her son-in-law, Allan. According to Krahe's transcript, Elizabeth claimed that Ruby had said, 'Do you have any poison? I want to give Allan a dose, the bastard'; 'I will do it in a way I won't hang for it'; 'Do you have any strychnine, I want to poison a dog or a fox'; and the particularly damning 'Police will never take me alive. I'll shoot it out with them.' They were extraordinary statements, worthy of a melodramatic work of fiction, and all were included in Krahe's interview transcript.

The detectives next spoke to Allan's mother, Margaret, who described the ongoing turbulence in the Norton home. Margaret claimed that Ruby had turned up one day looking like she had been in a fist fight. A terrible argument had broken out in the Norton household, and it had got physical. Ruby said that Allan had held Ruby's hands and arms down so she couldn't defend herself while her own daughter socked her in the jaw. Margaret said Ruby had spoken to her about Allan's behaviour. 'Allan gets cranky at Fay,' Ruby said, 'he's not treating her right.' Ruby said she would never give her consent for Fay to marry Allan, and as Fay was not yet the legal age to marry, Ruby's consent mattered.

Margaret also claimed that Allan had complained to her about his future mother-in-law. He said that Ruby was deliberately tormenting him. She had put four pounds of sugar in his petrol tank, he said. She had also put 'spirit of salts' – the lay term for hydrochloric acid – in his car engine. Many local farms kept acid on site because farmers used it to wash the pesticide off picked fruit. The Nortons had an orchard.

Not surprisingly, Allan's mother had a lot to say. Grief-stricken over her son's death, she was angry. Fergusson and Krahe did little to factor this into the credibility of her accusations. Instead, they asked her to detail every strange encounter she had ever had with the Nortons. She willingly obliged. At the end of the previous year, around Christmas time, Margaret had received a distressed phone call from her son, asking her to come round. When she arrived she found Allan unwell, propped up beneath a lucerne tree in the backyard. Fay sat next to him in the shade, dabbing moisture onto his lips with a wet spoon, the way one might with an invalid. Despite his exhaustion, no one seemed to think he was sick enough to go to hospital.

Muriel Hackett, a Noonbinna local, claimed that Ruby Norton had told her she was going to 'get rid of Allan'. She said that Ruby had even explained to her how and why the relationship with her future son-in-law had soured. 'He was a fine little chap when he first came, but the last twelve months he's getting unbearable in the house . . . I can't ask him to go.

The home belongs to my husband and he thinks the world of Allan ... If I can't get him out, I'll make it so hot for him he would have to get out.' Conflict in the Norton home was mentioned by another neighbour – Florence Hill – who had heard yelling in the middle of the night. She also happened to be Ruby's niece.

Another neighbour, pea farmer Walter McIllhaton, reported that Ruby had said to him on one occasion, 'I will stop Allan from marrying my daughter if it is the last thing I do.'

Annie Williams, from the nearby village of Wottamondara, visited the Norton property earlier that year. She reported to Fergusson that when Ruby's husband had climbed into a truck with Allan and driven away, Ruby had leaned over to her and said, 'I hope they run into a tree and kill themselves.' Annie also claimed that Ruby had referred to Allan as 'a pig and a bastard'.

Mr Dickson, the Noonbinna postmaster and storekeeper, claimed that Ruby had talked about Allan's illness and hospital stay when she was in the store to collect her mail. Ruby had said to him, 'If we ever see Allan back at Noonbinna I'll be very surprised.'

With the interviews completed and the toxicology results in, Detectives Fergusson, Krahe and Killen went to the Norton homestead and searched the premises, finding a tin of what was described as 'a proprietary rat poison containing thallium'. Ruby Norton was arrested at midday and taken to Cowra Police Station to be formally charged.

When it came to interviewing Ruby, country detective Killen deferred to the city experts, who had a reputation for knowing both interrogation and poison.

Ruby claimed that, 'He [Allan] did not have an enemy in the world and I never had an argument or cross word with him. There was never a serious row in the home. I can kiss the Bible on it. The rat poison I bought is the same as the woman who killed her two husbands with rat poison.'

In remote Noonbinna the only way that Ruby could have even heard about the case involving Yvonne Fletcher was by reading about it in the newspaper. The problem was that she couldn't read. The transcript included the fact that Ruby had added, 'George Worth used to read it to me in the papers. I followed that case.'

Fay Norton tried to defend her mother, telling the detectives that Allan had false teeth and painted his gums with a solution from a small glass bottle. Both Thall-Rat and the gum treatment were small medicinal bottles, and it was possible Allan had confused them. She also said that Allan had put the Thall-Rat on bread and butter and left it in the compartment of the car door because he had complained that rats had been eating the upholstery. It was possible, according to Fay, that Allan had eaten sweets out of the compartment of the car door, where the thallium on bread had also been placed.

The first sign that there might be a snag in Fergusson and Krahe's case emerged when the toxicology results came back from the government laboratories. On one hand, Fergusson and Krahe felt vindicated: Allan Williams had died of thallium poisoning. On the other hand, they received an unexpected and confounding result: George Worth had not been poisoned at all and had nothing more than a tummy bug.

When Fergusson and Krahe finished their interviews, Killen was impressed, at least to begin with. He was also more than a little intimidated by what the city detectives had been able to achieve in such a short period of time. In less than a week, Fergusson and Krahe interviewed thirty-one people in the local area using their transcription technique. Fergusson asked the questions, Krahe took notes in shorthand and the two men worked in a way that seemed to be seamless and efficient. They prepared 157 foolscap pages of witness statements for consideration by the Coroner. The statements were very direct. Each one conveniently linked Ruby May Norton to the poison and then to Allan Williams. The statements gave the impression that Ruby discussed her plans for murder with just about anyone in the town willing to listen.

The case moved to the Bathurst Supreme Court, where the defence counsel scrutinised the witness statements. This was when Fergusson and Krahe's case really began to crumble. It turned out that everyone who gave evidence had a long-standing vendetta against Ruby Norton.

In his typed statement, George Worth described his mother-in-law as a threatening and conflict-driven woman who could not be made happy. However, in court he said that the statement he had been asked to sign was false. He added that Detective Sergeant Fergusson had intimidated him while he was in hospital, telling him that he needed to make a statement because Allan, by this point, was already dead.

Muriel Hackett testified for the prosecution and the defence counsel swiftly exposed how much she despised Ruby. Muriel was separated from her husband and living in what was euphemistically described as a 'housekeeping' arrangement with a man called Thomas Smith. Ruby openly judged Muriel for her lifestyle, believing the woman was living immorally. In response to being shunned by Ruby, Muriel hatched an unusual and inspired form of revenge. The previous year, she had put pen to paper and crafted a 'dirty and scurrilous and nasty poem' about the Noonbinna Norton girls and their mother. Not content to just delight in the hilarity of her rude rhymes, she shared her delight with others, distributing the song around town like she was leaflet marketing.

Florence Hill's grievance with Ruby was deep and bitter and very personal, and this was all exposed in court as well. Ruby had judged Florence harshly for living with a man out of wedlock. When a child was born, Ruby turned up at Florence's home. Ruby had always wanted a son, she said, but had been unable to have one. Ruby then suggested something which she said would save the child from disgrace. When baby Boris was just ten days old, Ruby marched the 400 yards to Florence's home and took him. She then strode back to the Norton house and absorbed the baby into her own family as if it had always been this way.

Every day since her baby had been taken, Florence had watched on, as if a stranger. She listened to the sound of her baby crying as she walked past the Norton house and saw his nappies fluttering on the clothesline. The resentment that burned within her became evident when she made her statement to the police at the time of Allan's death. Fergusson had fished for some dirt on Ruby. Given the circumstances, Florence had plenty to say. She claimed to have heard arguing coming from the Norton house. The fact that she lived 400 yards (over 360 metres) away and well out of earshot made her claim impossible, although this seemed to matter little to Fergusson at the time.

Ruby's lawyer described the testimony presented as malicious and likened the locals to 'the High Court of Noonbinna' because of the way they believed they could pass judgement on others.

The prosecution fought hard to convince the jury that Ruby was a malicious threat. In response, the defence counsel argued, 'It is strongly in the favour of the accused that she told the police where she bought a bottle of this poison. We are not dealing with a cunning woman. Remember, gentlemen, you are not a pack of gossips in a small country village deciding among yourselves who did this crime. We are dealing with an illiterate woman.'

It took little more than an hour for the jury to come to a decision: Ruby Norton was found not guilty.

When she walked from the courtroom a free woman, journalists from Sydney were waiting. 'How did you feel?' asked one. 'Are you relieved?' asked another. 'Will you go on a holiday now to recover from the experience?' suggested a third.

Ruby's response exposed the insularity of her world. Despite living in and contributing to a firmament of hate in her town, she seemed happy to return to it. 'I have been arrested and tried as a result of wicked gossip . . . I had a very nice time at Long Bay – it was very comfortable . . . all I am going to do now is to settle down again in my normal way of living.'

In concentrating on Ruby Norton as the sole suspect, Fergusson and Krahe ignored all other possible lines of investigation. How and why Allan Williams was poisoned by thallium have never been explained.

Potato and bacon pie (1952)

Ingredients
1 pound liver
8–10 slices bacon, cut in lengths to fit in pie dish
1 onion, thinly sliced
Lard (to grease)
3 pounds mashed potatoes
Half cup breadcrumbs
Half cup grated cheese

Method
Preheat oven to moderate temperature (about 365°F). Grease the bottom of a pie dish with fat. Slice liver very thinly and layer across

the bottom of the dish. Then a layer of bacon, a layer of onion, a layer of potato. Layer this way until the pie dish is full. Pour half a cup of water into the dish, and dot the top with small dollops of lard. When almost cooked, top with breadcrumbs, more dollops of lard and cheese. Put back in the oven and cook until brown on top. Can be left in cooler overnight and will set. Can be sliced and packed for work lunch.

13

BAIT AND WAIT

WITHIN A FEW SHORT MONTHS, FERGUSSON AND KRAHE WENT from triumph to defeat. The techniques used to capture Yvonne Fletcher – which at the time appeared robust because they had helped to secure a guilty verdict – now seemed problematic. The very same techniques had been used to pursue a case against Ruby Norton and had proved a dismal failure. Fergusson and Krahe were now being lampooned in the press for their decision to aggressively target a country woman, whom the press characterised as ignorant and illiterate, when there was little concrete evidence against her.

Then came a further humiliation. Yvonne had been the first person in Australia to be convicted of murder by thallium and her legal team believed this strengthened her shot at an appeal because so much of the trial grappled with new and untested legal territory. First, they would argue that the detectives' over-zealous interviewing techniques had impeded the ability for Yvonne to obtain a fair trial. Second, they would contend the legal decision to consider the deaths of Desmond George Butler and Bertram Henry Fletcher together had been the wrong one, because it had prejudiced the jury against the accused.

An appeal was lodged with the NSW Court of Criminal Appeal.

The appeals judge, Justice Owen, offered up a broad ruling which tolerated police discretion around interrogation and the management of information gathered at interviews. Owen stated that the way in which police grouped the information about the two deaths was necessary because the jury needed an opportunity to consider the uncanny similarities: both were strong, healthy men; neither were suicidal; both had experienced matrimonial discord and there was evidence Yvonne resented each of them for it. These circumstances made the evidence relevant and admissible, argued Owen. The judge noted in his final ruling: 'When object was raised to the admission of the evidence, the trial judge took the proper course of hearing evidence on the voir dire, and having done so, he admitted it subjected to the deletion of certain passages which he considered might have been unfairly prejudicial to the appellant. I see nothing to suggest that he improperly exercised his discretion ... The only evidence given on the voir dire came from the officers who questioned her. She herself offered none then or later ... The argument of counsel for the appellant ultimately it seems to me, came down to this, that many of the questions put by the police officers would not have been admissible in the court of law. That the interview is a long one is undoubted, but there was much ground to be covered. Two deaths were involved and there was a matrimonial history going back for years to be investigated. There were several breaks in the interview, one at least for refreshment . . . I am of opinion that the appeal fails and should be dismissed.'

Yvonne Fletcher's guilty verdict was upheld, but the increased scrutiny on Fergusson and Krahe's tactics had undoubtedly shaken them. The year 1953, it might be argued, was when cracks began to form in the relationship between the two previously compatible officers.

•

While Krahe was a persuasive man who undoubtedly had influence, his rise had not been as meteoric as Fergusson's. He remained a lower-ranking officer, and it was around this time that he began to look for opportunities beyond his alliance with Fergusson. Krahe turned to Detective Sergeant Ray Kelly. Like Fergusson, Kelly's rise through the ranks of the police force had been rapid. Like Fergusson, separating myth from fact poses a significant research challenge. To this day, Kelly's reputation within the NSW police force remains notorious.

In the workplace culture of policing, the use of nicknames is common. Kelly's tags (he had more than one) provide a more accurate picture of his capabilities than any detailed profile of his personality characteristics might. Ray Kelly was known by some as 'Gunner'. The nickname was earned after a succession of shootouts in which Kelly had proven himself to be a little trigger-happy. Gunner Kelly was often the man firing the fatal shots. His other nickname also reveals much about his reputation. At one point in the 1950s, the rumours surrounding his ability to simply concoct evidence and confessions were so abundant that one barrister in a court case involving Kelly's testimony referred to him as 'Verbal Kelly'.

The close personal associations between Kelly and the criminal underworld are undeniable. While Kelly argued at the time that fraternising with informants constituted good police work, his critics argue that, along with Krahe, he profited handsomely from skimming criminal enterprises. Kelly's reputation as a crook was certainly alluded to, even by those in significant positions of power in the legal establishment. In a 1952 case involving a fencer of stolen goods, Judge Redshaw ridiculed the curiosity of Kelly's close criminal associations. At one notorious criminal's trial, Redshaw noted, 'Your best friend is Sergeant Kelly.'

By 1953, Kelly's power and influence in the force was growing and he was beginning to get more high-profile assignments and postings, including being appointed as head of the lucrative Safebreaking and Arson Squad within the CIB. The rumours surrounding the corruption of this unit were rife, as bank and security vault robberies provided easy takings for the police investigating the crimes. Then, in October of that year, Kelly was appointed as part of an elite contingent of twelve detectives to be personal bodyguards for the Queen and Duke of Edinburgh while on tour in Australia the following year.

By this stage, Krahe was turning away from Fergusson and towards a more expansive range of activities that would be much more lucrative and potentially influential. But they remained close colleagues. They had little choice: that very year, another thallium case would surface.

•

Johnny Lundberg was not a police officer, nor a doctor, but an ordinary citizen. He'd read the newspaper reports about Yvonne Fletcher and recognised the symptoms the journalist described. He believed someone was poisoning his mother – and believed he knew who was responsible.

At first, the constable who took Lundberg's call was sceptical. The CIB received hundreds of phone calls a day, including its fair share of crank calls. The man's accusations seemed outrageous, and the constable was reluctant to waste the time of a senior detective. Finally, he asked Lundberg to wait while he located the resident CIB poison expert: Detective Sergeant Donald Fergusson.

Lundberg said his mother, Eveline, had been sick, but the doctors were having trouble working out what was wrong with her. With no real diagnosis other than some seemingly unrelated symptoms (gastric upset, nervous anxiety, hair loss and arthritis), the family tried to do what they could to ease her distress. She'd taken a long holiday to Western Australia. She'd tried staying with relatives in warmer climates for extended periods. Her health would rally briefly, only to deteriorate after she returned to Sydney. She was only sixty-three yet she suffered crippling pain in her legs and lower body. She was often inexplicably nauseous. Lundberg said his memories of birthdays, Christmases and Easters for close to two years were bound to memories of Eveline's illness.

In March 1952, she was admitted to hospital to have her gallstones removed. It was hoped the operation would alleviate some of the unpleasant digestive symptoms she was experiencing. It did not. In June, she went for a long stay with her daughter in Macksville, north of Port Macquarie on the Nambucca River. Slowly, her strength returned. She began sleeping again. Her hair even began to grow back. Everyone assumed the change of scenery and time away from the city had helped to ease her melancholy. When she came home to Sydney, everyone was hopeful. Unfortunately, her symptoms quickly returned.

Lundberg said he knew who was responsible: members of the family called her Aunt Carrie, and she was his aunt by marriage.

Fergusson stuck a finger in his exposed ear, bent his head and leaned harder into the receiver so he might hear better. He could tell that Lundberg had more to say.

'Aunt Carrie spent a lot of time with my father before he died,' the man said. His voice was angry now. 'Aunt Carrie is now spending a lot of time with my mother.' He described how Aunt Carrie seemed to spend a lot of time with people in the family who wound up lame, then blind, then dead.

Fergusson smoothed down his tie and eased the receiver away from his ear. 'Mr Lundberg, how would you feel about coming in for an interview?'

Even though the victory in Yvonne Fletcher's case had emboldened Fergusson, he still had reservations. The failure to convict Ruby Norton showed that thallium cases were still a tricky proposition and could go horribly wrong. The last thing he wanted was to take on a weak case that would not be compelling enough to convince a jury. He called Krahe and said he needed him.

If the accusations that Lundberg had made about the woman known as Caroline Grills were true, she was not going to be easy to catch. She had no criminal record and was not part of the underworld of organised crime. She did not conform to prevailing criminal tropes: she was a married woman, a housewife and a charity worker. Her husband was no criminal either. The Grills were an ordinary Sydney family. Fergusson and Krahe were presented with an unusual scenario for an undercover operation. They would need to study a social order which had its own complex rituals and remained impervious to the understanding of anyone outside its hierarchy. What police faced was far more complex than any criminal syndicate. Fergusson and Krahe had to infiltrate a family.

•

By early 1953, Fergusson and Krahe believed they had a better understanding of thallium killing because they understood more about both key components to these crimes: the science of the drug, and the psychology of the killer. The detectives postulated that thallium killing was different to other kinds of killing. It was not violent, at least in the traditional sense. Thallium murderers did not usually seek to strike one devastating blow; it was not like taking aim and firing a weapon into lethal target zones like the brain or the heart. Thallium killers were capable of patiently exploiting the poison's manifold secrets. Thallium was a slow burn, and killing with it required a certain kind of disposition: deceitful. In turn, efforts to catch these criminals required a certain kind of investigation: deceitful.

Undercover operations had become an increasingly important part of policing and in the two years leading up to the pursuit of Caroline Grills, the CIB had employed them more and more. For circumstantial cases, which relied heavily on witness statements, undercover stings were an ideal way to gather the necessary evidence. Just that year, the CIB had used an undercover sting to expose the international smuggling of possum furs. Highly sought after for its soft and fine texture, and rare because of the difficulty faced by hunters sourcing it, possum fetched huge prices on the overseas market. In 1953, the CIB staked out the GPO letterboxes in Sydney city, waiting to witness the collection of a parcel of possum fur en route to an illegal trafficker overseas. The operation took months of planning. Dressed in overalls, and posed with a rag and polishing cream, an undercover officer pretended to remove the tarnish from the brass plates of post office boxes while watching people collect and send their mail.

In 1953, undercover operations fell firmly within the CIB's expertise, for both good and ill. Fergusson and Krahe, influenced by the custom and practice of the CIB at the time, began to hatch a plan to catch Caroline Grills. But with Krahe now spending more time with Gunner Kelly, Fergusson needed extra manpower. He needed an informant to be the eyes and ears of the police during the operation.

The two detectives met with Johnny Lundberg and his brother-in-law, tram driver Jack Downey, who was married to Lundberg's sister, Chrissie. Jack and Chrissie lived at 7 Great Buckingham Street, Redfern. Eveline had lived across the road at number 12 for more than twenty years, but now, almost blind, she stayed mostly with Jack and Chrissie. The location of the sting was set and the instructions the detectives gave their new informant Jack Downey were simple: take note of everything you can about Caroline Grills whenever she visits. Make a record of it, just like a real detective.

Jack Downey took to his new vocation as undercover detective with considerable enthusiasm. Caroline visited every Monday – usually to have lunch and play cards. Jack worked a Monday morning roster but got home just in time for lunch.

The timing was perfect.

•

After the interview with CIB, Jack and Chrissie sat down with Johnny at the kitchen table at 7 Great Buckingham Street and compiled a timeline of deaths that had occurred in the orbit of their family. They tried to remember every visit Caroline made, every cup of tea she poured and every card game that was played. At first, it seemed an impossible task, but the more they talked, the more they remembered. A picture began to slowly emerge. Chrissie had also been sick on and off throughout the previous year. When they tallied it up, the periods of her illness seemed to follow a visit by Caroline.

The circumstances of the death of Chrissie's father (John Lundberg senior) also seemed suspicious, though they had not seemed so at the time because doctors had been adamant he died because of a peptic ulcer. But John had gone to Woy Woy on holiday with Caroline and Richard Grills in 1948 and had returned to Sydney sweaty and ill with cramps in the back of his hands. He died later that year 'after he went totally blind and mental', according to Chrissie.

They also considered the deaths of Angelina Thomas, Caroline's sister-in-law Mary-Ann Mickelson, and Caroline's stepmother Christina. They knew all of this because the families knew each other well enough to stay in touch. They also knew all of this because Caroline seemed to delight in family gossip.

When the deaths were compared, the similarities seemed remarkable. A timeline slowly began to emerge across the Lundberg, Grills and Mickelson families. At first the deaths seemed unrelated. Those deaths could only be linked through their connection to two people: Caroline and Richard Grills.

Of these two people, it was Caroline who had time during the week and conducted a rotation of visits.

Chrissie was nervous about her brother and her husband getting involved. 'Shouldn't the police handle the investigation?' she asked.

'They are,' Johnny said. 'We're just getting the evidence they need.'

Chrissie was about to argue when she heard her mother call out from the other room. She pushed back her chair to get up, but Eveline appeared in the doorway. She had shuffled her way through the house, her arms outstretched, feeling the walls as she walked. The light was blinding she said, she could no longer bear it. With the intense pain in her forehead and in her eyes, and the blindness, she looked permanently startled. Chrissie, who only moments before had expressed her reservations about the police plan, now watched helplessly as her mother walked face first into a wall.

'I agree. We have to do something,' Chrissie said. She got up and guided her mother carefully out to the toilet.

14

JAM ROLY-POLY

Jack Downey started keeping a diary, tracking Caroline's every move.

29 March. Caroline brought a vast amount of food, far too much for only a handful of people. A dozen pikelets – Caroline made them herself. Crystallised ginger – bought from the grocer. Jam roly-poly – Caroline made herself.

The jam roll or roly-poly was a popular afternoon tea treat because it could be made cheaply with suet and tinned conserve from the pantry. A large sheet of cake batter was baked, spread with jam, and then rolled into a long log shape. To serve, it was sliced into round pieces of cake streaked with dark red lines. The unusual appearance led to its informal name: dead man's arm.

When Caroline arrived at the house that day she tipped a quantity of crystallised ginger straight into a large ceramic ginger jar on the mantle. She served the pikelets. 'I brought the roly-poly for your mother, I know she likes them,' she said.

Chrissie and Jack looked at each other.

'I don't know how she would eat it all,' said Chrissie. 'There's so much food.' She was determined her mother would not take a single bite of the dessert. 'We're headed over to my brother's this afternoon, I'll take this over there.'

But Caroline was adamant. 'Don't take it out there. It's for your mother. You could leave it for her for tomorrow.'

Chrissie wrapped a tea towel around the cake and put it aside in the kitchen.

•

Later that day, sometime around dusk, and after Caroline had gone home, Johnny Lundberg arrived. Chrissie immediately went to the kitchen and grabbed the jam roly-poly. She placed it on a chopping board, on the bench.

'This is what she brought today,' said Jack. Johnny turned the kitchen light on, so they could see it more clearly. The three amateur sleuths stood in a circle, staring at the dead man's arm.

Jack pushed back his sleeves, like a medical examiner anticipating the inspection of something irksome. 'Do you have a knife?' he asked. Chrissie grabbed a long boning knife from the drawer and passed it to him, handle first, like a medical assistant. She then got a flip-top notebook from the writing desk in the other room. She came back in, notebook open and pencil in hand, ready to take notes.

Jack carefully unwrapped the cloth from the cake, exposing its soft flesh. He picked up the knife and, with the precision of a surgeon made a long incision through the top layer. With the flat of the blade he bent the top layer of the cake away, as if skinning it. Three heads leaned over the body of suet and flour, like doctors conducting an autopsy on a severed limb.

'Wet,' said Johnny.

'Sticky,' said Jack.

Chrissie made a note of this.

Not knowing quite what to expect, and having no real idea of what they were looking for, they were silent. They stared into the depths of the sticky red filling, as if somehow any deadly mysteries held within the roly-poly might reveal themselves.

'Just looks like jam,' said Jack, disappointment in his voice. Chrissie didn't bother writing that observation down. When police asked about it later, Jack said simply, 'We put it in the dirt bin.'

13 April, Caroline arrived in a blue cottony frock, with pockets in the front. She brought eight meat pies from Sargents to share, and a dozen pikelets and a bun loaf.

Two weeks later, Jack saw his mother-in-law eating one of the pies that Caroline had brought. As Eveline was now almost completely blind, the pie had been mashed up in a soup plate so she could spoon it like a bowl of meaty porridge. Jack also noticed how actively involved Caroline had been with the serving of food and drink that day. She served water to everyone at the card game. She carefully poured glasses and one by one handed them to each person, walking back and forth between the kitchen and the verandah – one glass per trip.

20 April, Caroline wearing a brown flannel frock. She served sandwiches and bun loaf.

When Jack heard the sound of crockery in the kitchen, he ran down the hall and waited, watching carefully from some distance away. Caroline poured a cup of tea, then walked it through the house. She returned, poured another cup, and then walked it through the house again. At one point, he saw her pause. Just out of his line of sight in the doorway, she half-turned away and pulled something out of her front pocket. Her hand appeared to hover over the teacup for a moment, before she walked on.

Jack was convinced Caroline had poured something into the cup. Assuming she was gone, he rushed into the kitchen, desperate to inspect the space for evidence of something nefarious. But Caroline doubled back unexpectedly and came bounding into the room only moments after she had left. She was not startled to see him there. Her manner seemed completely casual.

'They want a drink, Jack,' she said. He jumped a little. 'And your fridge is playing up.' She kicked her foot bossily and thumped the metal door of the cooler with her heavy-soled shoe before turning on her heel and leaving the room once more.

Jack took a few deep breaths to calm himself then rushed down the hall to look through the front window. He wanted a clear view of the porch, but did not wish to be seen. He hid behind the curtains, the drapes falling around him like a cloak of invisibility, but his loafers still protruded very clearly from underneath. He watched. Eveline sat vacantly staring forward. Caroline placed a teacup into her hands. She assisted the vulnerable woman by bending her fingers around the cup to ensure she could grasp it.

When he was certain that Caroline was distracted, he peeked from behind the curtain. He spied Caroline's bag on the floor. With a flutter of the drapes he rushed to take a closer look, plunging his hands into the bag but careful not to disturb anything within. He was not entirely sure what he was looking for, but felt certain he would know when he found it. This time, there was little more than knitting and candy and old ladies hankies. He resumed his post, behind the curtain, and continued to watch.

Caroline took three or four empty cups from the table and brought them back to the kitchen. Jack waited for her to walk back down the hall. As soon as she passed, he ran as fast as he could on the tips of his toes after her. He pulled up fast again, in the hall, peeking around the corner, watching her for a moment, before falling back into another room so he wouldn't be seen. When he heard the back door of the house slam, he bolted up the stairs to the top floor. Caroline was going to the outhouse, and he was determined not to miss it.

In his haste, he slipped on the stairs. He grabbed his knee and hobbled forward to the window on the top level. He knew if he could reach it, he would have an unobscured view of the backyard. He watched, stealthily, by standing a few steps back from the window in the shadow, so he would not be seen in the light streaming in from outside. He got there just in time. Caroline swung open the door to the toilet. She closed it. The gap under the door allowed him to see her feet. They spun on the spot. He then saw her black, heavy-soled slippers, worn to support her bad ankles, come to a rest, pointing forward. Her feet remained there for some time. Jack knew this because he watched the clock. She sat for three minutes. When the door swung open again, she paused for a moment to tug at her underwear, then toddled back through the door and into the house.

Jack raced down to the toilet. He needed to get there before anyone else could use it and possibly destroy precious evidence. On his way across the yard, he snapped off a camellia branch. He swung open the dunny door. It banged loudly. He stared into the toilet bowl with the stick in his hand. His shoulders sank with disappointment. The bowl was empty. He poked about, hopeful the stick might dislodge some treasure of evidence, but nothing bobbed up. He hoped for a small brown glass bottle, but all he found was a dark brown skid. When Jack reported the matter to police later, he described it as 'a rust mark'. When police asked Jack to record Caroline's movements, no one expected that he would take the instructions quite so literally.

Jack ran back into the house. His shoes slid in a patch of mud. He corrected, straightening his back and steadying himself. He again hid behind the drapes, with a good line of sight to the porch. He saw Johnny Lundberg arrive but, eager not to miss a moment of surveillance, he did not go out to greet him. He waited. Eveline still sat holding the teacup that Caroline had given her. When Jack saw the swoop of Caroline's brown housecoat, and her feet toddle back towards the front door, he made his move.

He ran outside to his mother-in-law and grabbed the cup from her hand. She was staring, seemingly unaware of what was going on around her. 'Mother, your tea's gone cold,' he said. 'Let me just reheat that for you.' With the still-full cup, he walked briskly but carefully to the kitchen and hid the cup behind a chopping board. He took a deep breath.

•

Later that day, once lunch was cleared and he was sure everyone was outside, Jack rummaged around in the bottom of the cupboard for an old jam jar. He took the teacup Caroline had given Eveline, decanted the tea into the jar and hid it on the top shelf in the laundry.

When he returned to the hall on his way outside, he saw Caroline. He took his chance. 'Have you seen my tropical fish?' he asked. He put his arm around her shoulder and steered her into the sitting room. Along one wall was a large and very impressive glass fish tank. Caroline's bag was still on the floor. She headed towards it, but Jack directed her instead to the tank. He pointed at their brightly coloured swishing tails.

'They're worth so much I'm going to sell them,' he said.

'Is that right?' Caroline replied, completely uninterested.

'Can you see that one right at the back, it's the rarest one – very expensive, very exotic. Take a look at it, really, it's worth it.'

Caroline leaned forward to try to get a better look at whatever was hiding in the plant matter at the back of the tank. As she leaned over, so did Jack. Her housecoat pocket swung open, but he saw nothing at all. It was empty. Jack heard the sound of Chrissie and the other women outside. Outdoor chairs were being scraped across the ground, and crockery clattered as it was stacked.

As the door swung open, Caroline went over to her bag and cried, 'Someone has been in my bag!' Jack gulped. Caroline lifted up a roll of Lifesavers which had been sitting at the very top of her bag. 'Jack, how did these get here? These aren't mine.' She looked him straight in the eye and Jack's face filled with schoolboy guilt. She then grabbed her roll of knitting and brandished it high in the air as well. 'And this. Someone has moved this, the stitches have been slipped off the hook.'

At that moment, Chrissie entered the sitting room with teacups in her hand.

'Chrissie, someone's been through my bag,' said Caroline with an indignant tone. Chrissie could not control the look of shock that fell across her face. 'These aren't mine,' Caroline added, holding the offending Lifesavers up in the air.

Quick thinking, Chrissie answered without missing a beat. 'Sorry, Aunt Carrie. I thought they were yours, I must have put them there by mistake.'

'I only use Quick-eze, not Lifesavers,' Caroline said sternly, though she seemed to accept the explanation without further argument. She began repacking her bag in preparation to leave.

Jack exhaled heavily, walked to his bedroom and collapsed onto the bed.

Johnny appeared at the door. Starved of the only male company in the house, and finding Jack missing for most of the afternoon, he was suspicious. 'Right. Out with it, mate. What in the hell have you been up to?'

Jack motioned for Johnny to keep his voice down. 'You wouldn't believe me if I told you.'

'Try me.'

•

At regular intervals, Detective Krahe received food items collected by Jack Downey. But there was a delay. Jack worked a lot. The tea sat on his laundry shelf for fifteen days. From the jam jar it was moved to a rum flask. Jack dropped it off when he had time to travel to the city. The now lumpy and rancid liquid sloshed about in the flask as he carried it in his jacket pocket.

At different points during the investigative process, police had a vast amount of material tested: bottles of oysters, biscuits, chocolates, pies, pikelets, sandwiches, bun loaf, and cake. All the while, the crystallised ginger remained at the Downey home, untouched. At home one day, feeling peckish, Jack took a piece of ginger from the jar. It was not that he had forgotten who had brought it – he remembered clearly. He stared closely at the piece in his hand. It did not look like it had been tampered with. Not content to try it just once, he ate ginger for three straight days from 22 through 24 April.

Around the same time, Eveline suffered another painful attack. She was lethargic, weak and had terrible pain in her lower limbs. Rushed to hospital, she lapsed into a coma for a short period. Then Chrissie was struck down with a strange illness too, suffering gastric distress and other aches and pains. While in hospital, she wanted answers and asked to be tested for poison. The assistant medical superintendent of Sydney Hospital, Dr Farrar, agreed. Both Eveline Lundberg and her daughter Chrissie Downey gave urine samples. Both were found to have been exposed to thallium.

With this confirmation, the hospital now sought to develop a treatment. Most desperate to save Eveline, who was gravely ill and blind, they worked quickly. Just as the detectives were experimenting with new ways of investigating thallium poisoning, medical practitioners were exploring new ways to cure those affected. Doctors sought to neutralise the effects of the toxin and flushed Eveline's system with sodium iodide.

Her condition improved a little; however, doctors worried that too much damage had been done by the thallium for her to ever properly recover. Diagnosed with atrophy of the optic nerve, Eveline Lundberg's blindness was now permanent.

On Monday 11 May, Caroline visited the Downey home as she always did. This time, however, there were some unexpected guests. Detectives Fergusson and Krahe arrived before anyone had the chance to eat. Krahe confiscated the contents of Caroline's bags, which included meat pies, currant loaf, chewing gum, Minties, confectionery and pikelets. All of it was tested for the presence of thallium. All of it tested negative. So too did the crystallised ginger.

Over the next fortnight, Jack Downey began to suffer tightness in the chest and a deep pain across his legs and shins. 'I just feel queer,' he said to Chrissie. He understated his symptoms. Not sure how seriously to take it, Chrissie waited a few days. She wondered if the stress of the last weeks had been too much for him. He was distressed, but was also sick in the stomach. Chrissie was worried. She picked up the phone, but did not call an ambulance. Instead, she called the CIB HQ. A short while later Fergusson arrived, alone, and took Jack to hospital.

Within two weeks Jack's condition deteriorated. His symptoms were strange. The glands in his neck were tender and hard, like golf balls. He had tightness and pain in his chest, and his left foot was numb. When examined by the medical team, his urine tested positive for thallium.

Caroline Grills was charged with the murder of Christina Mickelson (d. November 1947), Angelina Thomas (d. January 1948), John Lundberg (d. October 1948), Mary-Ann Mickelson (d. February 1953), and the attempted murders of Jack Downey (her fifty-year-old nephew, by marriage), Eveline Lundberg (her sister-in-law) and Chrissie Downey (her niece, by marriage).

Bail was set at 2000 pounds.

Dead man's arm (early 1950s)

Ingredients
3 eggs
Half cup of white sugar
¾ cup S.R. flour
2 tablespoons of boiling water
Jam (whatever is available in the pantry)
A little caster sugar (optional)

Method
Preheat oven to 350°F. Prepare a swiss roll pan by greasing sides with butter or margarine and lining tray with baking paper.

Beat eggs in a commercial mixer until thick and foamy and pale yellow in colour. Slowly add sugar, making sure that the mixture remains foamy and thick. Ensure the sugar is being dissolved into the egg. Add sifted flour and water. Fold carefully. Pour into prepared swiss roll pan/tray. Bake in oven (ensure the oven is really warm) for only 10–15 minutes.

On the kitchen bench, lay out a tea towel and place a long piece of baking paper (dusted with caster sugar). Turn warm cake out immediately onto the baking paper/tea towel. Spread cake with jam. Using the tea towel and baking paper, roll the swiss roll so that it looks like a long sausage. Slice into pieces to serve.

15

EXPERIMENTING WITH NEW INGREDIENTS

MUCH LIKE THALLIUM SPREADS AND SETTLES UNPREDICTABLY in different sites throughout the human body, between 1952 and 1953 thallium seemed to spread and settle across a variety of sites in the city of Sydney. Two cases of gastric distress appeared at a northern Sydney hospital and were found to be thallium-related. One case of peripheral neuritis was diagnosed in the west. Inner-city residents appeared at Sydney Hospital suffering headaches, respiratory distress and paralysis – all determined to be caused by toxic levels of thallium. Between March 1952 and April 1953, ten deaths and forty-six hospital admissions were attributed to thallium. It was an alarming statistic given exposure to thallium could only be traced to one source – the product known as Thall-Rat.

While thallium could be bought in other states in Australia, its sale was subject to stricter regulations. The grain industry was considered important, so Thall-Rat was more freely available in rural areas. In Queensland, for example, thallium had formed an important part of the frontline defence of the canefields against attack by vermin. As a commercial preparation, marketed for mainstream sale in the cities, thallium was uncommon outside of New South Wales. Victoria moved quickly and at the end of 1952 legislated for heavy restrictions on the conditions of its sale. In Queensland thallium had been on the restricted poisons list for many years.

Only in New South Wales could thallium be purchased so easily and cheaply. You did not need to provide a name or address at the time of purchase. You did not need to sign for it and no one checked your identification. Anyone could sell it – from a pharmacist to a grocer – and it was at the seller's discretion to retain any record of sale.

Health staff were only slowly beginning to understand the potential dangers thallium posed should it fall into the wrong hands. By the end of October 1952, North Sydney Hospital had admitted three patients with what staff described as disturbing examples of thallium exposure. In all cases, thallium had been self-administered. Twenty-five-year-old Jack Goldsmith was admitted with symptoms consistent with thallium poisoning. When questioned, he claimed that he must have accidentally eaten poisoned toast, as he happened to prepare a rat bait at the very same time that he was making his breakfast. No one thought much of it until Goldsmith appeared with poisoning symptoms again, and again. In less than twelve months he was dead. Once the case was examined, more information came to light. Goldsmith was a troubled man. A girlfriend had ended a relationship of four years. He had taken thallium over and over again before it finally killed him. He'd slipped right under the medical radar.

In December 1952, a Czech migrant (whom authorities refused to publicly identify), walked into the Department of Immigration and begged for help in finding work. He had been living in a migrant hotel in Bathurst in central western New South Wales. Under the terms of his immigration he had been required to work under government direction, but this had only been for two years. He received a certificate of release and was now officially 'free'. This also meant he was unemployed and homeless, as the department no longer agreed to assist him to find work or house him. Destitute and unable to find work because he looked and talked like 'a foreigner', the man walked into the front office of the Department of Immigration to plead mercy. He staged a sit-in, refusing to leave the office until someone helped him.

When a staff member said it was not their job to find him work, he took a small dark bottle from his pocket and said, in carefully phrased English so there would be no confusion, 'If you will not help me, I will drink this.' He moved the bottle labelled Thall-Rat purposefully to his lips. A quick-thinking immigration worker leaped forward and smacked the bottle away from his mouth just in time. The man was handed over to police custody and sent to Reception House. The news media dubbed this thallium victim 'the unhappy migrant'.

Authorities suspected there were more cases of thallium poisoning going undetected; however, it was difficult to get an accurate picture. Symptoms were regularly attributed to other causes, including gastric upsets, heart trouble, respiratory distress, nervous conditions and delusional disorders. Identifying the presence of poison required knowledgeable medical staff to be on roster when a patient was brought in, and law enforcement personnel capable of recognising the signs of poisoning if police were called. Although the media had begun sensationalising the issue of thallium, there remained a poor level of knowledge about it across the community.

The year 1953 saw thallium use spike in clusters near to where pharmacists and grocers were known to sell it. Like any commercial preparation, it was not sold everywhere. A local pharmacy in the inner west (comprising Newtown, Marrickville and Earlwood) stocked it, and in March 1953 a young married woman from Marrickville (her name was not released) presented at Royal Prince Alfred Hospital as a potential suicide from thallium. Next an Earlwood man, Robert Bruce Bardon, presented at Regent Street police station claiming he had poisoned his father. He was prepared to face the death penalty, he said, because he had cut his father's cough mixture with thallium. At first police thought Bardon was delusional, until a medical assessment of his father revealed the man had indeed been poisoned. Bardon's case illustrated the complexities faced by authorities in managing the growing crisis. The state immediately sought to prosecute Bardon, but very quickly hit a wall. They could not get anyone from the local community to give witness statements. Bardon was a returned serviceman who had suffered terribly from neurosis, and everyone in the area knew and had great affection for the family. His workmates rallied to his defence, signing a petition attesting to his good character, and suggesting that his attempts to kill his chronically ill father were, in a strange way, a misguided attempt to help him. Robert's father even appeared in court on his behalf stating, 'I forgive him. It is my dearest wish that my son come home again.'

The inner city, both west and east, then experienced a spate of thallium poisonings. Twenty-year-old Edgar Azzopardi, from Darlinghurst, used thallium in a kind of terroristic threat against sixteen-year-old Gwenneth Turner. Gwenneth had spurned his advances so Edgar began sending packages of thallium to her in the mail. On 15 June, a 72-year-old pensioner from Glebe appeared in the Lunacy Court. He swallowed a bottle of thallium, he said, because he was suffering from chronic pain. On 17 June, a 27-year-old drank a bottle of thallium in front of his girlfriend. He survived, but was now in hospital under police guard. A third suicide attempt, of a sailor, was also being investigated by the CIB. He had argued with his wife, and had taken thallium some weeks prior to garner her sympathy. The thallium had taken a long time to affect the man's health, but was ultimately confirmed because medical staff now knew what to look for.

Dismayed at what appeared to be signs of a unique epidemic (albeit a slow and insidious one), the board of one major Sydney hospital contacted their local member of parliament. North Sydney had several local grocers and pharmacists who stocked thallium, and North Sydney Hospital received numerous ER admissions which were linked to thallium. James Geraghty, the local member for North Sydney, raised the matter in Parliament, asking the Health Minister (Mr Sullivan) what the government intended to do. Would they ban thallium? Would they amend the *Poisons Act* to include thallium in the schedule of poisons and, at a minimum, restrict its sale?

While the police prepared their case against Caroline Grills, yet another poisoning came to light. Beryl Joyce Hague was charged with having maliciously administered thallium to her husband. Police knew this for sure because it was Beryl who told them so.

On 15 June 1953, Leichhardt man Alan Hague arrived home drunk. Although this wasn't unusual, on this night he was particularly belligerent. Beryl Hague dished up dinner. Alan was abusive. He tipped the dinner down the front of her dress and threw his plate at the dog. An argument ensued, which culminated in Alan striking Beryl in the back of the head with the heavy handle of a large kitchen knife as he shouted at her to, 'Shut up!' Beryl walked out the door, leaving their three children Clifford (fourteen), Lynette (twelve) and Janice (nine) behind. The children looked on from the window as their mother walked down Marion Street. The children were not surprised that she was leaving; she had done so before when their father became unbearable. They were only surprised that this time she was not taking them with her.

Beryl fumed for about half an hour. She walked it off. When she returned, she seemed to have calmed down. She asked him if he would like a cup of tea. She gently suggested to Alan that perhaps it was best if he go to bed.

It was only after Alan was in bed, in his pyjamas, that Beryl ran suddenly into the room and began yelling at him. 'Alan, get up! We have to go to hospital!' Too drunk to ask questions, he assumed his wife was ill. He got out of bed, pulled on some clothes and went with her. Their eldest son Clifford looked after his two sisters as he watched his mother and father pile into a cab.

When the couple arrived at hospital, Beryl told staff what she had done. After she had returned from her walk following the couple's argument, she had seen the bottle of Thall-Rat on the shelf while making Alan's tea. She decided to teach him a lesson, but claimed she had not intended to kill him. Beryl's story seemed plausible. The woman was clearly agitated and remorseful. Nevertheless, Alan did not believe her. He felt nothing, he said. In front of doctors he said to Beryl, 'You're the one that's sick. You have a bad case of imaginitis.' Doctors insisted that Alan remain in hospital to be treated and pumped his stomach before the poison had the chance to be properly absorbed.

When trying to explain her actions that night, Beryl freely admitted what she had done. 'It was to give him a headache, for all the headaches he has given me.' In court, the case did not unfold at all in the way police planned. Alan supported the wife who had admitted openly that she had tried to kill him. He refused to give evidence against her and said they could not make him because they were married.

The prosecution tried to dig dirt on Beryl Hague. To their amazement, a check of the legal records led to an extraordinary discovery. The Hagues had been married – but had also subsequently divorced after a period of marital discord. They'd reconciled a short time later. When police told Alan, and then Beryl, that they were no longer husband and wife, both seemed genuinely shocked that the decree nisi had been made absolute. The Hagues had been living together again for over four years under the assumption they were still legally married. They were not. To Beryl's horror, she'd been living in sin.

Alan Hague remained staunchly loyal. He bailed Beryl out and took her home while she waited for her day in court. He worked with the defence, and not the prosecution. He blamed himself for the entire incident saying, 'The children had been sick. Beryl was nervy. I was more or less the cause . . . Possibly I had too much beer that day.'

The court case unfolded like a scene from *Romeo and Juliet*, largely because Beryl and Alan behaved like teenagers. The affection between the couple seemed strong, despite the obstacles of alcoholism, abuse, divorce, and now thallium. While giving evidence, Beryl openly admitted to wanting to hit Alan in the face with a frying pan on more than one occasion when he came home drunk. She then looked lovingly over at him. While the prosecution described the process of pumping his stomach, Alan smiled sweetly and winked at his wife. The dark comedy with which the Hagues approached their marriage muddied any debate about the dangers of thallium and the potential seriousness it posed.

On 30 July 1953, Beryl was sentenced to two years in prison. In passing sentence Justice Holden took into account her remorse, her nerve condition and her husband's loyalty too. Beryl may have poisoned her husband, said the judge, but that didn't make her a bad mother. Justice Holden also noted another mitigating factor: Alan could clearly not look after the children, so it was in their interests that their mother be released as soon as possible. If her behaviour was satisfactory in prison, she could be out that year.

As it turned out, Beryl Hague was home in time for Christmas.

•

By mid-1953, authorities had publicly acknowledged the problem that thallium posed. Aware that something needed to be done, and fast, an emergency meeting of poison experts was called. Clinical doctors and scientists from the Office of the Government Analyst met to pool the disparate pieces of information being gathered across many areas of service activity. Among the attendees were the Senior Medical Officer of Health, the Chief Veterinary Surgeon, and representatives of the Australian Dental Association, the Agriculture

Department, the University of Sydney, the Pharmacy Board, the Chamber of Commerce, the Chamber of Manufactures, and the Agricultural and Pastoral Associations. Now dubbed the 'poison experts' of the CIB, Fergusson and Krahe were considered essential to the discussions too. A set of recommendations about the restriction of sale of thallium were given to the Minister of Health. In addition, experts agreed to assemble again to discuss whether the scientific scope existed to develop an antidote. It was the first meeting of its kind ever held in Australia.

While the policy response to thallium was slowly beginning to form, the police response also grew in momentum. On 11 May, Fergusson and Krahe had quietly arrested Caroline Grills. She'd been formally charged on 12 May and was held on remand. Throughout June, Fergusson and Krahe began working on one of the most complex circumstantial cases they had ever assembled.

Pikelets (early 1950s)

Ingredients
1 rounded cup SR flour
1 tablespoon sugar
1 large egg
Milk (to mix)
1 dessertspoon of melted butter
A little extra butter for cooking
Jam & whipped cream to serve

Method

Place flour and sugar in a bowl and make a well in the centre. Drop egg into well and mix, slowly adding enough milk as you go to create a thick batter. When the mix is thick and smooth, add melted butter. Let rest on bench in the kitchen until small bubbles form on the top of the batter.

Heat a frying pan to a medium heat. Melt butter so the batter will not stick when cooking. Pour in enough batter to create a pikelet of desirable size. When bubbles form on the surface of the pikelet, flip it over and cook on the other side.

Serve with jam and cream.

16

ALL-IN-ONE METHOD

DETECTIVES FERGUSSON AND KRAHE DEVELOPED AN INVESTIGA-
tive approach to thallium cases that might best be described as
the 'all-in-one method'. Countless witnesses were interviewed
and the suspect was interrogated about multiple murders
at one time. While the detectives' method was challenged
by a judge at Yvonne Fletcher's trial, any reservations were
quickly forgotten. A guilty verdict seemed to be an implicit
endorsement of the method, and since the recipe had worked
before, the detectives repeated the steps in the hope of getting
the same result.

They conducted several interviews with Caroline Grills
as different phases of the investigation yielded evidence.
Fergusson asked the questions while Krahe took his shorthand
notes. And, just as they had in Yvonne Fletcher's investigation,

the officers went into lockdown post-interrogation as they cross-checked the transcript together.

Caroline was tiny and grandmotherly, yet she seemed unruffled, even when faced with Fergusson's intense gaze and Krahe's intimidating frame. Very quickly, she demonstrated an ability to deflect any attempt to unsettle her.

'Did you know what Mrs Lundberg was suffering from when she was admitted to the Sydney Hospital in May of last year?' Fergusson asked.

'I thought it was her nerves,' Caroline responded coolly.

'Who told you she was suffering from nerves?'

'I do not know now, it's a long time ago. I suppose it would be one of the family but I cannot remember which one.'

'Did you visit her while she was in hospital?'

'Yes, often. I used to go with my husband.'

'Did anybody ever tell you that she was suffering from any kind of poisoning?'

'Yes, they thought she might have had gallstones. That was twenty-seven years ago. She was being treated by a Mr Morrow, a chemist, and he was supposed to pass them for her. She was on the table ready to be operated upon and she said, "No, I will go and see Morrow". He'd been treating her for a long time and she'd had it for about twenty-seven years. She had one big stone.'

'I am not speaking of the occasions on which she was operated on for gallstones,' Fergusson said. 'I am referring to the occasion when she was admitted to the Sydney Hospital about this time last year. Is there any ill feeling between you and any member of the Downey or Lundberg families?'

'Not as far as I know, we have always been pals and friends.'

•

Fergusson and Krahe then interviewed Eveline Lundberg. As the victim of an attempted murder, she offered a unique perspective. Her view of the relationship with Caroline was especially important to the investigation. Like others, she had a bank of anecdotes in which she felt hurt or aggrieved. She recalled what Caroline had said to her in the weeks before her arrest. 'I had a dream about you. In the dream you died and you left all your clothes to me.'

Fergusson and Krahe asked Eveline about the quality of their relationship. She spoke of Caroline in unflattering terms. There was no connection between them. There was tolerance, but no love. Even Caroline's generosity was viewed with suspicion. 'She never goes to anybody's place empty-handed,' Eveline said.

Eveline's testimony also gives insight to the complex dynamics that existed between Caroline and Richard's family. When asked about the affection between the two women, Eveline answered, 'Well, I was [kind] for my mother's sake ... for the family's sake to keep the peace ... my mother asked me to always be kind to her.'

Eveline described her father (Caroline's father-in-law) as a difficult man who was abrasive with everyone, but appeared to have a particular dislike for Caroline. 'My father was very bitter,' she said.

'Did Mrs Grills need some kindness?' Fergusson asked.

Eveline was emphatic. 'Yes, she did.'

In contrast, when it came to Richard, Eveline could not speak highly enough. 'I think a lot of my brother,' she said.

Fergusson also asked Caroline about the deaths that had occurred within her own family. 'Do you know the cause of your stepmother's death?'

'Old age I suppose.'

'Do you think your stepmother was the type of woman who would have taken her own life?'

'No.'

'Do you know any person who would have reason to poison her?'

'No, I don't know of anybody. Grandfather wouldn't do it.'

'Was there any poison such as Thall-Rat kept at 12 Gerrish Street?'

'No, Grandfather used to use traps.'

'The government analyst has found thallium in the exhumed body of your stepmother.'

'Fancy that.'

'Can you offer any explanation of how the poison entered the body?'

'No.'

'We are going to arrest you for the murder of your stepmother.'

'All right.'

'We suspect that you murdered Mrs Mickelson by the administration of thallium.'

'I suppose you have to suspect somebody.'

Questions were asked about multiple deaths and multiple timelines, and lines of questioning that pertained to different cases overlapped and blurred. Just as they had with Yvonne's interrogation.

'Have you any knowledge of a rodenticide called Thall-Rat?' Fergusson asked.

'Yes, of course,' Caroline replied.

'Do you use it?'

'It is some time since I bought a bottle at Corbers. There was a rat gnawing at the bedroom and I said to Father, "I will have to get some more Thall-Rat".'

Fergusson asked Caroline about Mrs Lundberg and Thall-Rat. Her response was not what Fergusson expected.

'I got a bottle for Mrs Lundberg. She had big rats in her house . . . I also got a bottle for Chris Downey . . .'

'When did you purchase the bottle of Thall-Rat for Mrs Lundberg?'

'It's a long time ago now. She told me that it was successful too.'

'Have you any Thall-Rat at home?'

'Yes, I always keep it. There are always rats and mice about where there are fowls. I have no fowls myself but my neighbours have them.'

As the interview progressed, police asked about the death of Caroline's sister-in-law, Mary-Ann Mickelson, and Fergusson reported back to Caroline what Mary-Ann's daughters had said about her. They did not like her.

Caroline's observations of family members were often brutally delivered at brutal times, with little regard for the impact they might have on people in a state of shock and grief. Of her sister-in-law, Mary-Ann, she said, 'She had injured herself internally. She was a big woman – and had a job to walk.' The sharp and cutting commentary was then dulled with, 'Oh, but I was just like a sister to her.' The balance of saccharine sweet and sour was unsettling. When asked about the pain and numbness in Mary-Ann's legs, Caroline was quick to dismiss it. 'She always had trouble with her legs because of her weight.' Then, as if to assuage any bad impression of her, she added, 'She was a marvellous woman.'

Gladys Allan and Jean Lane, John and Mary-Ann Mickelson's daughters, were keen to report the insensitivity that Caroline had shown to them when their mother died. 'Your mother has only got about a fortnight to live,' Caroline had said. It was a hard thing for the two sisters to hear, and Caroline had delivered the statement with all the authority of a doctor. Not content to leave it there, she drove the point home. 'I just saw her jaw drop. They all go like that.' Caroline was referring to the mandibular movement that occurs among some people nearing death. There was a casual cruelty and dismissiveness to her observations that was difficult for others to ignore. But there was also a utilitarian logic that was equally jarring. 'Your mother hasn't got long to live,' was followed by, 'So you might want to get her money out of the banks.'

When Fergusson confronted Caroline with some of these recollections, she was quick to chastise. 'I'm surprised at those girls saying such things . . . after all I've done for them.'

'Well, you are suspected of poisoning Mary-Ann Mickelson, their mother,' Fergusson said.

'Well, I would have to be clever. I would have to be mighty clever.'

Fergusson and Krahe then interviewed those who had been close to Caroline's stepmother, Christina Mickelson. The woman had passed away almost five years earlier, but her relatives had not forgotten what Caroline had said to them. Mrs Jean Ralston was Christina's granddaughter from her previous marriage. She lived in Melbourne, but she had visited her grandmother intermittently and witnessed the progressive decline in her health in the last two years of her life. She described Christina as someone who keenly did housework and enjoyed the upkeep of the garden. 'Grandma was perfectly healthy and had a good head of hair,' she said, 'until January 1946.' She then described her miserable final two years. 'There were long stints in St Margaret's Hospital. She lost the use of her legs. Her hair fell out.'

Just as they had with Yvonne Fletcher's investigation, the detectives worked backwards, unearthing the past. The police had a long list of people who had been close to Caroline and had died within a very short period of time. Christina Mickelson (her stepmother), George Mickelson (her father), Angelina

Thomas (Richard's friend), John Mickelson (her brother) and his wife, Mary-Ann, and John Lundberg (her brother-in-law) had all died in less than four years. After consultation with the government analyst McDonald, police focused on those cases which could offer up scientific evidence. Both George Mickelson and John Mickelson had been cremated, and McDonald stated that it was not possible to test ashes for thallium.

Suspicious circumstances surrounded Angelina Thomas's death, and a good circumstantial case could be made based on interviews with neighbours, so Fergusson and Krahe began there. On 11 June 1953, Angelina Thomas's body was exhumed from Katoomba Cemetery. Both detectives were present, along with McDonald, and the two funeral directors who had overseen her burial five and a half years earlier. When the wooden coffin was exposed, there was just a single crack across the top. Remarkably intact, it was carefully lifted from the gravesite in one piece and taken to the morgue at the Blue Mountains District Hospital.

Though the outside of the coffin was well preserved, the same could not be said for the inside. The analysts who had assembled to assist in the collection of samples were scientists, but they were not morticians, and were unfamiliar in working with corpses. When the coffin was split open, a large yellow and white sac of organic material spilled out. McDonald was rattled.

Though Angelina had been dressed in a very dignified suit at burial, there was no trace of any clothes. A gelatinous body-shape was visible. Eerily, the scalp was also recognisable because it was noted to have a good growth of hair on it. Across the rest of the body, the skeleton was covered in what was described in the analyst's report as 'a firm cheesy integument'. It was the soapy or waxy material which forms during the process of decomposition, known as apidocere. The notes describe the tissue as 'pultacious' and 'mushy'. Decomposition had been contained by the gelatinous sac and it aided the analysts in gathering samples because they found it easy to open up the abdominal and thoracic cavities (the stomach and chest) and collect material from within. A section of the left femur (thigh bone) was removed and so too were samples of fingernail, toenail and hair. Specimens were removed from the surrounds of the coffin, including wood shavings and dirt. The specimens were sent to Sydney for examination.

On 23 June 1953, Fergusson and Krahe opened Christina Mickelson's grave, along with analyst McDonald and attendants as well. The team gathered four wooden boxes full of earth and filled bottles with liquid, separated them carefully and sent them for analysis.

Weeks later, when the results finally arrived at CIB headquarters, the police were impressed with the thoroughness of McDonald's analysis. From Angelina's burial site, there was no thallium found in the water and mud around the grave. From the abdominal cavity (approximately three pounds of sample) the analysis detected 0.44 milligrams of thallium per 100 grams. This is equivalent to about one-tenth of a grain of thallium. From the two pounds of muscle removed from the left and right thigh, 0.24 milligrams of thallium per 100 grams were found. In the wood shavings in the bottom of the coffin 0.07 milligrams of thallium per 100 grams were found. The tests detected approximately 1.2 milligrams of thallium per 100 grams of sample taken.

The analysis of Christina Mickelson's gravesite also provided police with a bonanza of evidence.

Labels: Christina Mickelson	Contents	Weight	Thallium count
Sealed glass jar no.1	Muscle	1 lb & 10 oz	0.33 mg/100 g
Sealed glass jar no. 2	Brain	1 lb & 8 oz	0.30 mg/100 g
Sealed glass jar no. 3	Left lung	6 oz	0.12 mg/100 g
Sealed glass jar no. 4	Liver	1 lb	0.18 mg/100 g
Sealed glass jar no. 5	Intestine	12 oz	0.3 mg/100 g
Sealed glass jar no. 6	Kidneys	3.5 oz	0.56 mg/100 g
Sealed glass jar no. 7	Portion of thigh & body cavity of bone marrow	Not stated	Traces

McDonald tested the pieces of evidence gathered by Downey and other family members, and items gathered from Caroline's home. In the rum flask containing 2 ounces of sour milky tea, he found one-tenth of a grain of thallium. He also examined two frocks: one blue, one brown. On the blue frock he found nothing. On the brown frock he found stains, like drops of rain on a felt hat. Traces of thallium were found in the pocket and on the bottom of the skirt as well.

In an attempt to understand how the commercially bought crystallised ginger could have become contaminated with thallium, McDonald conducted an experiment. He soaked the ginger in thallium and left it to marinate. He then rerolled the ginger in sugar. It appeared just as it would on the shelf of the grocer.

To ensure the evidence was translated in a way that lay persons on a jury might understand, McDonald also provided a summary of his analysis. In a 1-ounce bottle there are approximately ten grains of thallous sulphate. Based on the quantity of thallium found in Angelina's remains, and accounting for the fact that the grave would have been flushed with rain over a five-year period, McDonald estimated that Angelina had most likely been given a 2-ounce bottle of Thall-Rat prior to her death.

The last issue that police raised with Caroline was the matter of Jack Downey's attempted murder.

'I intend to charge you with having administered thallium to Jack Downey with the intent to murder him,' Fergusson said.

Caroline tsk-tsked. 'Why would I want to do that?'

Fergusson ignored her question.

'Probably done it to himself,' Caroline added.

Fergusson pressed on. 'I need to advise you that you will not be permitted to leave custody. You will be held in a cell until you appear in court.'

Without missing a beat, she had a comeback at the ready. 'You might want to keep an eye on Jack.' Fergusson looked surprised, wondering if perhaps an admission of guilt might follow. Instead, she shook her head in pity. 'That boy Downey is a nervous wreck, you know. Who was I supposed to give the tea to?' she added.

'Mrs Lundberg,' answered Fergusson.

Caroline tut-tutted. 'Chrissie always looks after her mother. You don't want to be fooled by them. What interest have I got? Why would I want to do anything wrong?'

When confronted with the results of scientific testing, Caroline challenged the police.

'The tea which was recovered from Mrs Lundberg's cup was submitted to the government analyst for examination and he has reported that he found an appreciable amount of thallium in it,' Fergusson told her.

'Well, why didn't he keep the cup and then you would have been able to tell whether I handled it or not?'

Caroline also had an explanation for the drops of thallium on her dress.

'Jack Downey was very strange with me that day. He asked me to go and look at goldfish in a bowl in the loungeroom. He could have leaned over and dropped it in my pocket. When I looked back at my bag, things had been moved in there. I carry Quick-Eze with me, but there was a packet of Lifesavers on the top. I said, "These aren't mine" and I handed them back to Jack Downey. I think Jack could have filled the holes of the Lifesavers with thallium and planted them in my bag.'

Caroline paused and then took a deep breath. 'Or it could have been when I was going to see my daughter. I was already dressed and ready to leave when the telephone rang. I saw a rat at the end of the backyard so I decided then and there to poison it. I got the thallium and laid a bait for it and another bait for a rat that had been gnawing at the bedroom wall. I noticed then I got some thallium on my hands, so I just used my handkerchief in my pocket to wipe it off and I put the handkerchief back in my pocket.'

•

With all of the interview material gathered, the detectives were ready for the Coroners Court. In August 1953, the Coroner reversed the original inquest decision and found that Caroline's stepmother, Christina Louisa Adelaide Mickelson, had died of thallium poisoning, and there was sufficient evidence for Caroline Grills to be referred for trial.

The inquests came in quick succession. The state pursued four murder cases and three attempted murder cases against Caroline Grills. Thallium, it was argued, had been the weapon used in each. Fergusson submitted to the court that under absolutely no circumstances should Caroline Grills be allowed out on bail. Bail was not granted. While waiting for trial on remand, she was given her own cell. Richard dropped off knitting and some magazines for her.

She chatted to wardresses in a relaxed way. The last movie showing at the afternoon matinées before her arrest had been the Irving Berlin musical comedy *Call Me Madam*, starring Ethel Merman and Donald O'Connor. Caroline recounted favourite scenes from the film with her captors, who found the diminutive lady, less than five feet tall, unlike any other prisoner they had met.

The trial proceeded uneventfully. The interview protocols used by Fergusson and Krahe which had previously been so controversial passed seamlessly into the trial proceedings.

On 15 October 1953, it took the twelve jurors just twelve minutes to convict Caroline Grills of the attempted murder of Eveline Lundberg. The verdict was delivered to an almost empty courtroom. Caroline's husband, Richard, who had loyally sat through every day of the proceedings, was outside on the lawn of the courthouse having a smoke when the verdict was read. Eveline had already gone home. The other trials unfolded quickly, and efficiently, and without incident.

On all charges, Caroline Grills was found guilty.

With legislative change now underway, New South Wales had taken steps to contain the threat of thallium. It was pulled from the shelves of many businesses. Where it was still available, pharmacists and grocers were required to document and keep a record of sale. But thallium had also already been sold for years, and these bottles were still in the community and in homes across Sydney. One major thallium case was still yet to break.

All-in-one cake (1950s)

Ingredients
4 oz butter
¾ cup sugar
2 eggs
1 rounded cup S.R. flour
¼ cup milk
vanilla

Method
Preheat oven at moderate (350–375°F). In one bowl, place all the ingredients. Beat for eight minutes. Pour cake batter into a well greased and lined cake pan. Bake in moderate oven for about half an hour. Cake should be golden, like sand, when cooked.

17

MILO: THE TONIC FOR THE TIMES

THE SAME YEAR CAROLINE GRILLS WENT TO TRIAL, AND ONLY a few kilometres away from her home on Gerrish Street in Gladesville, a couple of newlyweds were settling into their brand-new home on Hinkler Avenue, Ryde.

Judy Montanari had met Bobby Lulham in 1947 when she was just fifteen years old. The only child of prosperous Italian hairdresser Alfred Montanari (Monty) and elegant and aspirational Veronica Mabel, Judy was very close to her parents. A devout Roman Catholic, she attended Mass twice a week.

When she met twenty-year-old Bobby Lulham, there was an instant attraction. Each year, the rugby league association held trials so officials could assess and select potential talent for the upcoming season. Held at Gladesville Oval, local families used the event as free public entertainment. Judy, like many local teenagers, came to swoon at the public display of masculinity as young athletic men sprinted, wrestled and chased each other around the field.

Judy and Bobby began dating almost immediately. While they courted, Bobby spent a lot of time playing rugby league and he rose quickly through the grades. Within a few short years he'd developed into one of the most desirable and skilful players in the state. While he was a gifted sportsman and admired by many fans, this was the era before full-time professional salaries. During the day, Bobby still drove a truck as a contractor. He trained two nights a week and played games every Saturday when the competitive season was on. When he was picked to represent Australia in the international tests the following year, Bobby's career soared. He was away for months with the Kangaroo Squad as it toured Great Britain and France. Bobby and Judy exchanged love letters the entire time. The war had ended two years before and the two fantasised that they were having their own wartime romance: Bobby was fighting rugby battles on foreign soil, while Judy waited for him to return. On Judy's eighteenth birthday, they became engaged. But Judy, enraptured with the prospect of married life and starry eyed about her future husband, was shocked to discover her own parents' relationship falling apart.

In 1953, Judy and Bobby married. She was now the wife of one of the great rising stars of rugby league. Bobby's family was not wealthy, so Albert generously bought the young couple a brand-new house. Not yet twenty-two, Judy was his only daughter and he wanted to make sure she was well looked after. However, in keeping with the rigid and skewed perceptions of gender roles at the time, the home was put in Bobby's name, as he was the male head of the household, despite the fact that Judy's father had paid for it.

Judy worked as an office administrator. She had inherited her mother's taste for fine clothes and fashionable costume jewellery, and carried herself with the grace and poise of a woman far beyond her years. Bobby continued to work as a driving contractor while playing rugby on the weekends. The year 1953 signalled the start of Judy and Bobby's married life. It was also the year that her parents Albert and Veronica's marriage ended. Veronica walked out of the family home she'd shared with Albert and straight into the house on Hinkler Avenue, Ryde, to live with her daughter and son-in-law.

•

At Hinkler Avenue, Veronica cooked for the young couple. She washed their clothes. She even occasionally served them breakfast in bed. She decorated their home. She selected the fabric for the curtains and was responsible for sewing them up. She planted flowers in the front garden.

In her first year of marriage, behind the scenes, Judy also spent a good deal of time caring for her mother. The two women were close, but very different.

Judy was voluptuous with a tiny waist and curvaceous hips, full lips, and large, warm eyes. Veronica was more rigid, angular and stern. Her brows were arched and her features more hawk-like. It is unknown if it was intentional, but the pair represented highly stylised versions of two very different kinds of movie star. With her dark, shiny, bobbed hair, Judy bore a strong resemblance to the ingenue Liz Taylor, while Veronica assumed an aesthetic which bore an uncanny resemblance to Joan Crawford. Indeed, her hair, make-up and slim-fitting angular suits were identical to Crawford's severe styling both on and off screen. Veronica Monty was a dead ringer for the character Beth played by Joan Crawford in *This Woman is Dangerous* released only the previous year.

Veronica cut a tall, statuesque figure, but maintaining this mask came at great personal cost. She was nervous, neurotic and possessive. Her clothes, accessories and make-up were important to her: shoes, bags, hats and gloves were treated with great care, like each was a precious heirloom. She was an exacting woman, critical and obsessive. Rake thin, she was a compulsive buyer of nerve tonics: liquid extracts and powders that could be mixed with other foods. She was particularly fond of Milo. While it is now marketed as a children's drink, in the 1950s it was branded as a 'tonic nerve food' and 'the tonic for the times'. An extract of malt barley and chocolate fortified with vitamins and mineral salts, it was said to aid digestion, assist sleep, and soothe nerves. Veronica drank it religiously.

Judy marvelled at the kindness of her husband, who welcomed his mother-in-law into his home. She was relieved and grateful that she had married such a patient man. He didn't even call Veronica 'Mum'. The pair had bonded and Bobby called Veronica 'Tops', or sometimes 'Bluey' on account of her red hair. An observer of their relationship described it as 'attentive'.

Veronica talked frequently and in forensic detail with Judy and Bobby about her many physical health complaints. In this, too, her son-in-law seemed to endure the conversations with a remarkable patience. In June 1953, Veronica underwent surgery. Now in her fifties, she had experienced a uterine prolapse. While many women at the time were routinely scheduled to have a hysterectomy if they experienced the condition, Veronica wanted to save her uterus. She underwent a procedure called a Fothergill posterior repair, which aimed to shorten the cervix and repair the pelvic floor, but keep the uterus intact. She spent weeks recovering at home. Now living permanently in Judy and Bobby's spare room, Veronica was lovingly cared for by her daughter.

In return, Veronica also responded lovingly. Just how lovingly soon became clear. As Veronica herself would describe it, everything changed on 'the fateful night of the second cricket test'.

On 26 June 1953, Bobby, Judy and Veronica had planned to stay up late and listen to the cricket broadcast on the radio, live from England. It was a cold winter night, and the three sat in the soft, warm light of the sitting room. Bobby had lit a fire in the hearth. Judy had just come out of the shower and was sitting in her nightgown, her hair wrapped in a towel. Curled on a rug, she faced the fire. She stretched out her arms towards the open flames. Veronica sat at one end of the three-seater lounge reading *The Sun*. Bobby sat on the other end reading *The Mirror* in his pyjamas and bathrobe. The image of the trio that evening could have appeared on any advertising campaign for the wireless radio, or the Dunlopillo lounge, or the plush bathrobe worn by Bobby.

After a while, Judy unfurled the towel from her head. Her hair fell down onto her neck. She fingered at her dark, full hair, shagging it loose with her fingers so it might dry in the warmth of the fire. Bobby and Veronica exchanged newspapers. The three chatted happily between overs. Sometime before 9.30 p.m., the broadcaster announced that play was breaking for lunch. They would resume in an hour or so, weather permitting.

Judy yawned. It was a Friday night and she had been at work all day. Although she didn't have work the next day, she was disinclined to stay up. She was tired. 'I'm not waiting up any more. I'm going to bed,' she said. She went to the couch and kissed both her husband and her mother goodnight.

Judy and Bobby's bedroom faced the lounge room. Within only a few moments the bedroom door was shut, though the light within the room stayed on.

'I'm not inclined to stay up either,' Bobby said. 'Play might be delayed by rain as well by the looks of it. I'm off to bed too.' Bobby put the newspaper on the lounge next to him and went to leave.

'No. Wait, Bob,' Veronica called, almost limply. 'Come sit down. I want to talk to you about Judy. And talk about married life too.'

'What's wrong with our married life?' Bobby asked, a little unsettled by Veronica's directness.

'I'm worried. What's wrong between you and Judy? There's something wrong, I can tell.'

Bobby went to move off the lounge. 'I'll go talk to her about it then. If there's a problem . . .'

Veronica pulled softly at the crook in his arm. 'No, no. Don't disturb Judy. If there's nothing wrong, leave it till morning.'

The horizontal bar of light under the bedroom door went dark.

Veronica patted Bobby on the back of the hand, in a motherly way, and pulled his head down onto her shoulder. 'Oh, I don't know, Bobby,' she said slowly and a little dreamily. 'It's just neither of you are taking much interest in the house. I just don't want to see the two of you drift apart.' She kept her hand curled around his head, like a mother might with a son. Then, slowly, she began to run her fingers softly through his hair in long, slow movements.

Bobby did not pull away.

'I think we should talk to Judy about this,' said Bobby, leaning away from her.

'Oh, Bobby, don't take any notice of me. As you know, I've been through quite an ordeal.'

Bobby thought for a moment, but wasn't sure what she meant. Was she talking about the trouble with her husband? Was she talking about her surgery?

Veronica ran her hand down from his head and along his arm. She slid her fingers into his hand. Their hands locked, their fingers intertwined. They stiffened their arms and began pulling and tugging at each other, with the motion of a child caught in a Chinese finger puzzle. Veronica then moved to grab Bobby's other hand. They began wrestling. Their bodies tugged at each other, tense and stiff and charged.

Veronica popped the side studs on her pants in one swift movement then took Bobby's hand and slid it into her now open pants. She wasn't wearing any underwear. Bobby took a deep breath but did not stop. Veronica's surgery had been only a few weeks before and she had been shaved clean. While Bobby felt and squeezed and pressed his hand along and into Veronica, she moved her hand quickly into the fly of his pyjamas.

For a moment, their hands moved rhythmically and in perfect time. Of every motion she made on his body, he mirrored it. She rolled the top of her pants down, just enough to free herself, then spun herself up and bounced on top of him. They rolled onto each other and kissed.

It was Veronica who had the presence of mind to pause and ask, 'You won't say anything to Judy about this?'

He shook his head just as he came on the sofa.

Veronica spot-cleaned the Dunlopillo with a damp rag, taking extra care that the expensive upholstery would not mark. Bobby grabbed his bathrobe and covered himself in a false modesty, and ran towards his bedroom without saying a word.

●

The next morning, while Judy was in the other room, Bobby and Veronica shared a few whispered words in the kitchen. They agreed it had been a flight of madness and should never happen again.

'I'm sorry,' she said.

He touched her face, and she rustled his hair the way a mother might playfully clip the ear of a son. 'I'm sorry, too. We can't let it happen again.'

It happened again the following week.

But then, a few days after that, while Judy was in the shower, Veronica stomped through the house brandishing a collared shirt in her hand. She held it up to Bobby's face. 'What's this?' she demanded.

'A shirt,' answered Bobby, unaware of the point Veronica was making.

She bent the collar over and exposed a small red mark. 'Lipstick? It's that pretty daughter, isn't it?' Veronica demanded.

She was referring to Bobby's boss's daughter who often appeared in the society pages and was about the same age as Judy. Bobby denied any knowledge at all of even meeting the girl.

'You are a married man!' Veronica berated him with the tone of a woman scorned, and without any hint of irony in her voice. At that moment, the bathroom door opened and Judy came walking down the hall. Bobby took the reprieve and bounded off for a shower.

•

The next week, Bobby came home from work and threw his car keys down on the bench. Veronica was sitting at the kitchen table, with two teacups. It was as if she was waiting for him. Judy was out.

'You rely on Judy too much, Bobby,' Veronica said. 'You need to take more interest in her.' She peered over the rim of her teacup at him. 'Judy does all the banking and handles all the accounts. It's not fair on a woman.'

'Judy's all right,' Bobby said. 'It's what she does for a job. She knows what she's doing.'

'Oh, I don't know. She's all right now, but just look at me. I never thought I would end up in a situation like this.' She raised the teapot in the air, as if motioning him to join her.

'Go on, then,' he said.

She poured him a cup of tea. 'The house should be in Judy's name too. I'm only thinking of her.'

'Leave it alone, Tops,' Bobby said. 'I'll discuss it with Judy. You have to stop bringing it up. It's between me and her.'

'Bobby, if it's about the legal fees, I've told you, I can pay that. I'll pay the lawyer and he can arrange for the transfer of the title so she's protected. Judy needs that security.'

'Enough, Veronica,' Bobby said firmly.

•

The next few weeks passed as if nothing had happened. Bobby still kissed both his wife and mother-in-law goodbye as he left for work in the morning. He still playfully called Veronica 'Tops' or 'Bluey' and was openly affectionate and loving towards Judy while Veronica looked on.

One Sunday morning, Judy got ready for Mass. Bobby was still in bed. He watched her pin a large costume brooch to the lapel of her powder-blue suit. She pecked him on the cheek as she left.

Bobby lay in bed watching the sunlight as it crept through the closed curtain and made its way across the ceiling. The house was silent and he assumed that Veronica was still asleep in the spare room down the hall. Moments later, out of the corner of his eye, he saw the pattern of sunlight in the bedroom move and he realised that someone had silently opened the door. He did not stir.

Veronica stood in the doorway. She was wearing a sheer nightdress and a dressing gown. 'Where's Judy?' she asked.

'You know where she is,' Bobby said.

'Are you going to get up?' She pointed her toes and danced forward playfully, like a child simulating the movements of a ballerina.

'Veronica . . .' was all he said. He moved swiftly, slid out the side of the bed furthest from her, and made for the door. He ran to the bathroom down the hall and closed and locked the door. He urinated. He closed the lid of the toilet and sat down. He waited for ten minutes until he was sure the house was quiet and that she'd given up and left. He opened the bathroom door without making a sound and crept back down the hallway. When he turned the corner to his bedroom, Veronica was now seated on the bed. He walked past her without saying a word, yawned and stretched his arms pointedly, and crawled back under the covers. He pulled the blankets up to his chest and tucked himself in. He combed his fingers hard through his fringe and then gripped the top of the covers with the intensity of a man clinging to a cliff edge. Bobby was waiting for another confrontation about the lipstick on the collar. But Veronica did not want to talk. She slid up the bed, then slid her hand under the blanket. Her arm moved effortlessly like a serpent gliding beneath the surface of the water. Within moments, she had him cupped in her hand. Within seconds he ejaculated. He wiped the bathrobe across his leg as he ran back into the bathroom. He closed the door and waited again, sitting on the lid of the closed toilet while he thought about what he was going to do. He waited a long time, until he was sure she had gone. He opened the door and there she was, still sitting on the bed in the very same spot.

•

Judy seemed content that life at Hinkler Avenue had settled into a happy, if unorthodox, pattern. She worried about her father, but was relieved that her mother appeared more relaxed and stable. The three shared family meals. They listened to the wireless together. Judy and Veronica went to watch Bobby at training and at games.

One night while in bed, Judy and Bobby heard Veronica in the kitchen mixing her Milo drink. They called out, 'Can we have a Milo too?'

Shortly after, Veronica swept into the room carrying a tray with three mugs, just like an illustrated advertisement in the newspaper. Judy and Bobby took their mugs and Veronica sat on the edge of the bed. It had all the innocence of a child-hood slumber party. Veronica cupped the mug of Milo in her hands, sitting in the very same spot where she had cupped her son-in-law's genitals only days before.

That night, Judy went to sleep thinking how lucky she was. Despite her parents' separation and the tensions and anxie-ties that perpetually worried her mother, perhaps everything would turn out all right in the end.

Milo (1950s)

Ingredients
1 teaspoon Milo powder
1 cup water, brought to a rolling boil

Method
Boil water. Place teaspoon of Milo in cup and pour in boiling water. Stir vigorously until dissolved. Drink while steaming hot. Add milk before serving, if desired.

18

IT'S IN THE MILK

IN EARLY JULY 1953, THE BALMAIN TIGERS PLAYED THE MANLY Sea Eagles at Brookvale Oval and won 13–7. Although Bobby had scored every single victorious point, he'd felt sick before he even ran onto the field. By the time the game was over something was definitely wrong. He had a pain in his chest and a strange numb sensation in his feet that he'd never felt before. He spoke to his coach, Arthur Patton. Patton thought it was muscular and sent him to the club masseur.

The following Saturday, 11 July, the Tigers played St George. In the morning, Bobby couldn't get out of bed – the pins and needles in his feet were bad – but after warming up his muscles the pain seemed to ease a little. Bobby went on to score seven goals and the team won 26–12. But he felt even worse than he had the previous week. Again, he spoke to the coach, who referred him to the team doctor this time. Unable to work out what was wrong – and in the absence of any other explanation – the doctor sent him home with a prescription for some stomach ulcer medication. Bobby felt so sick he couldn't even eat. When he finally tried the medication, he only took half a tablet. It made him violently ill.

At the next game on 18 July, Bobby's performance was woeful. He usually impressed with his quick reflexes and his speed. But that day, he was sluggish. When he tried to focus, he seemed distracted.

From his first season with the Tigers, he'd been one of the team's most popular players. Born on the mid-north coast in the tiny town of Tuncurry, he looked more like a surfer than a footballer with his compact and lean frame, and tousled, sun-bleached hair. In 1947, he scored a club record of twenty-eight tries. It was an unprecedented high for a debut player, and one that has never been matched by anyone playing for the club since.

But on 18 July 1953 at Leichhardt Oval, Bobby was out of sorts and everyone noticed. He struggled to run and seemed to have trouble concentrating. A player usually known for his quick and deceptive footwork and his fast reflexes, he seemed uninterested. When the Tigers lost to Canterbury Bankstown 7–14, fans blamed Bobby. He was booed. Even children hooted 'Rookie!' as he left the field.

It was now clear that something was very wrong. Judy and Veronica, who attended every single game, fretted as they watched Bobby publicly crumble.

●

The next Monday, Bobby came home from work early feeling worse than ever. Judy was still at work, but Veronica, as always, was at home. Frustrated that the ulcer medication did not seem to be helping, Bobby convinced himself he just needed to sleep off the awful feeling in his back and legs and stomach. He went to his bedroom and immediately stripped to his undershorts and a shirt. He took a moment to steady himself. He felt dizzy. He pulled on his pyjama pants and dressing gown, ran to the toilet and vomited. Veronica was waiting for him when he opened the toilet door. She felt his forehead, just like a mother might, checking to see if he had a temperature. She went to kiss him, but he dodged, and she kissed the corner of his mouth. He tasted like vomit.

Bobby's stomach was in knots and he fought the urge to be sick again. He went to his bedroom and flopped onto the bed.

Veronica followed.

Dressed in a buttoned silk suit, she popped it open to reveal suspenders, stockings and scanties. She lifted up her skirt and unfastened the clips on her suspenders. She climbed on top of him. He began grinding up against her. His dressing gown parted and his penis popped out through the open fly of his pyjama pants. 'We can't do it properly on account of my operation,' she said. They improvised with frottage.

Moments later Veronica was back in the kitchen, leaning over the sink with the look of a mad woman, feverishly cleaning her silk suit with a wet flannel.

•

The following Monday, Bobby felt a bit better so he left for work very early. Veronica waited and waited for Judy to finally leave the house. When she saw the figure in deep blue velvet with a matching velvet hat and silk stockings cross the yard and close the gate, she knew Judy would not be returning. Veronica, already dressed, and in full make-up, walked down to the telephone booth on the corner. She dialled the police. 'I need to speak to a detective at the Central Investigative Bureau, please. I have important information.' She waited while the operator connected the call. When a voice answered she said quickly, 'There's another thallium poisoning. It's in the milk.' The staff member on the other end of the phone had just enough time to say, 'Who is this?' before Veronica hung up. A note was made of the call. It occurred at 11.10 a.m. But with no further information, the police at HQ simply shrugged their shoulders and dismissed it as a prank.

Veronica went home. In the broom closet in the laundry behind the buckets and bleach, she retrieved a stack of newspapers. She took the papers to the kitchen table, grabbed some glue and scissors from the roll-top writing desk and sat down. She flicked through the newspapers until she got to the articles about Caroline Grills and carefully cut out the word 'thallium' and 'victims'. She then proceeded to snip out single letters of different sizes and fonts. She carefully assembled the words then glued them onto a piece of card. While her craft project dried on the table, she went to the writing desk and took an envelope and addressed it to the CIB, Police HQ. She shoved the snips and scraps in the bottom of the bin and covered them up with garbage. She pushed the newspapers back into their hiding place.

Veronica then carefully finished applying her make-up, adjusted her hat and straightened the seam in her silk stockings. She caught a bus to the GPO at Martin Place and posted the letter.

•

Later that week, at the CIB HQ, a junior staff member opened a letter, postmarked Sydney. Inside was a piece of card, with newspaper lettering carefully spelling out the message: 'More victims. Hinkler Ave Ryde. Thallium in milk.'

But no action was taken.

By this stage, Bobby had become ill again. He was still playing rugby, but not well. He couldn't run. He stumbled. A persistent pain in his stomach had him doubled over in agony. And the strange feelings in his legs and feet, the deadness, was the worst thing that could happen to a star player whose job it was to run.

He went to see Dr Bentivoglio, another team doctor, who prescribed some tablets for the pain. Bobby felt worse. He was convinced the medication was making him nauseous.

He spent the entire day after the game in bed. Judy wanted him to see Dr Greenberg, a consulting doctor for the Balmain Tigers (and also Veronica's personal physician), but Bobby had lost faith in doctors entirely. He tried to go to work on Monday 20 July but soon realised he couldn't continue. He had to keep stopping the truck so he could vomit on the side of the road. He drove all the way to the Darling Harbour goods yard, but he barely made it. By the time he got there, he had to turn around and go home again. He was simply too sick.

While Bobby was out, Veronica walked again to the public phone booth. She had already tried the police directly, and nothing had happened. This time, she rang Dr Greenberg. She assumed a deep, husky voice and spoke with a slow staccato into the receiver. 'My name is Mrs Wilkins,' she said. 'My husband put rat poison in Bobby Lulham's beer.' Then she hung up.

Dr Greenberg was alarmed and immediately reported the incident to the police.

Around the same time, yet another card arrived at the CIB HQ. This one was even more explicit, and the tone had changed in part because Veronica had run out of large-font headline-sized words like 'thallium' and 'poison'. The tone may also have been indicative of the rising intensity of feelings within her. Veronica snipped and glued a more desperate and more malevolent threat than ever before. Mailroom staff had been alerted to look out for letters that resembled those sent in previous weeks, and so this time they were quicker to identify and open any worrisome deliveries.

'Get him yet. Hate Lulham. Bombing their home. Thallium in milk. Death. Victims. Destroy all.' There was also an address.

At CIB HQ, Fergusson and Krahe were in the middle of preparations for Caroline Grills's trial. Given the seriousness of the cards arriving at the CIB HQ, it was decided the case should be immediately allocated to Detective Sergeant George Henry Arthur Davis and Detective Constable Keith Robert Paul instead, who would be closely guided by the poison expertise of Fergusson and Krahe as necessary.

When Bobby arrived home that day his condition was grave. Judy was scared. Her fear increased when she opened the door to two detectives.

Police spoke briefly with the couple, but because of Bobby's condition they left almost immediately for hospital.

Judy collapsed in the lounge room. On the very same Dunlopillo lounge that her mother had picked out for her – the very same lounge she had used to have sex with her son-in-law – Veronica comforted her daughter. She petted Judy on the hand and stroked her hair. Judy rested her head on her mother's shoulder, just as Bobby had done.

'I just can't understand what's happening,' said Judy. She started to cry.

Veronica held her daughter's hand and solemnly said, 'Judy, there's something that I have to tell you. Bob and I have been intimate.'

Judy lurched forward, as if some unseen force had thrown her. 'What?' she cried.

'Twice,' said Veronica.

'Mum!' Judy put her hands over her ears. 'Stop!'

Once Veronica had decided to unburden herself, it seemed she couldn't stop. 'He has kissed me, passionately!'

Judy recoiled from her mother's embrace, which now felt bony and clawing. She ran to her room.

After Bobby was taken to hospital, the calls to CIB continued. Veronica's voice was husky, and broken: 'My husband is jealous of the lot of them. He's out to get the lot of them. There is thallium in milk at Lulham's house.'

The atmosphere in the home was now unbearable. Judy could not be around Veronica. She avoided her. She could not speak to her. She went to her father's and stayed with him.

The police came for Veronica on 6 August and arrested her on a charge of attempted murder. She was supposed to remain locked up until her trial. Unable to stand being around her mother, but finding the notion of her locked away in prison also too much, Judy asked her father, Albert, for money to post her bail. She went to the police station and counted it out in fifty-pound notes.

Veronica spent but one night in gaol.

When released, she went straight to the now empty house at Hinkler Avenue. From the top drawer of her bedroom vanity, she removed a small brown glass bottle. She shook it to see if it was empty. It was not. She unscrewed the lid and drank what remained.

On 8 August 1953, Veronica Montanari was admitted to the very same hospital as her son-in-law, Bobby.

•

Both Bobby and Veronica confessed to their affair, but each offered differing accounts of the specific sexual acts that had taken place. Veronica claimed that there was penetration. Bobby admitted to everything *except* having sexual intercourse with his mother-in-law.

Judy visited Bobby in hospital. His sandy surfer hair was gone, and his Tuncurry tan as well. He was pale and weak and bald. 'Mum told me there were intimacies between you two,' Judy said, hoping that he might spare her the embarrassment of an interrogation and simply confess.

'Yes,' he said. 'I was going to explain it all when I came out of hospital.' Then he lowered his voice and put his finger to his lips. Nurses walked behind them in the corridor and the openness of the hospital with its bare walls made the sound echo.

Bobby left hospital on 19 August and went home. Judy soon joined him. Veronica was discharged on 22 August. She did not return to live with Bobby and Judy, and did not return to her husband, but went to stay with a friend elsewhere in Sydney.

Judy wanted to continue the conversation that she had started with Bobby in hospital, but she didn't know how or where to begin. Bobby was still sick, even after he was discharged, and this made it more difficult. For the first few days she focused on his recuperation. She looked after him. She cooked for him. She helped him to the bathroom when he was feeling unwell. But there was an awkward silence between them.

Albert moved into the house in Hinkler Avenue to help the young couple. Shortly after, a detective from the CIB visited Judy at home and confirmed the affair between her mother and her husband – and that Bobby was suffering from thallium poisoning. Veronica had admitted she was responsible, but claimed it had been accidental. She had planned to kill herself but had mixed up the Milos, she said. When the detective asked Judy why she hadn't discussed her husband's infidelity with him, she said, 'I waited until I thought Bobby was well enough to talk about it. He'd been so ill.'

Emboldened by a new confidence after speaking with the detective, and knowing that Bobby was feeling stronger, Judy finally raised the issue again. 'Bobby, now you're home, tell me. What went on between you and Mum?'

'It was just one of those things that happens. When an opportunity is thrown up at a man, he accepts it.' Feeling better, he ate his lunch and drove off in his truck, eager to return to work.

19

PROOFING THE DOUGH

WHILE FERGUSSON AND KRAHE'S WORK MAY HAVE LED TO THE capture and conviction of Yvonne Fletcher and Caroline Grills, the jury believed Veronica Montanari's claims that she'd poisoned her son-in-law by accident. She was found not guilty and promptly released.

Yvonne Fletcher and Caroline Grills both received a mandatory capital sentence, although in both cases the death penalty was eventually commuted to life imprisonment. By the early 1950s there was strong opposition to capital punishment, and the mercy shown to both Yvonne and Caroline was in line with prevailing public sentiment. Indeed, the death penalty would be officially abolished in 1955.

The presiding judges were scathing of the women's actions. They were calculated killers. The strategic way in which they had planned and then executed their murders was heartless and cold blooded. In passing sentence on Caroline Grills, Justice Brereton described her as 'inhuman, diabolical, felonious and malicious'. At Yvonne Fletcher's trial, Justice Kinsella characterised her as an 'atrocious and horrible person'. Their convictions were applauded by the community. Killers of this calibre should be locked up forever, it was said.

•

By 1955, under the assumed name of Vera Morgan, Veronica Montanari was working as a housemaid and renting a room at the Union Hotel in North Sydney. Judy and Bobby's home in Ryde had been sold. Bobby's rugby career was over. His health never fully recovered and he was considered too weak to play at the A-grade level. Alfred had divorced Veronica and Judy had divorced Bobby. Veronica was desperately trying to start her life over. Only the month before she had been through the divorce courts – twice. It was a gruelling process in which she had been required to discuss every embarrassing infidelity, all of it printed in the newspapers in gritty and sordid detail.

On Sunday 17 April, with the Union Hotel closed, the owner took his family out for the day. When the hotelier returned he found Veronica lying on the bed in her rented room. She was fully clothed and a bottle of brandy was on the floor. The floor of the hotel room was scattered with newspaper clippings. In the half-light, for a moment he thought she was asleep. When he crept closer he saw the small bullet hole in her head. Veronica had found the pistol that he had hidden in a cupboard in his office and had taken her own life.

•

Caroline Grills remained in prison for close to eight years. She died behind bars from a gastric rupture and a bacterial infection (peritonitis) in 1960.

Yvonne Fletcher was a model inmate. She worked in the prison kitchen and was released for good behaviour just before Christmas 1964. At the age of forty-five, and not wanting to spend the rest of her life alone, she married 49-year-old Leonard Wailes at St Patrick's in September 1967. Like Desmond Butler, Leonard had a criminal record. Like Bertram Fletcher, he had a reputation as a playboy. Like both of her previous marriages, life with Leonard was not what Yvonne imagined it would be.

While Yvonne was in prison, Leonard had earned a reputation right across the country as a womaniser and small-time swindler. In 1954 he was convicted of stealing fifty-four pounds from a Thelma Burley in Launceston, Tasmania. Leonard had waited for Thelma to go to work then stolen a money box which was hidden behind a panel inside her wardrobe. He was also known to police further north in Brisbane. Described by some as 'debonair', a prosecutor summed him up when he faced a charge of vagrancy: 'He is one of those unprincipled individuals who would rather live on women than work.' When Leonard met Yvonne, he too had a string of broken relationships behind him, had been married twice and had been in and out of prison.

Yvonne and Leonard were married for a little over five years. He died of pneumonia in January 1973 after a three-day illness and a long history of what was described as 'chronic obstructive airway disease'. From the evidence available, it appears that Yvonne and Leonard had been separated for a period of time before his death.

•

Detectives Fergusson and Krahe's relationship with thallium did not end there. Their reputation for capturing and convicting insidious and hard-to-catch killers helped to sustain an upward career trajectory for both of them. The pair worked closely on every thallium case that the state brought to trial between 1952 and 1955, and while not the lead officers in all cases that were prosecuted, the perception of them as the 'CIB poison experts' meant they played a regular role in offering strategic advice.

Over time, they became powerful and influential officers within the CIB. Although their working relationship spanned many functional areas of CIB activity, they managed to ride the 'thallium wave' for many years and appeared to exercise a high degree of discretion over the cases they pursued. Their cases following Caroline Grills's trial share some common characteristics. Almost all of the deaths they investigated had occurred many years before, having been sourced from the archives of the Coroners Court. The detectives were not interested in just any unsolved murders. Working closely with the Office of the Government Analyst, they combed through the Coroner's findings, guided by a question with broad scope: were there any deaths which showed indications of thallium poisoning? They weren't interested in cold cases so much as old cases which meant digging up bodies all over the state. Lots of them.

John Pearson was eighty years old when he was laid to rest beside his wife. A wealthy farmer, his estate was estimated to have been worth about 10 000 pounds. There were rumours about greedy, opportunistic relatives and this, it seemed, was enough to spur Fergusson and Krahe's investigation into his death. Pearson had been in the Armidale Cemetery for five years when he was exhumed.

It was a quiet and peaceful day in the northern NSW tablelands when the detectives from Sydney arrived. After heavy summer rains, there were patches of new growth and the usually dry and dusty graveyard was gradually transforming from brown to green. The Pearson family plot looked picturesque and settled, as if nature had intervened to lovingly memorialise the New England grazier and his wife.

The serenity of the cemetery was soon broken by the herd of policemen and gravediggers armed with spades and shovels. Pearson's resting place was now filled with the squeaky pitch and rhythm of spades as they pierced the pristine lawn. Gravediggers worked in a spiralling circle like a human Ferris wheel as they shovelled and spun the dirt away from the excavation.

Within hours the coffin was retrieved. Fergusson and Krahe were graveside, supervising every shovel of dirt, picking through bones and sorting teeth, and gingerly stepping over Pearson's wife who, after a patient wait of twenty years for her husband to die, now seemed reluctant to let him go.

The CIB committed months to the Pearson investigation. Traces of metallic poisoning were found in the man's remains but laboratory testing did not identify the substance to be thallium. Medical experts linked Pearson's exposure to heavy metal to the copious amounts of medication he took at the end of his life. His health had been poor and he had self-medicated with a cocktail of remedies and drugs to ease his symptoms. After four months, the investigation into his death was abandoned as an utter waste of time. John Pearson's death was, for the second time, attributed to natural causes.

In the tiny town of Baradine, west of Tamworth and over three hundred miles north of Sydney, Fergusson and Krahe organised their next exhumation. This time, it was a timber worker by the name of Les Ruttley. Ruttley had been sick for days with gastroenteritis before he died, but this was a common complaint which often led to infection, so there appeared little justification for reopening his case.

Nonetheless, once again rumour propelled Fergusson and Krahe's activities. Ruttley was young, strong and single. Locals had nicknamed him Hercules because of his impressive ability to dead-lift felled timber. He was hardworking and well off, but also a bit of a loner. His sister, Mary Hitchen, was convinced that someone had poisoned her brother, and adamantly denied any suggestion that he may have taken his own life. Another sister, Esme Rice, an ex-nurse, said she had never seen someone die in so much pain, and this seemed very suspicious to her. A friend, Alan Burton, said he had seen Ruttley suffer for months with gastric problems, dysentery and headaches. Others, however, suggested he'd only been sick for a few days prior to his death.

Both Fergusson and Krahe vastly underestimated the scale of the job at hand. In the city there were challenges to digging up the dead. Discretion was required. City cemeteries were busy places and there were schedules and services to consider. Baradine, however, was little more than a section of cleared forest on a lonely country road. Les Ruttley had also only been dead and buried for two months. With the coffin barely in the ground, and most likely still very much intact, the detectives believed this disinterment would be a doddle.

They were dead wrong.

On the morning of Ruttley's scheduled exhumation, it started raining a little. Then it rained a lot. And then it poured. This was a remote cemetery, built by the community, with only rudimentary attention paid to landscaping. With the rapid infill of water, the graveyard quickly turned into a pit of sticky mud. The exhumation had now become more than just inconvenient for the city officers – it was downright dangerous. Investigators slipped and fell in the slimy clay. Others found their boots trapped, the muddy graveyard seemingly unwilling to release its grasp on the officers. The exhumation stalled, then it resumed, then it stalled again. Fergusson insisted on proceeding. When the body was finally retrieved, and after weeks of preparation and collecting and testing, not to mention interviewing and paperwork, it all came to nothing. No evidence of anything suspicious was found.

Of all the old cases that Fergusson and Krahe revisited, the investigation into Aileen Jefferson's death made the most sense. At the time of her death, a post-mortem examination had concluded that toxic exposure to *something* had most likely been responsible, but testing procedures at the time could not identify the precise agent involved. The Coroner, and others, surmised that hair dye might have been responsible: Aileen was a hairdresser and in the habit of dying her hair, and she had recently gone from blonde to brunette. Medical evidence showed her death had been painful and had dragged on for weeks. It started with pins and needles in her feet and legs, then progressed to more severe nerve pain and, finally, hysteria. All of this had been well documented prior to her death.

If Fergusson and Krahe had what might be called poisonous instincts, in this case, at least, they paid off. Traces of thallium *were* found in Aileen's remains. The detectives rolled out their usual methodology, interviewing relentlessly. In the end, however, it yielded nothing. Aileen had been dead for almost fifteen years. It was too hard to reassemble the last weeks or months of her life to understand what exactly had occurred, because simply too much time had passed.

Still, Fergusson did not see the decision to pursue the investigation into Aileen Jefferson's death as a mistake. The exhumation had been a success, he said, because his work represented the forefront of innovative policing. With this particular case, Fergusson had done something no other police officer nor medical expert had ever done before: he made a movie of the exhumation, the first recording of its kind ever taken in Australia. While it might be argued that a recording of the event offered an opportunity to train other officers in the procedures, it might also be argued that filming the disinterment of human remains in all its grisly detail just allowed him to further indulge his morbid passions.

●

In 1953, the newly established Poisons Advisory Committee was charged with making recommendations about the thallium problem. The committee engaged in a lengthy process of consultation and policy analysis which culminated in amendments to the *Poisons Act* and strict regulation of the sale of thallium. As a result of the amendments to the Act, pharmacists were required by law to take down the purchaser's name and address so there was a record of sale. The new provisions did not prevent the sale of thallium, but regulated it through the creation of a poisons log book which had to be signed off by the retailer. It was a fast way to reduce demand for thallium quietly, and with little push-back from the manufacturers, because it sidestepped the issue of consumer demand entirely. Forcing retailers to record thallium's purchase posed the biggest deterrent to its continued sale. These restrictions fell into line with those which had already been implemented in Victoria and South Australia. Thallium sales and thallium-related deaths soon began to subside, and in 1956 three notable thallium-related incidents brought the crisis to a close. Two of these incidents demonstrated that the state's new approach to the challenge of thallium was working.

By now, doctors knew what to look for. In August 1956, Tasuola Makrides was admitted to hospital suffering symptoms consistent with thallium poisoning. Doctors could not save her, but tests of her remains found traces of thallium. Police swooped in to conduct an investigation and quickly discovered that her husband, hamburger shop owner Panagiothis Makrides, had purchased Thall-Rat using a fake name in the weeks leading up to his wife's death. He was charged with murder.

Doctors also now knew how to better treat thallium poisonings and knew the importance of acting quickly. In mid-1956, a Dee Why man drank 6 ounces of thallium at his home. It was well beyond a lethal dose. He also attempted to slash his wrists. Taken to the emergency room at Manly Hospital, prompt response in triage saved his life. In September 1956, after three months of treatment, he was discharged from hospital.

In the same month, it might be said the thallium crisis drew to a very sad, if inevitable conclusion. After years of struggling with ill health, Caroline Grills's last victim, her sister-in-law Eveline Lundberg, finally died. Permanently blind, and requiring a high level of care due to the effects of the thallium she had ingested, she died at home, aged sixty-nine.

By the end of 1956, the thallium crisis in Sydney was over. Fergusson and Krahe remained in policing, but moved on to other pursuits. Fergusson's rise through the ranks steadily continued: from 1967 to 1969, he was promoted from 1st Class Inspector to 1st Class Superintendent in record time. Beyond Superintendent there was only one more level to conquer. If his rise had carried on at the same rate, he was only a handful of promotions away from being the most powerful police officer in New South Wales. Krahe, too, achieved promotion and went from Detective Constable to Detective Sergeant. He did not rise as rapidly through the ranks as Fergusson, however, and for good reason. It might be argued that his ambitions were better served by maintaining a close connection to the street.

Primary sources such as inquest and trial transcripts provide us with a picture of the prowess and skill of these two police officers. Secondary sources in the form of newspaper articles and other media highlight the public acclaim for police work in bringing cold-blooded killers and calculating criminals to justice. But there are further sources of evidence too. Rumours surrounded the lives of the women that Fergusson and Krahe brought to justice. Rumours also surrounded the lives of the detectives who caught them. It is almost universally acknowledged that Fergusson and Krahe were criminals who profited from the proceeds of crime for years.

Investigative journalist Tony Reeves aligns Fergusson and Krahe to every corrupt leadership team in the NSW police force, including Commissioner William John Mackay, Ray 'Gunner' Kelly, and another high-ranking police official, Fred Hanson. Reeves gives Frederick Krahe the unforgettable nickname 'the killer cop'.

Informants, underworld figures and crooks, reputable police officers and investigative journalists are all in agreement: Fergusson and Krahe were key figures in the institutionalised corruption of the NSW police force from the 1940s through to the 1970s. Furthermore, writers such as Duncan McNab, Barry Ward, David Hickie, Peter Rees, Peter Cox, John Silvester, N Jameson and Evan Whitton all link Krahe to organised crime and a trail of money that flowed from the high-density development of Kings Cross during that period.

The answer to the question of what bound Fergusson and Krahe together for so many years – despite their very different personalities – cannot be found in the archives, but in anecdotes. At the most basic level, investigative journalists who have studied the culture of policing in New South Wales suggest the pair had shared motivations. Both wanted money. Both wanted power.

Investigative journalist Evan Whitton has written some of the most definitive accounts of police corruption in New South Wales. He notes that Fergusson, along with Ray Kelly and Krahe, ran extortion rings that ensured money was systematically skimmed from profitable criminal enterprises. Whitton claims that Fergusson effectively levied 10 per cent on every abortion performed in Sydney. Based on Whitton's evidence, it appeared that this practice might have persisted from the postwar period right up until the end of the 1960s. Journalist Matthew Condon has also written extensively on police corruption in both New South Wales and Queensland and contends that Krahe 'had an enormous number of contacts in the underworld, and lived off his reputation as a hard and feared man'.

Police corruption is not all the same; in fact, criminal behaviour among police officers can vary so much that academics have developed specific typologies to understand the kinds of criminals that police can be. There are opportunistic police, who might steal from a house that has already been burglarised; or police who take a cut of the drugs that they seize from a vice raid. Shakedowns are a different kind of opportunistic criminal activity for police because when the opportunity presents itself to take a bribe, they just do it. Fergusson and Krahe represented yet another kind of police criminal because the pattern of their activity was well organised and systematised, falling into a category known as protection of illegal activities. They benefitted from gambling, illegal drugs, abortion rings, pornography and dodgy clubs – and offered police protection so that these criminal activities could continue.

Fergusson and Krahe participated in and led a 'collaboration of corruption' in the NSW police force, according to the journalists who have exposed them. As American academics of police criminality characterise it, 'A high degree of organisation is usually present in this type of collaborative corruption. For successful protection, several members of the police organisation must know what places, business, and persons enjoy immunity; systems of ongoing communication must be insured; payoffs and kinds of police protection must be negotiated. Protection of illegal vice operations may be so complete in some departments that officers who inadvertently arrest protected operators must pay a fine to the corrupt officers who have illegally licensed the vice operators.'

In Sydney in the postwar period criminals controlled and ran their enterprises. Money flowed to police to allow these activities to flourish unencumbered by liquor licensing laws, or laws prohibiting illicit drug use, gambling, soliciting and abortion. At a Commonwealth inquiry into corruption, the methodology for these criminal enterprises also reveals the dual business profile that existed for many enterprises in Kings Cross, in which 'black' and 'white' accounts were kept. Corrupt police maintained a similar double life as they outwardly engaged in legal police work while simultaneously and secretly profiting from criminal activity.

While Fergusson maintained a more covert criminal profile, Krahe's activities belonged to another criminal typology entirely. Krahe is what has been described as a 'direct criminal', meaning he led and engaged directly in criminal operations and organised others to gather money at the bottom which would rise to him at the top. In an account written by journalists James Morton and Susanna Lobez, the description of Krahe gives some insight to the reputation of the man: 'A good detective involved in a number of major cases, such as the first thallium poisoning, like a number of others Krahe organised abortion rackets and armed robberies, as well as standing over prostitutes and bricking criminals.' George Freeman, the colourful racing identity and illegal casino operator, is said to have described Krahe in the following way: 'After he'd arrest you the paying began. You'd pay him to get bail, you'd pay some more later for a reduced sentence, you'd pay more for remands, you'd pay for whether or not he gave verbal evidence against you, and you'd pay again if he decided not to give evidence . . . And believe me everybody paid.'

It has been said that Krahe was known as 'the Big Till', that when he knocked at your door, you needed to have a handful of money or you were going to gaol.

By the mid-1960s, Krahe had moved into the honey-pot areas of policing like armed robberies and large-scale heists, which provided the opportunities for even bigger payoffs. By the late 1960s he was involved in pursuing criminals responsible for some of the most lucrative heists ever committed in the state of New Soouth Wales.

The rumours surrounding Krahe's criminal activities are compelling but from a conventional research standpoint almost impossible to prove. What we do know is that he had a close association with some of the most infamous crime figures in Sydney's history. Indeed, journalist John Silvester names Krahe as mentor to one of Sydney's best-known crooked cops, Roger Rogerson. Silvester also notes Krahe's vast contribution to institutionalising corruption in the NSW police force by setting 'the gold standard'.

Krahe was linked to the disappearance of Kings Cross campaigner Juanita Nielsen, who went missing in 1975 in the midst of a heated and acrimonious conflict with an ambitious inner-city property developer. Heiress to the Mark Foy's department store empire, Nielsen had bought a local newspaper called *NOW* and used this publication to print and circulate material to undermine the rampant development that threatened the historic precinct. For greedy developers, Nielsen was seen as an irritating obstruction.

Her body has never been found, but a subsequent inquest concluded that she had most likely been murdered. At the time, Krahe was working as a security consultant for Victoria Point Pty Ltd, a family-owned development company run by a man called Frank Theeman. The company had borrowed to buy key properties along Victoria Street, Potts Point, intending to tear them down and build multistorey apartments. Nielsen and others dug in their heels and refused to leave the properties. Theeman was losing thousands of dollars every day – until Nielsen disappeared. While there are many theories as to how she died, many contend Krahe was responsible.

Krahe's name was also raised in connection with the murder of another woman. Shirley Brifman, a key informant on the sex industry in both Queensland and New South Wales, gave evidence about police corruption at several government inquiries. In an interview with the ABC's *This Day Tonight* programme in June 1971, she publicly implicated several key figures in the network of corrupt police. No recording of the Brifman interview is now known to exist. The ABC archives report the tape to be missing. What is known is that less than twelve months after Brifman began talking about exposing corrupt police, she died in suspicious circumstances in her Brisbane home. Witnesses who saw her the evening of her death describe secretive and tense phone calls, a late-night visitor who was never identified, and a small glass vial being delivered to her home. Her cause of death was recorded as an overdose of barbiturates.

Many argue that the reliability of Brifman's testimony is not the issue. The fact that she was speaking so brazenly about corruption – and seemed so willing to implicate so many people – sealed her fate. Journalist Phil Dickie writes that Shirley Brifman named over fifty corrupt police officers in New South Wales and Queensland. Fred Krahe was near the top of the list.

After Brifman's death, according to Tony Reeves, Krahe was quietly retired from the NSW police, cited as unfit for duty thanks to a thrombosis in his leg. Reeves claimed that then Premier Neville Wran had even privately joked that Krahe's health problem 'could have come about from kicking too many people to death'.

Towards the end of his life it's widely acknowledged that Krahe was simultaneously on the payroll of a man called Abe Saffron and a high-profile Sydney tabloid newspaper. Abe Saffron (aka Mr Sin) was one of the most well-known organised crime figures in Kings Cross and he and Fred Krahe were contemporaries. They were both born in 1919 and for many years their careers seemed to operate in close parallel. In 1947, Saffron took over the Roosevelt nightclub in Orwell Street. By the time of the NSW Liquor Royal Commission in the early 1950s, his empire had grown to include several other hotels which he used as 'dummy' operations. Such operations, noted a Commonwealth inquiry into corruption, made it difficult to track and expose illegal activities because it was impossible to work out who really owned what. Preventing publicity of criminal activities was also important, and it is rumoured that Krahe's employment by *The Sun* news-paper formed a vital part of the infrastructure which allowed corruption to flourish.

Journalist N Jameson described Krahe simply as a 'vicious thug, thief, standover merchant, organised crime figure and probably a murderer. When not up to his eyeballs in criminal activity he was serving as a senior detective. In a long line of corrupt coppers stretching back to the Rum Corps, Krahe was as bad as it gets. Everybody was afraid of him.' And journalist John Silvester reiterated the folklore surrounding Krahe's life in an article in *The Sydney Morning Herald* as recently as four years ago.

While illness might have forced Krahe out of the police force, Fergusson's rise through the ranks continued unabated. In 1969 he was awarded the Queen's Commendation for Brave Conduct after his involvement in the 'Glenfield Siege', in which a man took his wife and baby hostage in a suburban home in south-west Sydney. Fergusson even rose to the very same rank that his own father, George, had held: Superintendent of Police in New South Wales.

His career progression seemed to have no ending. That is, until Valentine's Day 1970, when he was found dead in the private toilet adjacent to his office at police headquarters with a 0.38 bullet in his brain. The bullet matched his service revolver, which sat on the toilet floor along with a note.

There was considerable speculation as to exactly what had happened. Journalists James Morton and Susanna Lobez contend that the tensions in the relationship between Krahe and Fergusson, which had simmered for some time, finally boiled over. The abortion racket, which had sustained Fergusson's profiteering from criminal activity for years, was about to be exposed. While it was claimed that Fergusson had been worried about a brain tumour, the autopsy determined that he had 'no trace of any organic disease'.

Dr Stephen Lantos gave evidence at the investigation into Fergusson's death. He claimed that he had been trying to convince Fergusson for over a decade that he did not have a brain tumour. 'He was by no means reassured,' said Dr Lantos. City Coroner J J Loomes prohibited the publication of the note that was found near Fergusson's body, although in view of the considerable publicity the case received, he felt obligated to state that Fergusson believed he was suffering from something 'incurable'. The cause of death was officially recorded as 'the effects of a bullet wound of the head, and self-inflicted whilst in a state of mental depression'.

In an interview journalist Tony Reeves conducted with an unidentified morgue worker, the worker described the idea that Fergusson had committed suicide as absurd: 'He must have had very long arms and quick reflexes.' It is also claimed that the original autopsy report identified *two* bullet wounds to the head, which was subsequently and very discreetly amended. None of this can, of course, be verified because the official records are not available for public scrutiny.

However, in almost every account ever written, Fergusson's death is attributed to Krahe.

•

Robert A. Deilenberg, a specialist writer on the history of NSW policing, notes that police culture in the 1950s and 1960s underwent a profound transformation. The lure of hard drugs and the money that could be made from them caused rifts between countless corrupt police officers who had once been allies.

Evan Whitton thinks that Fergusson and Krahe had a big falling out late in the 1960s. He suggests an informal code known as the 'clean quid and the dirty quid' governed the behaviour of many corrupt police officers. Other accounts of police corruption note the difference between perceptions of 'dirty' money and 'clean' money among officers willing to engage in intimidation, extortion and bribery. By Whitton's reckoning, Fergusson had no moral problem extorting money from abortionists, but he drew the line at hard drugs and refused to engage in criminal activities linked to the importation and selling of heroin, in particular. As Whitton notes, Krahe was what you might call 'less delicate'. It's rumoured that Krahe wanted to strengthen connections associated with criminal enterprises trading in hard drugs and Fergusson objected. Not only that, Fergusson's promotion took him out of the CIB and into a senior tier position, which meant he could no longer directly shield his old partner. Of course, money remained a central motive for both detectives in pursuing their criminal activities. Krahe's success relied on maintaining a close connection to the street, but he needed associates in power, who were just as crooked, to cover up his nefarious activities.

Financial gain was certainly one motive for the three most famous thallium killers in Sydney – Yvonne Fletcher, Caroline Grills and Veronica Montanari. But there were other motives as well. While much has been written about the diverse and complex psychology that underpins the willingness to commit murder, one recent ex–NSW police officer suggests there is a simplicity to the psychology of killers that many people overlook. Retired Detective Inspector Gary Jubelin has more than thirty years' experience in the NSW police force, and more than a decade spent exclusively in homicide. Jubelin warns against applying too much theoretical 'academic' reasoning when it comes to murder. 'It's not a logical act to kill someone. If you try to put too much logic into a murder investigation I think you will sometimes go astray.' Jubelin does argue, however, that one thing seems to unite all murderers. He says they almost always all hold steadfast to one universal yet simple truth about their victims: 'My life would be better without you in it.'

Rumours continue to surround Sydney's thallium killers and the two detectives responsible for their capture to this day. The rumours about Yvonne Fletcher, Caroline Grills and Veronica Montanari were pivotal to the criminal investigations against them. The rumours about Donald Fergusson and Fred Krahe, however, have never been proved – and not a single charge has ever been laid.

If what is rumoured about Fred Krahe is true – and someone were to write his life story – part of it would be easy to tell because it has already been told. Indeed, the psychology underpinning his behaviour bears an uncanny resemblance to that of a murdering Sydney housewife back in 1947. The opening lines of Krahe's story could even be copied directly from Yvonne Fletcher's . . .

In February 1970, retired policeman Frederick Claude Krahe planned the perfect murder. He didn't arrange an alibi, because he wouldn't need one. In fact, he felt so confident of getting away with murder he left the victim's body out in plain sight and didn't bother to hide it. Krahe believed the perfect murder was possible if it could be made to look like something else entirely and no one even realised that a crime had been committed . . .

ENDNOTES

CHAPTER 1: THE BONOX HABIT

p. 3, 'A thick, brown, concentrated paste': 'Strong he-men and doctors recommend', *The Herald*, 27 April 1938, p. 20

p. 3, 'Doctors recommended Bonox because': Advertising, *Australian Women's Weekly*, 15 July 1939, p. 42; Advertising, *Australian Women's Weekly*, 30 August 1947, p. 14; Advertising, *Australian Women's Weekly*, 14 August 1943, p. 2

CHAPTER 2: JITTERBUG AND JUGS

p. 12, 'At Merrylands a local woodcutter': 'Sly grog seller fined', *The Broadcaster*, 25 April 1945, p. 2

p. 13, 'Podgey was short but strong': 'Two husbands died from thallium poison', *Truth*, 29 June 1952, p. 8

CHAPTER 3: BLACK TEA

p. 41, 'Professional fitters instructed women on how best to squish': 'Correct corsets', *The Labor Daily*, 5 July 1929, p. 8

p. 45, 'Caroline's son Bill died in 1940': 'Footballer killed', *Cumberland Argus and Fruitgrowers Advocate*, 17 January 1940, p. 1

p. 45, 'With little street lighting': 'Cow causes cyclist's death', *Weekly Times*, 20 January 1940, p. 3

p. 45, 'An ambulance rushed him to Marrickville Hospital': 'Man killed when cycle hits cow', *Daily Telegraph*, 14 January 1940, p. 5

p. 45, 'Interviewed at the time, his father said': 'Man dies after recovering body', *Daily Telegraph*, 23 February 1943, p. 5

p. 46, 'He had most likely contracted typhoid': 'Beach inspector's death', *Army News*, 3 March 1943, p. 4

p. 46, 'More than 4000 people attended his memorial': 'Life saver's ashes scattered at sea', *Evening Advocate*, 12 April 1943, p. 3

p. 46, 'Harold's ashes were scattered': 'Tribute to dead surfer', *Daily Telegraph*, 26 March 1943, p. 12

p. 50, 'From there the family travelled to local Catholic cemetery': Family Notices, *Sydney Morning Herald*, 2 December 1947, p. 22

CHAPTER 4: PORK ROAST

p. 57, 'Mrs Hurry had come in to check on Angelina': 'Supreme court woman bail', *Daily Examiner*, 15 August 1953, p. 3

p. 60, 'On the morning of 17 January 1948, Angelina Thomas died': 'Supreme court woman bail', *Daily Examiner*, 15 August 1953, p. 3

CHAPTER 5: CRACKLING AT CHRISTMAS

p. 62, 'In New South Wales at the time it was illegal to commit': Jowett S, Carpenter B & Tait G, 'Determining a suicide under Australian law', *UNSW Law Journal*, 41, 2, 2018, pp. 1–25

p. 63, 'The road leading into the area known as Lilyfield': Lawrence J & Warne C, *Pictorial History: Balmain to Glebe*, Kingsclear Books, Sydney, 1995

p. 64, 'The area on which Callan Park was located': Lawrence J & Warne C, *Pictorial History: Balmain to Glebe*, Kingsclear Books, Sydney, 1995

p. 65, 'With its own power station, a large boiler room': 'Callan Park Conservation Management Plan', Part 2, report prepared by Tanner Architects, 2011

p. 66, 'The Broughton Hall estate had been absorbed by Callan Park': Rosen A & Manns L, 'Who owns Callan Park? A cautionary tale', *Australasian Psychiatry* 11, 4, December 2003, pp. 446–51

p. 66, 'How staff interacted with vulnerable patients': 'Callan Park Man Dies', *The Herald*, 27 September 1948, p. 1

p. 66, 'The cruelty shown to 28-year-old ex-serviceman Leslie Winter': 'Callan Park struggle described to court', *Newcastle Sun*, 16 December 1948, p. 3

p. 66, 'Winter's bowel had been ruptured': 'Revelation in Callan Park case', *Daily Advertiser*, 23 December 1948, p. 1; 'Callan Park Inquiry', *Barrier Miner*, 22 December 1948, p. 1

p. 66, 'No doctor had been called': 'Callan Park struggle described to court', *Newcastle Sun*, 16 December 1948, p. 3; 'Callan Park patient died after struggle', *Daily Examiner*, 18 December 1948, p. 3

p. 66, 'Winter's depositions, taken from his death bed': 'Investigate Callan Park incident', *Newcastle Morning Herald*, 18 September 1948, p. 3

p. 66, 'The man had been at Callan Park for only eighteen months': 'Callan Park patient dies', *Goulburn Evening Post*, 27 September 1948, p. 5

p. 66, 'Reporter Victor Valentine investigated the abuse': 'Callan Park overcrowded', *The Herald*, 10 August 1948, p. 3

p. 67, 'That year a public inquiry was opened': 'Inquiry into Callan Park', *Glen Innes Examiner*, 16 July 1948, p. 1

p. 67, 'The details of the allegations were horrifying': 'Callan Park report displeases', *Lithgow Mercury*, 11 August 1948, p. 2

p. 67, 'Patients who were skilled tradesmen': 'Scandal at Callan Park', *The Sun*, 4 July 1948, p. 6

p. 67, 'Those suffering sexual disorders were allowed to prey': 'Inquiry into Callan Park adjournment', *Northern Star*, 20 July 1948, p. 5

p. 68, 'There were no psychologists or social workers': 'Doctor confirms Callan Park staff shortage', *The Sun*, 18 July 1948, p. 5

p. 295, 'A few years before Desmond's arrival': 'From the courts', *Daily Telegraph*, 24 February 1942, p. 6

p. 72, 'Dr Kirkwood had heroically worked ninety hours straight': 'Beyond 1914: The Great War and University of Sydney project', University of Sydney's Chancellor's Committee and State Library of NSW, 2014

p. 73, 'With the influx of war veterans, Dr Wechsler (in medical partnership': Prendergast F & Wechsler Z, *Medical Journal of Australia*, 17 October 1970, p. 753

p. 74, 'By the 1940s camphor oil was replaced with a synthetic chemical preparation': Payne N & Prudic J, 'Electroconvulsive therapy part I: a perspective on the evolution and current practice of ECT', *Journal of Psychiatric Practice*, 15, 5, 2011, pp. 346–68; Cooper K & Fink M, 'The chemical induction of seizures in psychiatric therapy: were flurothyl (indoklon) and pentylenetrazol (metrazol) abandoned prematurely?', *Journal of Clinical Psychopharmacology*, 34, 5, 2014, pp. 602–07

p. 74, 'On 17 July 1946, Dorothy Nellie Graham was diagnosed': 'Coroner finds no risk in shock treatment', *Newcastle Morning Herald and Miners' Advocate*, 10 August 1946, p. 6

p. 74, 'The Coroner found that she had died from exhaustion': 'Coroner interrupts inquest after barrister's charge', *The Sun*, 9 August 1946, p. 3

p. 75, 'Desmond's treatment had been deemed safe after extensive testing': Rzesnitzek L & Lang S, 'Electroshock therapy in the Third Reich', *Medical History*, 61, 1, 2017, pp. 66–88; Wright B, 'An historical review of electroconvulsive therapy', *Jefferson Journal of Psychiatry*, 8, 2, 1990, pp. 68–74

p. 75, 'For Christmas 1947, the hospital held musical concerts': 'Xmas comes to old soldiers', *Daily Telegraph*, 22 December 1949, p. 12

CHAPTER 6: HEAD CHEESE

p. 85, 'As gender studies essayist and American feminist scholar Heather Fireman notes': Fireman H, 'The dark past keeps returning: gender themes in neo-noir', winning essay of the Louis Kampf writing prize, MIT program in women's and gender studies, MIT, 2003

p. 85, 'In *Possessed* (1947) Joan Crawford plays a woman who coldly commits murder': *Variety* magazine review of *Possessed*, 31 December 1946

p. 86, 'Academic critiques of gender roles in film noir': Barnes-Smith D, 'Fatal woman, revisited: understanding female stereotypes in film noir', Scholar Works at University of Montana, 2015; Theses and Professional Papers 38, University of Montana

CHAPTER 7: CURRY AND BOILED VEGETABLES

p. 93, 'Patients at Callan Park were encouraged to engage in activities': 'Helping sick minds back to health', *Australian Women's Weekly*, 27 April 1935, p. 10

p. 94, 'Gardening and animal husbandry were seen as particularly sanative': Callan Park Conservation Management Plan, Part 2, report prepared by Tanner Architects, 2011, p. 19

p. 94, 'By the time of Desmond's admission': Callan Park Conservation Management Plan, Part 2, report prepared by Tanner Architects, 2011, p. 25

p. 98, 'The dense and dusty texture of common wheat flour and powdered chocolate': 'Cockroach control', *The Land*, 31 January 1947, p. 18

p. 101, 'Mrs Withers chimed in immediately': 'Didn't want her husband', *The Herald*, 26 June 1952, p. 3

p. 101, '"I'm not going to have him," Yvonne replied': 'Poison has base of thallium', *Sydney Morning Herald*, 18 September 1952, p. 6

p. 113, 'Dr King did not know why the man's condition had deteriorated so quickly': 'House of death', *Truth*, 6 July 1952, p. 9

CHAPTER 8: SPLIT PEAS

p. 119, 'One game had even been uncovered in a home on Ferndale Street in Newtown': 'Second two-up raid on same premises', *Daily Telegraph*, 11 September 1946, p. 8; 'Fined for two up', *The Sun*, 9 May 1949, p. 3; '167 arrested in four two-up school raids', *Daily Telegraph*, 7 September 1946, p. 1

p. 120, 'The war had been good to Yvonne': '2000 women for change of jobs', *The Sun*, 20 March 1944, p. 3; 'NSW drive for 2000 more single women', *Advocate*, 22 March 1944, p. 5

p. 120, 'But some contracted and changed their hiring practices': Advertising, *Sydney Morning Herald*, 28 July 1947, p. 14

p. 121, 'As J H Holman, General Manager of Butterfield and Lewis': Daily Telegraph Midweek Magazine, *Daily Telegraph*, 4 September 1947, p. 13

p. 122, 'On 1 January 1951 he proposed': 'Two husbands died from thallium poison', *Truth*, 29 June 1952, p. 8

p. 123, 'But it would only be a repetition in a year or two of what I have already gone through.': 'Real life court dramas', *Daily Telegraph*, 22 June 1952, p. 38

p. 124, 'Bertram's service record was not the kind that earned him respect': Anderson N, 'The offending M – Army service numbers Australian Army History Unit', 2016, Department of Defence, Canberra

p. 126, 'In an article printed in *The Sun* newspaper': 'Broken home', *The Sun*, 17 December 1939, p. 2

p. 127, 'When Dottie and Harry Bogan divorced in 1927': 'In divorce', *Sydney Morning Herald*, 2 November 1927, p. 12; 'Another bloke', *The Sun*, 1 November 1927, p. 12

p. 130, 'They could help her take out a summons for an assault': 'Says husband gave her a terrible time', *Advertiser*, 17 June 1952, p. 3

p. 130, 'By the time Monday rolled around, Henry had talked Yvonne out of pressing charges': 'Rat poison interview', *The Herald*, 17 June 1952, p. 2

p. 131, 'Bertram brought a bottle of Thall-Rat home the following day': 'Court told of woman's row story', *Daily Telegraph*, 17 June 1952, p. 12; 'Denies poisoning two husbands', *Daily Advertiser*, 23 September 1952, p. 1; 'Real life court dramas', *Daily Telegraph*, 22 June 1952, p. 38

p. 132, 'As she ran, the neighbour heard Yvonne yell clearly': 'Woman denied using thallium', *Newcastle Sun*, 22 September 1952, p. 3

p. 132, 'Yvonne claimed Bertram had punched her so hard': *Sydney Morning Herald*, 20 September 1952, p. 6

p. 132, 'Yvonne prepared a breakfast very common for working-class families': 'Woman denied toast poisoned', *Newcastle Morning Herald and Miners' Advocate*, 18 June 1952, p. 5

p. 133, 'Lionel watched Bertram eat his soup from his aluminium thermos': 'Real life court dramas', *Daily Telegraph*, 22 June 1952, p. 38

p. 135, 'He banged his feet on the floor, as if desperately trying to wake them up': 'Women denied using poison', *The Age*, 16 June 1952, p. 3; 'Real life court dramas', *Daily Telegraph*, 22 June 1952, p. 38

p. 136, '"I tell you how silly she is, Flo,"': 'Real life court dramas', *Daily Telegraph*, 22 June 1952, p. 38

p. 137, 'In that moment, Bertie's words returned to her': 'Doctor suspected man poisoned', *Daily Examiner*, 19 June 1952, p. 1

p. 139, 'Doctors knew that heavy metal poisoning caused hair loss and gastric symptoms': Trestrail III J, *Criminal Poisoning Investigational Guide for Law Enforcement, Toxicologists, Forensic Scientists and Attorneys*, Springer, New York, 2000, p. 62

p. 139, 'Dr Goldie ordered the tests for arsenic and lead immediately': 'Doctor's evidence on death of second husband', *Sydney Morning Herald*, 20 September 1952, p. 6

p. 139, 'On 23 March 1952, Henry went to see his son': 'Grinned, waved at husband's funeral', *Advertiser*, 19 June 1952, p. 3

p. 139, 'Bertram Henry Fletcher's funeral procession': Funerals, *Sydney Morning Herald*, 25 March 1952, p. 18

CHAPTER 9: STOMACH, HEART, LUNG, LIVER AND KIDNEYS

p. 142, 'Early in his career, he had even been shot in the face': 'Midnight shots', *Evening News*, 7 March 1923, p. 7; 'Telegrams', *Goulburn Evening Penny Post*, 28 April 1923, p. 4; 'Sentenced', *Northern Star*, 28 April 1923, p. 5; 'Policeman's pluck', *Evening News*, 7 June 1923, p. 10

p. 142, 'He had lived to tell the tale': 'Promoted', *The Sun*, 8 April 1933, p. 3

p. 143, 'As chief of the CIB, Wiley was required to report': 'CIB Chief praises men on year's work', *Lithgow Mercury*, 24 December 1952, p. 2

p. 144, 'Dr Stratford Sheldon and Dr Percy, the government medical officers': 'Remand for woman on two murder charges', *Northern Star*, 20 May 1952, p. 1

p. 144, 'It took more than two weeks for the laboratory tests to be completed': 'Wife hears analyst say poison in two husbands', *Brisbane Telegraph*, 16 June 1952, p. 3

p. 145, 'Wiley assigned the investigation to Detective Sergeant Donald George Fergusson': 'CIB Chief praises men on year's work', *Lithgow Mercury*, 24 December 1952, p. 2

p. 145, 'As Tony Reeves, investigative journalist, notes': Reeves T, *The Real George Freeman: Thief, race-fixer, standover man and underworld crim*, Hybrid Publishers, Ormond, 2011

p. 146, 'It was a mad scramble of an operation': 'Police arrest ex-detective in luxury flat', *Sydney Morning Herald*, 12 August 1948, p. 3; 'Police seize four trucks of goods', *Daily Telegraph*, 19 June 1948, p. 1; 'Night swoops in escapee hunt', *The Sun*, 3 January 1948, p. 4

p. 146, 'Dr Richard Evans, lecturer in criminology at Deakin University': Evans R, 'The police are rottenly corrupt: policing, scandal and the regulation of illegal betting in Depression-era Sydney', *Australian and New Zealand Journal of Criminology*, 2014, pp. 1–16

p. 146, 'Investigative journalist Evan Whitton, who has written extensively on the underbelly': Whitton E, *Can of Worms II: A Citizen's Reference Book to Crime and the Administration of Justice*, Fairfax Library, Sydney, 1987; Whitton E, *Can of Worms: A Citizen's Reference Book to Crime and the Administration of Justice*, Fairfax Library, Sydney, 1986

p. 147, 'George Fergusson's arrogance did not stop there': Museum of Applied Arts and Sciences Australian Olympic Team Uniform for 1936 Berlin games; 'NSW Crew Ashore in Uniform', *Sporting Globe*, 27 May 1936, p. 11

p. 147, 'Of the thirty-three Olympic athletes to compete for Australia that year': 'Manchester Unity Ball', *Newcastle Sun*, 8 June 1938, p. 3; Guerin A, 'History of Australian Rowing Olympic Games Berlin 1936', https://www.rowinghistory-aus.info/olympic-games/1936-Berlin; 'Country strong in Olympic Team', *Sporting Globe*, 27 May 1936, p. 11

p. 148, 'By 1952 Krahe was a high-profile officer in the homicide squad': 'Homicide squad officer spending holiday here', *The Kyogle Examiner*, 29 August 1952, p. 1

p. 148, 'In one of the first cases of its kind, Krahe had managed to secure': 'Extradition to NSW', *West Australian*, 25 July 1950, p. 19

p. 150, 'In Mackay's words, police were not people but "crime-hunting machines"': 'Police cadets NSW police best in world', *Daily Telegraph*, 7 August 1946, p. 11

p. 151, 'David Dixon has written of the role that corrupt police played': Dixon D, *A Culture of Corruption: Changing an Australian Police Service*, Hawkins Press, Sydney, 1999, pp. 9 & 148

p. 151, 'Media reports written after the 1950s retrospectively claim that Fergusson's': Whitton E, *Can of Worms II: A Citizen's Reference Book to Crime and the Administration of Justice*, Fairfax Library, Sydney, 1987; Whitton E, *Can of Worms: A Citizen's Reference Book to Crime and the Administration of Justice*, Fairfax Library, Sydney, 1986

CHAPTER 10: INGREDIENTS

p. 154, 'In 1936, Thomas Alan McDonald was one of two analysts appointed': *Government Gazette of State of NSW*, 4 September 1936, no. 138, p. 3631

p. 154, 'Raspberry jam was found to be made of apple pulp': 'Technical offence', *Nepean Times*, 3 July 1941, p. 3

p. 155, 'Occupational diseases also fell within the remit of the Analyst': 'Crime in a test tube', *Sydney Morning Herald*, 15 March 1952, p. 9

p. 155, 'In 1951 alone, the police department had called on the Government Analyst': 'Crime in a test tube', *Sydney Morning Herald*, 15 March 1952, p. 9

p. 156, 'The suspect was convicted because he had never left Australia': 'Government analyst traces crime and guards public health', *Sydney Morning Herald*, 26 May 1949, p. 2; 'Crime in a test tube', *Sydney Morning Herald*, 15 March 1952, p. 9

p. 156, 'When Thomas Alan McDonald was given responsibility for the Fletcher analysis': 'Remand for woman on two murder charges', *Northern Star*, 20 May 1952, p. 1

p. 158, 'Thallium tricks the body into thinking it is potassium': George D, *Poisons: An Introduction for Forensic Investigators*, CRC Press, Boca Raton, 2017

p. 159, 'They made an application to court to exhume Butler's body': 'Remand for woman on two murder charges', *Northern Star*, 20 May 1952, p. 1

p. 162, 'Gordon Bruce Wooster, the superintendent of Callan Park': 'Poison has base of thallium', *Sydney Morning Herald*, 18 September 1952, p. 6

p. 166, 'In the United States, the burrowing of prairie dogs': Munch J & Silver J, 'The Pharmacology of Thallium and its Use in Rodent Control', *USDA Technical Bulletins*, 1931

p. 168, 'In August 1946, *The Sun* misreported that William Alan Cunningham Brocksopp': 'Drug given child to be sent to analyst', *The Sun*, 13 August 1946, p. 5

p. 168, 'On 17 July 1946, three-and-a-half-year-old William Allan Cunningham Brocksopp': 'Maitland boy's death: coroner sends drug', *Newcastle Morning Herald and Miners' Advocate*, 14 August 1946, p. 4

p. 168, 'It was a cheaper and quicker way to attain the same result': 'Tell me doctor', *Sunday Herald*, 29 July 1951, p. 13

p. 170, 'He returned an open verdict': 'Open verdict in child's death', *Daily Advertiser*, 4 September 1946, p. 2; 'Open finding on child's death', *Sydney Morning Herald*, 4 September 1946, p. 4; 'Open finding given on death of Maitland child', *Newcastle Sun*, 3 September 1946, p. 2; 'Maitland boy's death: coroner sends drug', *Newcastle Morning Herald and Miners' Advocate*, 14 August 1946, p. 4

p. 170, 'In an orphanage in the town of Carmarthenshire': Roche Lynch G, 'The toxicology of thallium', *The Lancet*, 20 December 1930, p. 1340; Lewis D & Lloyd A, 'Treatment of ringworm of the scalp with thallium acetate', *British Medical Journal*, 15 July 1933, p. 99

p. 171, 'in an institution in Granada, Spain': Timbrell J, *Poison Paradox*, Oxford University Press, 2005

p. 171, 'It should not be recommended to the public as a rodent poison': Munch J & Silver J, 'The Pharmacology of Thallium and its Use in Rodent Control', *USDA Technical Bulletins*, 1931

p. 172, 'Women could no longer see their facial hair because Koremlu had sent them blind': Greenbaum S, 'Reports of thallium acetate poisoning following the use of Koremlu', *JAMA*, May 1931, p. 1868; Duncan W & Crosby E, 'A case of thallium poisoning following the prolonged use of a depilatory cream', *JAMA*, 96, 1931, pp. 1866–68

p. 172, 'As early as the 1920s, researchers knew that thallium exposure': 'The action of thallium', *British Medical Journal*, 1, 1929, 3568, p. 962

p. 173, 'In a paper examining the history of therapeutic goods regulation in Australia': McEwen J, *A History of Therapeutic Goods Regulation in Australia*, Attorney-General's Department, Commonwealth of Australia, 2007, p. vi

p. 173, 'As one review of the legislative history in this field notes': McEwen J, *A History of Therapeutic Goods Regulation in Australia*, Attorney-General's Department, Commonwealth of Australia, 2007, p. 15

p. 174, 'the pain in her legs had become so severe': Duncan W & Crosby E, 'A case of thallium poisoning following the prolonged use of a depilatory cream', *JAMA*, 96, 1931, pp. 1866–68; Greenbaum S, 'Reports of thallium acetate poisoning following the use of Koremlu', *JAMA*, May 1931, p. 1868

p. 174, 'After a prolonged case, the company was ordered to pay well over two million dollars': Greenbaum S, 'Reports of thallium acetate poisoning following the use of Koremlu', *JAMA*, May 1931, p. 1868

p. 175, 'McDonald estimated that about half a teaspoon': 'Thallium murderess sentenced', *The Advertiser*, 24 September 1952, p. 1

CHAPTER 11: GRILLING

p. 181, 'In a lengthy statement, Justice Kinsella': Kinsella J, Central Criminal Court, Regina v Yvonne Gladys Fletcher, Judgement on Admissibility of Evidence (in the absence of the jury), Central Criminal Court, 15 September 1952, p. 1

p. 182, 'They involve discussions with many people and may have very many aspects.': Kinsella J, Central Criminal Court, Regina v Yvonne Gladys Fletcher, Judgement on Admissibility of Evidence (in the absence of the jury), Central Criminal Court, 15 September 1952, p. 1

p. 184, 'Instead, she displayed a hard-edged pragmatism': 'Woman's appeal poison case', *Daily Advertiser*, 25 September 1952, p. 3

CHAPTER 12: POTATO AND BACON PIE

p. 186, 'It transpired Allan worked as a truck driver': 'Inquiries on Cowra death', *Sydney Morning Herald*, 26 July 1952, p. 4; 'Woman charged with murder, Cowra', *Barrier Daily Truth*, 30 July 1952, p. 1

p. 187, 'While her future son-in-law did not appear to have enemies': 'Charged with murder', *Brisbane Telegraph*, 14 August 1952, p. 1

p. 187, 'Less than a month before, Cowra had faced a catastrophic flood': 'Man missing in floods at Cowra', *Sydney Morning Herald*, 18 June 1952, p. 3

p. 187, 'Meanwhile, at Cowra Hospital, George Worth had been admitted': 'Collapse at thallium poison trial', *Daily Mercury*, 23 October 1952, p. 1; 'Cowra mystery continues', *Cootamundra Herald*, 29 July 1952, p. 1

p. 189, 'According to Krahe's transcript, Elizabeth claimed that Ruby had said': 'Poison request story at murder trial', *The Sun*, 22 October 1952, p. 2

p. 190, 'Many local farms kept acid on site': 'The Orchardist's Interests', *The Farmer and Settler*, 5 December 1935, p. 10; 'Further evidence in poison pie case', *Daily Advertiser*, 19 August 1952, p. 1

p. 190, 'Instead, they asked her to detail every strange encounter': 'Cowra Inquest', *Sydney Morning Herald*, 19 August 1952, p. 5

p. 191, 'Another neighbour, pea farmer Walter McIllhaton, reported that Ruby': 'Detective says woman expected arrest', *Daily Telegraph*, 23 October 1952, p. 10

p. 191, 'Annie also claimed that Ruby had referred to Allan': 'Detective says woman expected arrest', *Daily Telegraph*, 23 October 1952, p. 10

p. 191, 'With the interviews completed and the toxicology results in': 'Woman charged with murder', *Daily Telegraph*, 30 July 1952, p. 1

p. 191, 'Ruby Norton was arrested at midday and taken to Cowra Police Station': 'Murder charge', *Armidale Express and New England General Advertiser*, 30 July 1952

p. 192, 'Ruby claimed that': 'Detective says woman expected arrest', *Daily Telegraph*, 23 October 1952, p. 10

p. 192, 'The rat poison I bought is the same as the woman': 'Detective says woman expected arrest', *Daily Telegraph*, 23 October 1952, p. 10

p. 192, 'The transcript was sure to include the fact that Ruby had added': 'Woman's denial on poisoned pie', *Daily Telegraph*, 15 August 1952, p. 9

p. 192, 'Fay Norton tried to defend her mother': 'Woman's defence at murder trial', *Sydney Morning Herald*, 24 October 1952, p. 4

p. 192, 'She also said that Allan had put the Thall-Rat on bread and butter': 'Elderly woman on charge of murder', *Central Queensland Herald*, 14 August 1952, p. 15

p. 192, 'It was possible, according to Fay': 'Woman denies murder charge', *Daily Examiner*, 24 October 1952, p. 3

p. 192, 'The first sign that there might be a snag': 'Woman faces murder charge', *Daily Examiner*, 30 July 1952, p. 1

p. 193, 'They prepared 157 foolscap pages of witness statements': '31 Crown witnesses to be called in murder trial', *Newcastle Sun*, 21 October 1952, p. 4

p. 194, 'The previous year, she had put pen to paper and crafted': 'Woman claims wicked gossip led to trial', *National Advocate*, 24 October 1952, p. 2; 'Nasty poem by poison witness', *Newcastle Sun*, 22 October 1952, p. 3

p. 194, 'Not content to just delight in the hilarity of her rude rhymes': 'Cowra Inquest', *Sydney Morning Herald*, 19 August 1952, p. 5

p. 194, 'Florence Hill's grievance with Ruby was deep': 'Woman on trial for murder', *National Advocate*, 22 October 1952, p. 2; 'Woman's trial', *National Advocate*, 22 October 1952, p. 5

p. 195, 'Ruby's lawyer described the testimony presented as malicious': 'Woman to face murder trial', *Daily Telegraph*, 20 August 1952, p. 9

p. 195, 'The prosecution fought hard to convince the jury': 'Woman's defence at murder trial', *Sydney Morning Herald*, 24 October 1952, p. 4; 'Poison charge fails', *The Age*, 25 October 1952, p. 7

p. 196, 'Ruby's response exposed the insularity of her world': 'Freed woman to return home', *Daily Telegraph*, 25 October 1952, p. 7; 'Welcome to freed woman', *The Sun*, 26 October 1952, p. 7

CHAPTER 13: BAIT AND WAIT

p. 198, 'Then came a further humiliation': 'Woman sentenced to death', *Sydney Morning Herald*, 24 September 1952, p. 1

p. 199, 'The appeals judge, Justice Owen, offered up a broad ruling': 'Appeal dismissed', *Cairns Post*, 14 February 1953, p. 1; 'Woman poisoner appeal fails', *Central Queensland Herald*, 19 February 1953, p. 17; 'Woman's appeal dismissed', *Northern Star*, 14 February 1953, p. 1

p. 200, 'I am of opinion that the appeal fails and should be dismissed': Reg. v Fletcher, Court of Criminal Appeal State Reports, 13 February 1953, p. 80

p. 201, 'At one point in the 1950s, the rumours surrounding his ability to simply concoct evidence': Morton J & Lobez S, *Bent Uncensored: Australia's Crooked Cops*, Melbourne University Publishing, 2016

p. 201, 'At one notorious criminal's trial, Redshaw noted': 'Detective is best friend of criminal who lapsed', *The Argus*, 24 July 1952, p. 5

p. 201, 'By 1953, Kelly's power and influence in the force was growing': 'Detectives switch jobs', *Sydney Morning Herald*, 6 December 1952, p. 5

p. 201, 'Then, in October of that year, Kelly was appointed': 'To guard the Queen', *Northern Star*, 19 October 1953, p. 1

p. 205, 'In 1953, the CIB staked out the GPO letterboxes in Sydney city': 'Shadow Fahy traps world wide fur ring: ex policeman in racket', *Sunday Mail*, 19 July 1953, p. 19

p. 206, 'Jack Downey took to his new vocation as undercover detective': 'Tram driver's poison fear', *Daily Telegraph*, 20 August 1953, p. 9

p. 207, 'But John had gone to Woy Woy on holiday with Caroline and Richard Grills': 'Relatives held Aunt Carrie's hand at the court', *Truth*, 23 August 1953, p. 44

CHAPTER 14: JAM ROLY-POLY

p. 218, 'Not content to try it once, he ate ginger for three straight days': 'I feared thallium on that ginger', *The Argus*, 20 August 1953, p. 9

p. 218, 'Both were found to have been exposed to thallium': 'Witness suspicious of Caroline Grills', *Advocate*, 13 August 1953, p. 5

p. 219, 'Over the next fortnight, Jack Downey began to suffer tightness in the chest': 'Relatives held Aunt Carrie's hand at the court', *Truth*, 23 August 1953, p. 44

p. 220, 'Bail was set at 2000 pounds': 'Cup of tea contained thallium', *Newcastle Sun*, 11 August 1953, p. 2

CHAPTER 15: EXPERIMENTING WITH NEW INGREDIENTS

p. 223, 'Victoria moved quickly and at the end of 1952 legislated': 'Thallium sales', *Cairns Post*, 4 December 1952, p. 1

p. 223, 'In Queensland thallium had been on the restricted poisons': 'Thallium not sold freely', *Brisbane Telegraph*, 14 December 1952, p. 13

p. 223, 'When questioned, he claimed that he must have accidentally eaten': 'Ate thallium by mistake', *Daily Telegraph*, 26 October 1952, p. 4

p. 224, 'He staged a sit-in, refusing to leave the office until someone helped him': 'Woman foils poison bid', *Daily Telegraph*, 2 December 1952, p. 1

p. 225, 'The news media dubbed this thallium victim "the unhappy migrant"': 'Poison knocked out of unhappy migrant's hand', *The Argus*, 2 December 1952, p. 1

p. 225, 'The year 1953 saw thallium use spike in clusters': 'Thallium case suspected', *Sydney Morning Herald*, 4 March 1953, p. 3

p. 226, 'The state immediately sought to prosecute Bardon, but very quickly hit a wall': 'Son's alleged bid to poison his father', *Sydney Morning Herald*, 11 August 1953, p. 5

p. 226, 'Robert's father even appeared in court on his behalf': 'Son forgiven, says father', *Daily Examiner*, 5 September 1953, p. 3

p. 226, 'The inner city, both west and east, then experienced a spate of thallium poisonings': '2 men charged over thallium', *Daily Telegraph*, 11 August 1953, p. 16

p. 226, 'On 17 June, a 27-year-old drank a bottle of thallium': 'Girl sees man take thallium', *Courier-Mail*, 18 June 1953, p. 1

p. 227, 'James Geraghty, the local member for North Sydney, raised the matter in Parliament': 'Wants thallium banned', *Maryborough Chronicle*, 20 June 1953, p. 5

p. 227, 'Beryl Joyce Hague was charged with having maliciously': 'More than 50 cases', *Sydney Morning Herald*, 19 June 1953, p. 3

p. 227, 'An argument ensued, which culminated in Alan striking Beryl': 'In the courts', *Daily Telegraph*, 28 July 1953, p. 14

p. 228, 'You have a bad case of imaginitis.': 'Dramatic turn in thallium in tea charge', *The Sun*, 23 June 1953, p. 2

p. 230, 'On 30 July 1953, Beryl was sentenced to two years in prison':
'Thallium case: gaol sentence', *Goulburn Evening Post*, 30 July 1953, p. 1

p. 230, 'Beryl may have poisoned her husband, said the judge': 'A new life
began at gaol gates', *The Herald*, 3 December 1953, p. 3

p. 230, 'By mid-1953, authorities had publicly acknowledged': 'New control
tomorrow of poisons sale', *The Sun*, 31 March 1953, p. 13

p. 231, 'Now dubbed the "poison experts" of the CIB': 'Remand for woman
on two murder charges', *Northern Star*, 20 May 1952, p. 1

p. 231, 'In addition, experts agreed to assemble again': 'Data on thallium
poisoning', *Daily Examiner*, 28 April 1953, p. 3

CHAPTER 16: ALL-IN-ONE METHOD

p. 234, '"I thought it was her nerves," Caroline responded coolly': 'Thallium
found in tea, police say', *Sydney Morning Herald*, 12 August 1953, p. 4

p. 238, 'Caroline's observations of family members were often brutally
delivered': 'Mrs Grills didn't care', *Examiner*, 18 August 1953, p. 6; 'Mrs
Grills didn't care: says police', *Newcastle Sun*, 17 August 1953, p. 2

p. 240, 'Both detectives were present, along with McDonald': 'Taken to Long
Bay Gaol: Bail refused woman on thallium', *Morning Bulletin*, 14 August
1953, p. 1

p. 241, 'Specimens were removed from the surrounds of the coffin': 'Body
exhumed', *Advocate*, 12 June 1953, p. 5

p. 243, 'McDonald estimated that Angelina had most likely been given a
2-ounce bottle': 'Poison has base of thallium', *Sydney Morning Herald*,
18 September 1952, p. 6

p. 243, "Probably done it to himself,": 'Tram driver's poison fear', *Daily
Telegraph*, 20 August 1953, p. 9

p. 244, 'When confronted with the results of scientific testing, Caroline
challenged the police': 'Tram driver's poison fear', *Daily Telegraph*, 20
August 1953, p. 9

p. 245, 'With all of the interview material gathered, the detectives were
ready': 'An artist's view of a sensational inquest', *Daily Telegraph*, 23
August 1953, p. 5

p. 246, 'On 15 October 1953, it took the twelve jurors just twelve minutes to
convict': 'Woman smiled at death verdict', *The Courier Mail*, 16 October
1953, p. 3

CHAPTER 17: MILO: THE TONIC FOR THE TIMES

p. 251, 'While it is now marketed as a children's drink': 'A nation's industry:
Nestlé's', *The Sun*, 25 March 1937, p. 10

p. 251, 'it was said to aid digestion': 'Gambling on mice', *The Sun*, 1 July 1936, p. 19; Advertising, Milo Nestlé Product, *Whyalla News*, 30 July 1948, p. 6

p. 252, 'As Veronica herself would describe it, everything changed': 'Mrs Monty', *Truth*, 13 December 1953, p. 6

CHAPTER 18: IT'S IN THE MILK

p. 266, 'While Bobby was out, Veronica walked again': 'Story of mother in law petting', *Mirror*, 19 September 1953, p. 6

CHAPTER 19: PROOFING THE DOUGH

p. 272, 'On Sunday 17 April, with the Union Hotel closed': 'Suicide of Mrs Monty', *Central Queensland Herald*, 12 May 1955, p. 31

p. 273, 'Leonard had waited for Thelma to go to work': 'Theft admitted by Sydney man: for sentence', *Examiner*, 26 October 1954, p. 10

p. 273, 'He was also known to police': 'Appearances deceptive', *Truth*, 5 June 1949, p. 14

p. 273, 'Described by some as "debonair"': 'Appearances deceptive', *Truth*, 5 June 1949, p. 14

p. 273, 'When Leonard met Yvonne': 'Gaol sentences for theft', *Advocate*, 12 November 1954, p. 10

p. 274, 'Detectives Fergusson and Krahe's relationship with thallium': 'Grazier's death was due to natural causes', *Manning River Times and Advocate of the Northern Coast Districts of NSW*, 9 April 1954, p. 3

p. 275, 'John Pearson was eighty years old when he was laid to rest': 'Inquiries opened five years after burial', *The Sun*, 20 January 1954, p. 7; 'Poison probe', *Daily Mercury*, 8 April 1954, p. 19

p. 276, 'John Pearson's death was, for the second time': 'Grazier's death was due to natural causes', *Manning River Times and Advocate of the Northern Coast Districts of NSW*, 9 April 1954, p. 3

p. 276, 'This time, it was a timber worker by the name of Les Ruttley': 'Rain stops death probe', *Daily Telegraph*, 12 July 1954, p. 7; 'Exhuming of body today', *Sydney Morning Herald*, 12 July 1954, p. 5

p. 276, 'His sister, Mary Hitchen': 'Man murdered', *Daily Mercury*, 14 July 1954, p. 16

p. 277, 'Another sister, Esme Rice': 'Family say man who died in agony poisoned', *Cootamundra Herald*, 13 July 1954, p. 1

p. 277, 'A friend, Alan Burton': 'Mystery death may be poison murder', *Truth*, 18 July 1954, p. 2

p. 278, 'Of all the old cases that Fergusson and Krahe revisited': 'Woman's death baffles doctors', *Truth*, 14 December 1941, p. 21; 'Thallium killed her', *The Argus*, 31 August 1955, p. 3

p. 278, 'Aileen was a hairdresser': Family Notices, *Newcastle Morning Herald and Miners' Advocate*, 1 November 1941, p. 2

p. 279, 'With this particular case, Fergusson had done something': 'Samples taken at exhumation of 1942 corpse', *Canberra Times*, 30 July 1955, p. 1; 'Film made of exhumation', *Central Queensland Herald*, 4 August 1955, p. 24

p. 279, 'In 1953, the newly established Poisons Advisory Committee': 'Control of thallium sales', *Sydney Morning Herald*, 24 June 1953, p. 2

p. 279, 'As a result of the amendments to the Act': 'Thallium sale curbed', *Newcastle Morning Herald and Miners' Advocate*, 17 September 1953, p. 8; 'Thallium poisons on sale', *Daily Telegraph*, 23 July 1953, p. 2; 'Thallium sale restrictions tomorrow', *Sydney Morning Herald*, 17 September 1953, p. 1

p. 280, 'Police swooped in to conduct an investigation': 'Alleged murder with thallium', *Central Queensland Herald*, 11 October 1956, p. 22

p. 280, 'Doctors also now knew how to better treat thallium': 'Survived despite 6oz thallium', *Canberra Times*, 18 September 1956, p. 4

p. 282, 'Investigative journalist Tony Reeves': Reeves T, *The Real George Freeman: Thief, race-fixer, standover man and underworld crim*, Hybrid Publishers, Ormond, 2011

p. 282, 'Furthermore, writers such as': McNab D, *The Dodger*, Macmillan Publishers, Sydney, 2007; Reeves T, *The Real George Freeman: Thief, race-fixer, standover man and underworld crim*, Hybrid Publishers, Ormond, 2011; Hickie D, *The Prince and the Premier*, Angus & Robertson, Sydney, 1985; Rees P, *Killing Juanita: a true story of murder and corruption*, Allen & Unwin, Sydney, 2004; Whitton E, *Can of Worms: A Citizen's Reference Book to Crime and the Administration of Justice*, Fairfax Library, Sydney, 1986

p. 283, 'Based on Whitton's evidence': Whitton E, *Can of Worms II: A Citizen's Reference Book to Crime and the Administration of Justice*, Fairfax Library, Sydney, 1987

p. 283, 'Journalist Matthew Condon has also written': Condon M, *The Night Dragon*, University of Queensland Press, Brisbane, 2019

p. 283, 'Police corruption is not all the same': Roebuck J & Barker T, 'A typology of police corruption', *Social Problems*, 21, 3, 1974, pp. 423–37

p. 284, 'Protection of illegal vice operations': Roebuck J & Barker T, 'A typology of police corruption', *Social Problems*, 21, 3, 1974, pp. 423–37

p. 284, 'At a Commonwealth inquiry into corruption': Parliament of the Commonwealth of Australia, *The National Crime Authority and James McCartney Anderson*, 37th Parliament, A report by the Parliamentary Joint Committee on the National Crime Authority, released March, Commonwealth of Australia, 1994

p. 285, 'George Freeman, the colourful racing identity': Morton J & Lobez S, *Bent Uncensored: Australia's Crooked Cops*, Melbourne University Publishing, 2016

p. 285, 'By the mid-1960s, Krahe had moved into the honey-pot areas of policing': 'Inquiries at Gold Coast', *Canberra Times*, 11 March 1970, p. 8

p. 285, 'The rumours surrounding Krahe's criminal activities': Silvester J, 'Why crooked cops are just dumb', *Sydney Morning Herald*, 28 October 2016

p. 286, 'Krahe was linked to the disappearance of Kings Cross campaigner': Rees P, *Killing Juanita: a true story of murder and corruption*, Allen & Unwin, Sydney, 2004

p. 286, 'While there are many theories as to how she died': McNab D, 'Sydney heiress Juanita Nielson 44 years on', *7 News*, 14 December 2019

p. 286, 'Krahe's name was also raised in connection with': 'Shirley Brifman: a timeline of a brothel madam and whistleblower', *ABC Sydney News*, 19 January 2017, https://www.abc.net.au/news/2017-01-19/shirley-brifman-a-timeline-of-a-brothel-madam-and-whistleblower/8194602?nw=0

p. 287, 'After Brifman's death': Reeves T, *The Real George Freeman: Thief, race-fixer, standover man and underworld crim*, Hybrid Publishers, Ormond, 2011

p. 288, 'Such operations, noted a Commonwealth inquiry into corruption': Parliament of the Commonwealth of Australia, *The National Crime Authority and James McCartney Anderson*, 37th Parliament, A report by the Parliamentary Joint Committee on the National Crime Authority, released March, Commonwealth of Australia, 1994, p. 103

p. 288, 'Journalist N Jameson described Krahe': Jameson N, 'Abe Saffron's life as a charismatic crook', *Newcastle Herald*, 18 June 2000

p. 288, 'And journalist John Silvester reiterated the folklore': Silvester J, 'Why crooked cops are just dumb', *Sydney Morning Herald*, 28 October 2016

p. 288, 'In 1969 he was awarded the Queen's Commendation for Brave Conduct': Report to Parliament of NSW Police Department, 1970

p. 289, 'While it was claimed that Fergusson had been worried': 'Depressed, CIB chief killed self', *Canberra Times*, 9 April 1970, p. 9

p. 290, 'In an interview journalist Tony Reeves conducted': Reeves T, *The Real George Freeman: Thief, race-fixer, standover man and underworld crim*, Hybrid Publishers, Ormond, 2011

p. 290, 'Robert A. Deilenberg, a specialist writer': Deilenberg R, 'Police Culture in New South Wales in the 1960s–70s', supported by a 2014 grant from the Royal Australian Historical Society, 2014

p. 290, 'Other accounts of police corruption note': Roebuck J & Barker T, 'A typology of police corruption', *Social Problems*, 21, 3, 1974, pp. 423–37

p. 290, 'By Whitton's reckoning': Whitton E, *Can of Worms II: A Citizen's Reference Book to Crime and the Administration of Justice*, Fairfax Library, Sydney, 1987

p. 291, 'Retired Detective Inspector Gary Jubelin': Interview Gary Jubelin, 'I Catch Killers', podcast episode, 27 May 2020

Other sources: Central Criminal Court transcripts, *Regina v Yvonne Gladys Fletcher*, Justice Kinsella, 15 September 1952; Central Criminal Court transcripts, *Regina v Caroline Grills*, Justice Brereton, 7 October 1953; Supreme Court of NSW in Divorce *Lulham v Lulham*, Justice Dovey, Petitioner Judith Anne Lulham, Respondent Robert John Lulham, 28 February 1955

ACKNOWLEDGEMENTS

I WOULD LIKE TO THANK THE FOLLOWING FOR THEIR ASSISTANCE in the writing and production of *The Husband Poisoner*: the archivists at the NSW State Archives, Kingswood, Sydney; the National Library of Australia's 'Trove' online portal; the family history databases Ancestry and FindMyPast, and the NSW Registry of Births, Deaths and Marriages.

Thank you to my publisher, Sophie Hamley; copyeditor, Rod Morrison; and the wonderful team at Hachette, including Fiona Hazard, Karen Ward, Jenny Topham, Daniel Pilkington, Chris Sims, Sarah Holmes, Bella Lloyd and Christa Moffitt.

AUTHOR'S NOTE

All of the dishes referred to in this book were for ordinary meals, which would have been regularly prepared in most Australian homes in the postwar era. As each Australian housewife would have had their own individual way of preparing these meals, I have taken the liberty of including the versions of these recipes which existed within my own family. These recipes have been drawn from the family cookbook compiled by my mother, Joan, who was herself a postwar wife and mother. Needless to say, my mother was not a murderer and her cooking never killed anyone.

Tanya Bretherton has a PhD in sociology with special interests in narrative life history and social history. She has published in the academic and public sphere for twenty years, and worked as a Senior Research Fellow at the University of Sydney for fifteen years. Currently she works as a freelance researcher and writer. Her first book, *The Suitcase Baby*, was shortlisted for the Ned Kelly Award, the Danger Prize and the Waverley Library 'Nib' Award. Her second book, *The Suicide Bride*, was shortlisted for the Danger Prize. Her third book, *The Killing Streets*, won the 2020 Danger Prize.